I'd Like To Thank The Cartel For Getting Me Out Of The Cult

A Memoir

Dr. Robyn Lynette

I'd Like to Thank the Cartel for Getting Me Out of the Cult

ISBN 978-0-9846581-4-5

Disclaimer
This is a work of nonfiction based on the author's recollections of her
life experiences. Some events may have been combined, compressed,
reconstructed or left out for narrative flow. The views and opinions
expressed are solely those of the author. This book is not intended to malign
any person, group, or organization, but to share the author's personal story
and perspective.

Published by Champion Performance Development

Cover Art by Russell Bruzzano
www.RgBDesignGroup.com

Book Design by Russell Bruzzano
www.RgBDesignGroup.com

For those living in the chaos, and those who carry the scars:
You are not alone.

Table of Contents

Prologue

Parts of my life sound like fiction and there were times I didn't realize how much danger I was in.

Would I want to repeat it? No. Would I wish it on my worst enemy? Also no. But I wouldn't change it. It made me who I am today, and I like who I am and the life I have now.

I want to start this story in the present, where I am happy and thriving, because parts of it get heavy and dark.

I am currently married to Russ, who is a great partner for me.

He is a former competitive bodybuilder and trainer on the Mr. Olympia tour. He is slow to anger and quick to forgive.

He was patient with the trauma responses I brought with me into our relationship.

He is self-sufficient; he doesn't need me, he wants me. Most importantly, he is confident in his masculinity. He isn't threatened by me being in the spotlight.

After my TEDx talk, someone came up to me and said, "I want to find a man who looks at me the way Russ looks at you."

He is my biggest cheerleader and isn't at all threatened by other men.

In fact, we have an agreement: I defend our relationship against anyone who hits on me, and he defends it against anyone who hits on him (if he notices).

It is the kind of relationship that twenty years ago I would have told you was boring. Now I realize this is what peace and calm look like.

Having a good partner has allowed me to explore and learn who I am professionally.

I now know who I help, how I help them, and why it matters. I no longer feel like I have to be everything for everyone.

I also want to answer the question: "Do you still talk to your family?"

The short answer is: sort of. I call my parents on their birthdays and for Mother's Day and Father's Day. I have lunch with them when I find myself in Central California. We talk about things that matter to them and what is going on in their world.

I am closer to some of my seven siblings than I am to others, but I wouldn't wish ill on any of them.

Each of them has their own lives and their own traumas to figure out. I respect that, even if they choose not to do the same for me.

Another common question is, "Which cult were you in?"

It isn't one of the big ones you've heard of. It is based on the teachings of John Calvin and is very conservative and patriarchal. My father is fanatical in those beliefs and has left to start new churches more than once over religious disagreements.

An example can be summed up in something I heard my father say when I was a teenager: "Women shouldn't have to vote. But we have to let our women vote because the heathens do."

I'm not going to go into detail about my parents' lives or the cult. The fact that I was married off was considered extreme, even within the church. But sadly, no one stepped in to stop it.

Some people have bristled that I use the word "cult," arguing that it is just an "ultraconservative and dogmatic religion." I am not here to argue semantics. What I survived wasn't about religion. It was using the Bible to create isolation and deep-seated control, specifically over women.

With the exception of myself and my husband Russ, every name in this book is an alias. I could say it's to protect people's privacy, and for some, that is true. But for many, it is because I don't want to give them even a second of recognition or the chance to try to gaslight their way out of how they behaved.

Do not for a moment think that getting here was easy. I worked *hard*, did a *lot* of therapy, and still bump into trauma responses.

On the days when the part of my brain that used to keep me safe starts to worry and freak out, I remind her: We are okay. We have a little dog named Nebula I teach to do circus tricks; we get to hike and bike ride and do work I love. I have friends who care about me.

She doesn't have to keep me safe anymore.

As you read my story, try to remember:

I made it through.

It's okay.

We are safe

Chapter 1

Born into a Cult

I didn't know I was born into a cult. In those earliest years, our faith was strict but not fanatical. Sunday services, grace before meals, daily devotions in the kitchen. It hadn't yet hardened into the suffocating rules that would later define my childhood.

My very early childhood seemed pretty "normal" based on the pictures I've seen. There's even one of me in a bikini as a toddler. Something that would have been absolutely unthinkable for my younger sisters.

From the time I was very young, I had to sit through "big-people church." My dad didn't believe in kids going to children's church.

I was so little that my feet didn't reach the floor, and I would swing my legs because they would go numb. Sometimes my shoes would kick the back of the pew in front of us.

One Sunday evening, Dad's hand clamped down painfully on my knee. He leaned in close, his breath hot in my ear as he hissed: "If you kick it again, I'll take you out and spank you."

I tried *so* hard to sit still. I tried to focus on not moving my legs. But they hurt. I thought I could just carefully shift my leg to make it stop tingling.

But I wasn't careful enough and my toe hit the pew.

Dad grabbed my arm and stormed out of the church, dragging me with him.

Outside, it was cold, and my little sweater was left sitting next to Mom and my brother inside.

I remember Dad lecturing me about how naughty I was.

When he realized I was shivering, he took his suit jacket off and put it over my shoulders. It was warm and I thought, "He loves me. He's not going to hit me." I was wrong. He did spank me. And the whole congregation heard it through the open window above us.

After church one of the other parents thanked my dad because it made his kid stop wiggling.

Even typing the story now, I feel so much compassion for that little girl and the trauma she endured because her father wanted to be the perfect parent.

In my dad's mind, evidence of a perfect parent is a perfect child. And I was far from a perfect child.

When I was between three and four years old, my parents decided to move from Southern California up to the Central Valley.

I feel like that move was particularly hard on my mother. She left behind her sisters, her parents, her safety net, and was now trying to raise two small children without help.

She would often send us outside just to get some alone time.

Before we moved, my aunt used to take me on little adventures. After we moved, Dad would take me with him to do chores just to get me out of the house and give Mom a break.

But it wasn't enough. Mom was still overwhelmed.

My dad had given up his job teaching high school music, was trying to start a dairy, and later he opened a landscaping business. Neither business worked out.

We wore hand-me-downs. Mom had to stretch recipes and left cheese out because it cost too much. Once, when a chicken was hit on the road, she called Dad to get instructions on how to pluck it so she could serve it for dinner.

We couldn't afford to heat the whole house so when it was cold, Mom only bathed us on Saturdays. My hair, matted from a week of not being brushed, would be a tangled mess. I spent many Saturday nights sobbing as one of my parents tried to get a comb through it.

In frustration, Mom would regularly threaten to chop my hair short. And sometimes she did actually cut it. That just made me cry harder.

As poor as we were, my parents still thought it was important for me and my brother to go to the private Christian school.

The only way they could afford it was for Dad to take a job as a janitor and bus driver there for the tuition discount, even though he had a master's degree in music.

I was a dirty little girl in hand-me-down clothes with unbrushed hair attending a fancy private school with well-groomed, fashionably dressed children.

I didn't fit in and was bullied for it. I didn't know it was bullying, but I knew it made me feel bad. Now I know that feeling was shame.

Perhaps unexpectedly, I was a deeply kind and soft-hearted child. My mom shared this story about me:

When I was in first grade, Mom put a small candy bar in my lunch. Which was an incredible luxury for us.

When I got home from school, I didn't mention it, so Mom asked, "How did you like the surprise I put in your lunch?"

I didn't understand. "The surprise?"

"The candy?"

"Oh, I didn't eat it. I gave it to Claire."

"Why?"

"She said it was her favorite and she never gets to have it."

Claire, with her perfectly styled hair and designer clothing, was from one of the wealthiest families. She picked on me mercilessly. But I wanted her to like me so badly that I gave her my candy.

My mom told me it made her cry. I sometimes cry for the little girl I was too. The child who would become an adult trying to earn acceptance by giving away pieces of herself.

How do you teach a child to be empathetic and kind without making them a target for bullies? I still wonder about that today.

****

My very early childhood wasn't all bad, though.

One of the dairymen from church had a small Shetland pony named Stardust that his children had outgrown

The dairyman told my dad she could live on the grass outside the fence. "Just tie her out on a rope."

And so, as a very little girl, I had a pony I learned to ride bareback with no shoes on.

I don't know how old I was when the dairyman came back and told me he needed to take Stardust back because his grandchildren were old enough to ride her.

I cried and cried and cried. But Dad explained it was the right thing to do, so I had to give her back.

As an adult, I realized Stardust was getting really old and the dairyman was trying to protect me from her dying. I think it would have been easier to accept her death than having her taken away.

Around my eighth birthday, Dad decided to take a job teaching music at the local public high school. He called it "an opportunity to bring God to the heathens."

Maybe it helped the finances; I'm not sure. Life didn't feel that much different to me.

It could have been that Dad didn't share the financial numbers with Mom so she didn't know we were doing better.

There always seemed to be money for his projects: buying cattle, random projects outside, taking the boys camping. But Mom was still pinching pennies, washing baggies to reuse, saving butter and yogurt containers, never buying herself a new dress. Even when Dad gave her money to do so. She carried scarcity deep inside her and couldn't put it down.

Once in a while, Dad's money priorities worked in my favor: he bought me a pony for $200 from the school janitor (Dad was always trying to convert him to Christianity).

The pony's name was Whiskey, but Dad was adamant that was an ungodly name, so we changed it to Thunder.

Thunder could be ornery with other people, but for me, he was my best friend. He came with a small saddle, but I had learned to ride Stardust bareback so I didn't use it.

We learned to take small jumps together. He could pull a buggy and many of my siblings learned to ride on him.

Dad often bragged to his friends about what a great little horsewoman I was.

I soaked it up. It made me feel loved. I didn't realize I was starved for his approval.

I was in my twenties, living in North Carolina, and at work when my dad called to let me know they had to put Thunder down.

Even now, as I type this, there are tears rolling down my cheeks and a painful lump in my throat. My dog Nebula just got up and put her front paws on my leg. Animals just have a way of knowing when we are sad.

I still love that pony with my whole soul.

****

In fifth grade, I was moved to a tiny co-op school where the parents were the teachers.

My brother and I took the city bus to school and got there well before classes started. We would entertain ourselves outside until someone arrived to let us in.

We had PACEs (Packet of Accelerated Christian Education), small booklets we had to read and basically teach ourselves. Except for Bible. That was taught to the whole school first thing in the morning by one of the main parents.

I graduated from eighth grade, part of a class of two.

I was then sent to the high school where my dad taught, and that's when I started to notice how strange our family was.

There were so many rules I had to follow that other kids thought were weird.

My dad would say, "We are [our family name]. We are better than that."

I didn't realize that he was creating an identity tied to a last name I wasn't going to be allowed to keep.

Chapter 2
High School

The first day I walked onto campus as a student, I felt like an outsider. I spent the next four years trying and failing to fit in.

I had been on campus before, but only as a teacher's kid. Now I had to navigate it alone while surviving the crazy politics of teenage life.

I was a strange combination of mature for my age yet completely naive, my world tightly controlled by my parents.

Everything in my life had to be pre-approved: being sent to the co-op school run by devout Christian parents, the handful of families I was allowed to babysit for, and a constant reminder that time with outsiders put my soul at risk.

I could interact with adults really well.

At one of the political events my dad took me to, someone asked me about school and I confidently told him I was a freshman. He replied, "Where are you going to college?"

He looked stunned and embarrassed when I explained I was a freshman in high school.

Dealing with kids my own age? I was completely lost.

Add together my being a teacher's kid, having a homeschool-style education, my family's staunch Christian beliefs and far right politics, plus my dad's constant mantra of "You're better than that," and you can imagine how judgmental and holier-than-thou I was.

Not to mention the rules Dad demanded I follow. Rules that weren't just about me, but about keeping our family "set apart" because outsiders were morally suspect.

1. If I wasn't in class or at track practice, I had to be in his classroom. I wasn't allowed to be out mingling with "the heathens," a term we used without irony for anyone outside our belief system.

2. If a boy asked me out, I was not allowed to say yes or no. I had to say, "You have to ask my dad." A few boys were brave enough to do it. They got what I called "the God speech." A mini-sermon about purity, God's will, and the dangers of dating. And after listening politely were always

told no. (This is important to remember for later.)

3. No dancing, no secular music, and absolutely no time alone with boys.

Let's keep piling it on. I was also a straight A student. I graduated valedictorian with a GPA of 4.25 (I took college-prep classes that were worth more than four points on the scale.)

Years later, when I was in college in my thirties and studying psychology, I realized my dad had traits on the autism spectrum.

I learned to communicate like he did. I was blunt, honest, and open with my opinions. Just like my father treated me. In our world, this was considered "just speaking the truth," even if it crushed you.

The idea that words could hurt was brushed off as weakness; truth mattered more than feelings.

Besides, if it was true, it *shouldn't* hurt your feelings. Unless you were "too thin-skinned," a phrase I heard a lot.

If you thought I was a misfit at the private grade school, this was ten times worse.

Kids put gum in my hair on purpose and refused to play tag with me when I was in grade school. Why would I expect my peers to be kind to me in high school?

The rejection wasn't new. Just meaner. There was a group of girls who regularly jerked down my gym shorts while laughing and pointing. It happened so often I started to choose my underwear based on its ability to stay up when I got pantsed.

But I didn't realize that life could be any different. My dad portrayed the outside world as a moral wasteland. Public school kids were to be pitied or avoided. Kindness toward them was fine as long as I didn't start thinking or acting like them.

Life moved on, and I tried to be the ideal daughter by the standards I'd been taught: holy, obedient, quiet, unseen.

It wasn't just about pleasing my parents. It was about proving my worthiness to God and avoiding eternal damnation.

Failure as a daughter meant risking punishment from an angry, vengeful God.

And the church elders, whose regular home visits dripped with judgment, were quick to quote the Bible to reinforce exactly how I was expected to live.

****

Being treated like the third 'adult' in the house was normal for me. I often took my youngest siblings with me when I drove to the dairy to get six gallons of milk twice a week, or on small grocery runs thirty minutes into our one-stoplight town.

Words can't convey how stressful grocery shopping with a toddler was.

I had a woman scream at me that I was everything that was wrong with America; having a child out of wedlock. When she finally came up for air and said, "What do you have to say for yourself?" I replied in a shaky voice, "This is my brother." She just stormed off without apologizing.

When I was about fifteen, Mom was recovering from a medical issue and I was expected to do all of the weekly grocery shopping for the family.

Mom would go through the weekly flyer, make a list in aisle order, separate the coupons, write the check, sign it, and send me on my way.

I wasn't old enough to be driving legally yet and was terrified about getting pulled over.

But I felt the most like a fraud at checkout when the cashier, who knew me, made me put my thumbprint on the check. My stomach knotted and heart pounded. I was sure everyone was watching and thinking I was a criminal.

The grocery budget was so tight that Mom got angry when I came home with two five-pound bags of sugar, instead of one ten-pound bag.

The list just said, "10lbs sugar."

They were out of ten-pound bags, so it made sense to me to get two five-pound bags instead. I hadn't realized the larger bags were on sale.

When I got home, Mom frowned as she unpacked the groceries, asking sharply if they'd given me the sale price on the sugar.

When I said no, she huffed, rolled her eyes, and demanded to know why I hadn't asked for a raincheck, then berated me about "wasting money."

I bowed my head, trying not to cry, feeling like a complete failure.

Mom wasn't being malicious. She was overwhelmed with so many children, dealing with her health and running a household. It was just how things were.

The School Play

I have some intensely devastating memories of my father (who, I want to remind you, does actually love me) saying incredibly hurtful things to me. This one happened after a school play.

I had wanted to take an acting class, and because it fit into my schedule and fulfilled the credit requirements, my father gave me permission to take it.

I had so much fun. The creative expression. The little bit of freedom that came with rehearsals and set building after school.

It was enough to overcome the fact that a couple of girls in the class weren't very nice to me.

Sadly, I only got to take it for one semester. Dad found out that I was using the "freedom" I had to see a boy I liked after rehearsal.

But that one semester left me with an emotional scar so deep I still carry the hurt of it today.

This is what happened:

The night of the production, I excitedly got ready for my very first time being on stage, other than singing in church.

I had two parts. A small part as an old lady sitting on a park bench talking with her friends and the main part of a "flirty" bank teller who, it was hinted at, was a streetwalker by night.

Dad sat in the audience with three of my younger siblings.

The show went off with only a few hiccups and after the applause and breakdown of the set Dad said we could go to McDonald's for sundaes. An unexpected treat.

We had to share one sundae between two siblings, which meant agreeing on the flavor or getting nothing.

On the twenty-minute ride from school to McDonald's, Dad talked about the performance, the lighting, the different actors, and how well my siblings did sitting through the show.

I waited expectantly for him to say something positive about me.

He was bragging on one of my friends as we were finishing our sundaes and I couldn't take it anymore. I said, "Dad, you've complimented everyone in the show but me…"

I trailed off expectantly, assuming I would get quick grin and hear, "Of course you did a great job!"

What he actually said was, "It's not acting if it's who you really are."

My breath caught in my throat. My chest burned. My face heated with shame. My father, the one person in the world I desperately wanted approval from, had just called me a streetwalker.

It was all I could do not to cry. But crying was for sissies. If he saw me cry, he would scoff that I was too thin-skinned.

I pressed my tongue hard against the roof of my mouth, took a long deep breath through my nose, and held it while I fed the last of my ice cream to my sibling.

It was a hard way to learn not to fish for compliments.

That wasn't the first time he had been needlessly mean. He had once "playfully" hit me so hard with a croquet mallet at a picnic that it left a welt on my leg.

When I went to the car to cry in secret, he followed me to say, "That's for a time you did something wrong, and I didn't catch you."

As an adult I told him it was sinful not to ask for forgiveness when you did something wrong, like hurting someone by accident.

Later he would call me a "juvenile delinquent," say I won our small-town beauty pageant because I ran against "cows," and claim I was valedictorian only because "It's easy to look like an eagle when you're being compared to turkeys."

The message was clear: You are nowhere near good enough.

You only succeed when other people don't try.

You aren't special.

Being proud of yourself is a sin.

I've spent decades unlearning those lessons. And I might need a lifetime to truly stop believing them.

Chapter 3:
My First Real Job

trigger warning — sexual assault

I don't remember my very first paid job. It was probably cleaning out the family Suburban for a dollar or pulling weeds for neighbors. But I do remember the first time I had a "real" job.

I was in tenth grade when a man on a beautiful buckskin horse rode up the road and onto our property.

I saw him through the window talking to Dad. A few minutes later, my brother came in and told me Dad wanted to see me.

I went outside and learned that the guy was looking for a farmhand type person to help him train roping horses. He had asked my dad about my brother, but while he *could* ride, he wasn't into horses the way I was.

Dad suggested me instead.

He told Dad to bring me to the horse ranch a few days later and he would see how I did. Dad agreed and took the address before the horse and rider went back the way they came.

On the appointed day Dad and I took the truck to the ranch. We had passed the driveway many times but had never had a reason to go up it.

It was long, curving up the hill and splitting off, with one part going to the right and up to a massive house and the other continuing back to an enormous horse barn.

They bred and raised Arabian horses, but the guy who would become my boss lived in a trailer near the barn and used the grounds to train world-class cutting and roping horses.

As Dad drove up and parked near the fence next to the barn, I noticed that same gorgeous horse saddled and standing lazily near the gate to the arena.

I soon learned his name was Obi-John and that he was a multiple-time national champion stud.

My "interview" was to ride Obi-John so the boss could decide if I had what it took to work for him.

Okay. Easy enough.

I hopped on, they adjusted my stirrups and I headed into the arena.

From the fence the boss yelled commands at me.

I had never ridden such an amazing horse in my life. We cut back and forth, changed leads, galloped full speed, and slid to a stop.

Even if I didn't get the job, it was worth the trip just to ride that horse.

My dad and the boss were in for a surprise when I finally trotted back over to the fence.

It turned out that the girth, the strap that goes under the horse to hold the saddle in place, hadn't been tightened properly and was hanging loose.

The boss said, "You're clearly a very well-balanced rider to be able to do all of that and not have the saddle slide out from under you."

He tightened the girth. I dismounted, and he offered me the job.

Just like that, I had my first job with regular hours.

I liked my boss. I thought of him like a grandpa. We got along well and it was fun to work with the horses.

Because I was strong and light, I was often the first person to get on a young horse, and my boss would say ridiculous things like, "Don't let 'em throw you!" as I hung on to a bucking two-year-old for all I was worth.

I would think, "It's not my *plan* to get thrown."

Before long, my job expanded to include going up the road to a different farm that bred racehorses.

Our job there was to barn-break the foals. Teaching them basic manners like how to be led with a halter, have their feet cleaned, and get a bath without losing their minds.

Working with the babies was fun, and I learned a lot about training animals, skills I now use to teach Nebula to do circus tricks.

Sadly, this story isn't as lighthearted as you might hope.

One Saturday afternoon, we had just finished working with a colt I nicknamed "Punkin," and I was in the stall with his mother when my boss came in behind me. I thought nothing of it. We worked in close quarters together all the time.

I turned toward him to see what he wanted and he was *way* too close to me. I tried to back up to get out of his way but I was against the stall wall.

On my left I had a broodmare and my boss was blocking any movement to the right.

I wasn't scared. My brain just couldn't compute what was happening.

He pushed his hips into me and shoved me into the wall with his body weight as one hand wrapped around my head. His mouth came down aggressively on mine, forcing my lips apart with his tongue.

His free hand came up under my shirt, his fingers shoving under my bra to painfully knead and squeeze my small breast.

I was in so much shock that it felt like I stood there and let it happen for minutes. In reality, I'm sure it wasn't more than a few seconds.

I pushed him off. "What are you *doing*?"

I don't remember what he said, how we got the horses put away or riding in his truck to go home.

I didn't tell anyone because I knew my dad would blame me.

I had heard him talk too often about women "deserving" what they got because of how they were dressed or where they were or whatever victim blaming thing he would come up with.

My dad and my boss were becoming friends, so that wasn't strange when my dad announced he had invited my boss over for dinner, but it was *super* weird for me.

I thought I would just sit on the other side of the table and it would be okay. But then Mom said: "Hey why don't you sit next to Boss?"

What was I going to do? Make a scene there in front of everyone? (Side note from adult Robyn: Yes. Yes, you absolutely make a scene.)

The moment I took my seat, his leg, in jeans he paid me to iron, pressed into my thigh.

As Boss and Dad talked about horse training, rope braiding and whatever other inane thing they were discussing, I was desperately trying to keep my boss's hand from working its way up my leg to my crotch.

I was so trained to be a "good girl" and not make men uncomfortable that I sat at my parents' dinner table and let him try to grope me.

After dinner, when I couldn't get away from him fast enough, my mom finally noticed something was off.

I told her what happened, although not with any detail. I think I said something vague like, "He tried to kiss me at the barn and he kept putting his hand on my leg under the table."

Until well into adulthood I had no idea what happened after that. All I knew was that Dad had talked to him and my boss claimed I had been flirting with him.

I was only fifteen or sixteen. He was well over sixty. I was most certainly *not* flirting with him.

I expected my dad to be angry. Maybe at me first, but then for sure at my boss. On TV, dads get mad and want to beat guys up for assaulting their little girl.

That isn't what I got.

Dad explained flatly that he told my boss not to do that again, and I should go back to work.

Years later, when I asked why he made me go back, Dad defended himself. At the time he thought my life's work might be with horses and I needed the experience. He told me he never let me go there alone again, as if that made what happened okay.

I don't remember him being there. But if he said he was, maybe he was. I do know my boss never groped me again.

That was the first time something like that happened to me. But sadly, it wouldn't be the last. It happened twice more before I was eighteen.

Chapter 4

The Second Time I was Assaulted

trigger warning — sexual assault

It was a hot spring day in the Central Valley, and my track coach had just told us we were going to run *another* 200-yard sprint.

I was the only girl on the track team, so of course I was running with the guys. And it wasn't uncommon for me to beat several of them.

We lined up, shoulder to shoulder. Hot. Sweaty. Exhausted.

I saw the smoke from the starter pistol before I heard the pop it made.

We launched ourselves off the line and started jockeying for position near the inside lane.

As we came around the corner, I realized the guy running to my right was starting to pinch into me. He wasn't far enough ahead of me to cut in yet!

I yelled, "Don't cut me off!"

It was too late. In slow motion I watched as the cleat of my right shoe caught in his heel, pulling my foot out from under me.

I skidded down the track, hip, elbow, then shoulder scraping raw.

I came to a stop and knew I was hurt pretty badly. I could hear the coach calling out times as my teammates crossed the finish line.

I pulled myself off the ground. My hip was on fire and I couldn't see. I was going into shock, although I didn't know it then.

I started walking toward the sound of my coach's voice, doing my best to feel the side of the track with my left foot.

I remember the boys laughing. Someone told me later he had been driving past when it happened and had to pull over because he was laughing so hard.

(I have never understood why people think it's funny when someone gets hurt.)

When I got to the finish line, my teammates were milling around as Coach set up the next exercise. No one checked on me and my coach barely looked at me when he told me I could be done for the day.

I walked, by myself and still barely able to see, several hundred yards to the locker room.

What I remember next is standing naked from the waist down in the tub at home, using a hand mirror to see as I picked sand, stones, and grit out of the deep, blood-red raspberry on my hip.

The skin was raw and oozing.

My mom was in the kitchen trying to make dinner and, I'm sure, dealing with a toddler. I heard my dad almost yell, "[Mom's name], get in there and help your daughter!"

Mom stormed in. She was clearly flustered and annoyed.

She grabbed a plastic-bristled scrub brush and began scrubbing my raw, bleeding skin. Her jaw was tight, as if I was an inconvenience.

I couldn't breathe. I sucked in air through my nose as I gritted my teeth and tried to keep from twisting away.

When she stopped, she said, "There. It's clean enough." The brush clattered into the tub as she threw it down before walking out and slamming the door behind her.

I still have a scar on my hip and if you look closely, you can see where the flesh was torn away by the brush along with the rocks and sand.

I cleaned the open wounds on my elbow and shoulder, breathing through the stinging pain. Then I sprayed it all with an antibiotic spray meant for cattle that Dad had given me. It was bright neon yellow and burned like fire, worse than when I first fell.

It made the oozing mostly stop. And according to the package it had a second benefit of keeping flies out of lacerations. But hey, it worked.

The next day I showed up at track practice in baggy shorts, my hip wrapped as best I could in an Ace bandage, yellow cow-antibiotic showing around the edges.

My coach asked me to unwrap it so he could assess how injured I really was. He took one look and said, "You can't run like that. Go home."

My teammates snorted and rolled their eyes. One said, "I thought you were ugly before. Now you're hideous." They were all laughing as I walked away.

But, as traumatic as that injury was, it might have saved me from something even worse.

****

The following Saturday, I had the opportunity to babysit for someone new. She was a referral from a teacher at school who I babysat for pretty often.

I had said no at first because there wasn't a vehicle for me to drive, and it was too far for me to ride my horse. (She was a beautiful palomino named Moriah who I exercised for a friend of my parents.)

But as luck would have it, the teacher friend said I could borrow her Jeep named "Tickld Pink."

So, on Saturday morning I drove up to a large house in a nice neighborhood a little before the requested time of 8 AM.

I parked in the street and walked up to ring the doorbell.

An attractive woman in the early 30s answered the door. I stuck my hand out as I introduced myself. She shook it absentmindedly, said her name was Julie, and invited me in.

The next several minutes was all the usual stuff. Meet the baby: a little girl who wasn't quite walking. Toys and diapers are here. Please feed the baby breakfast and eat whatever you want. Yep. Normal.

As she was gathering her things to leave, she told me she was going boating with friends and should be back sometime in the early afternoon.

If I had listened to my intuition, I would have noticed she didn't have a beach bag. She wasn't wearing a swimsuit, and her clothing was more picnic than boating. But my conscious mind didn't catch that.

She walked out the door, casually turning back before closing it and said, "Oh, my husband is still sleeping. He will get up at some point and go to work."

Wait. What?

But before I could get my brain to process what she said and open my mouth to reply, she closed the door and walked to the street to get in the passenger seat of a car idling at the curb behind the Jeep.

I should have gone after her. My gut was screaming at me.

But the part of me trained to obey adults, to be nice and friendly, kept me frozen behind the closed door as I watched them drive away.

Now I was in charge of the baby, so I might as well make the best of it.

I fed her, changed her, and was sitting on the living room floor playing with her when I heard a male voice behind me say, "Hi. Who are you?"

I spun around to see a full-grown man, wearing only boxer briefs, standing in the kitchen holding a coffee cup and grinning at me.

(Thinking about it now, how weird is that? A stranger is in your house playing with your baby, and you're just… making coffee and grinning about it?)

I was embarrassed because he was mostly naked but stammered out, "I'm Robyn. I'm the babysitter."

He smirked, "Are you now?" and turned back to the coffee pot.

As the smell of fresh brewed coffee wafted through the room, he came over, still in just his underwear, to sit on the couch near where I was on the floor with the baby and said, "Where's Julie?"

Even my teenage brain thought it was odd that his wife had made plans, scheduled a babysitter, and left the house while he was sleeping without telling him.

But I replied, "She told me she was going to the lake with friends and would be back this afternoon. That you're going to work."

He looked at me in that creepy way men look at girls and said, "I might not have to go to work right away."

I started to get up. "If you're going to be home, I can just go."

"No, no. I need to shower and have phone calls to make. Please stay." He stood and walked away sipping his coffee.

I should have left. But once again, respectful, polite Robyn, who hadn't been taught to trust her gut, stayed.

As I continued to play with the baby, I wondered what I was supposed to do. I couldn't just leave with the baby. Kidnapping was not something I wanted to explain and I had no way to reach Julie.

Even if I could use the house phone without him catching me, my parents were both out at events with my siblings.

I didn't know the home phone number for the teacher who had referred me to this job.

Besides, he hadn't "done" anything. Maybe I was just being paranoid.

I heard the shower running and then him talking on the phone, not loudly enough for me to hear the conversation. Just enough to know he was in the house.

The baby needed to be changed again, and I was thinking I would see if there was some fruit or something I could eat when he came back into the living room.

He sat on the arm of the couch, this time wearing shorts and a t-shirt. "I wonder what my wife was thinking, hiring such a beautiful woman to babysit."

I frowned, thinking, *I'm not really a woman*. But out loud I said, "Thank you?"

I picked up the baby to go change her. But to do that I had to walk past him. He noticed the abrasion on my elbow and shoulder.

"What happened?" He touched my arm to stop me.

"I got tripped at track practice." I dodged away and walked to the nursery.

When I got done, he was sitting on the couch. I went to the kitchen, holding the baby on my hip and opened the fridge to look for something to eat.

He stood up. "You look good with a baby on your hip." Then added, "Are you hungry? I can make you breakfast."

He came into the kitchen and stood way too close to me, blocking me in because the refrigerator door was open.

"No thanks. That's okay."

I used the baby to push him out of the way so I could close the fridge and escape back to the living room.

He made himself a full breakfast of eggs, bacon, and toast and sat at the kitchen bar facing me as he ate and drank more coffee.

He rambled about being a good cook, and having a good job.

I played with the baby, facing the kitchen, and thinking about how this situation was going to play out after I fed her lunch and put her down for a nap.

But it wasn't going to come to that.

After he finished eating, he came into the living room and sprawled on the floor next to me. He smelled like coffee, toast and cologne.

I asked if he wanted to play with his daughter and moved to get out of the way.

He grabbed my hand. "No. I want to play with you. You are so beautiful."

As I shifted to get away from him, he moved suddenly, pulling my hand toward him while pushing my other shoulder toward the floor.

Just like the last time a grown man put his hands on me, my brain froze, then panicked. I was pinned to the floor and he was trying to kiss me while working his knee between my legs.

The taste of his breakfast made me want to gag.

He whispered something about not wanting to hurt me, just wanting to kiss me and how amazing I was while holding me down with his body weight.

Then he grabbed my butt and lower hip, I guess to try to shift me. I screamed in pain as his fingers dug into my raw flesh through my shorts and the bandage.

He shoved himself off of me and jumped to his feet. "What the hell is wrong with you?"

I scrambled over the couch without replying, my heartbeat pounding in my ears.

He held up his hands and moved to block the door, "Wait! Let's just talk!"

I stood clutching my bag to my chest, eyes wide with panic.

Right then the front door slammed open, crashing into the table next to it, sending the decorations on top shattering across the floor.

Julie stood in the doorway, fury etched on her face.

The next few moments were chaos. Both of them screaming, the baby crying, and me desperately trying to get out of the house.

Julie raged that she had suspected him of cheating, that she had used me to try to catch him in the act, and that she had been watching through binoculars from the neighbor's house.

When she moved toward him, I made a dash for the Jeep.

She yelled from behind me, "Wait! Let me pay you!"

I stopped. I grew up poor and I wasn't going to pass on getting paid.

She ran out, pushed cash into my hands, and went back into the house, slamming the door without another word.

I jumped in the Jeep and drove off as fast as I could. But at the bottom of the hill, it stalled. My heart pounded as I frantically tried to restart it. The engine turned over but wouldn't catch.

I was afraid he was going to come after me.

I paused, closed my eyes, took a breath to calm my panic. It started. I drove home. It was over.

But less than a week later, I was riding Moriah down the road when I heard a car coming up behind me and slowing down.

Not uncommon. Sometimes people did that, being respectful of the horse. Other times it was guys who wanted to catcall.

This time it was him, driving a fancy little red sports car with the top down.

As he came up next to me, he said, "I thought that was you. You know, I can afford to take really good care of you. My wife doesn't need to know."

My stomach lurched, and I'm sure I made a disgusted face. I mumbled, "No thank you," as I turned Moriah into the walnut orchard, pushing her into a fast trot to get away from him.

Eventually, I could recognize the sound of that car long before he got close. It always made my stomach drop as a wave of fear passed through me.

He drove by several times over the next few months. I made sure I was never in sight of the road or that I took my horse into the fields and orchards when I heard him coming.

Thankfully, I don't think he ever figured out exactly where I lived.

I never told my parents. Why bother? What could they do at that point, except blame me?

My hip healed from the track injury, but the scar remains. Reminding me of the girl I was and that the woman I am now is able to handle herself very differently.

If I hadn't been injured, who knows what would have happened.

About a year later, Julie called to say she was getting divorced and asked if I would babysit.

I declined.

Chapter 5
The Last Time Each of My Parents Hit Me

I was spanked *a lot* as a child. I remember being spanked for hitting my brother. Even as a kid, I knew it was hypocritical.

My parents hit me when they were mad, so I hit other kids when I was mad. I didn't have any other regulation tools.

Many of the spankings, often with a wooden spoon, have blurred together and disappeared into the recesses of my memory over time.

I can still hear the sound of the kitchen drawer being jerked open, jamming, slamming shut, and then back open again.

That sound meant only one thing: Run!

But the last time my mom hit me stands out. It was the first time I got brave, and took a sliver of control.

****

I had a sharp tongue and good language skills, and talking back was my only weapon.

As an adult, my middle sister told me that she used to wonder why I fought with them so much.

She asked, "Why didn't you just do what they said, rather than getting into it with them and losing all the time?"

But fighting with them was what I chose to do, and this story starts with Mom and me going back and forth about something.

I was a teenager, fourteen, fifteen, sixteen. I don't really know. But I was close to the same height as Mom was.

She was sweeping the kitchen floor; there was always so much dirt tracked in from outside, and I was standing near the back door.

My mom always seemed to live on the edge of overwhelm. She had too much on her plate. Multiple kids, a house to manage, and a Christian marriage that demanded meek, godly submission.

I clearly said something that sent her over the edge because she flipped the broom up, grabbed it near the bristles, and started swinging it at me.

When I backed into the corner to protect myself, she couldn't swing it from the side and instead brought it over her head and came straight down toward me.

I reached up and caught it with both hands before it hit me.

For a moment we stood, struggling over it, until I wrenched it away from her.

She backed away. We both knew I had the weapon now.

I stared at her for two heartbeats. Then threw the broom across the floor.

I growled, "I'm leaving," as I stormed out the door.

I have no idea where I was going or what my plan was. I just started walking down the road away from the house.

I wasn't going anywhere in particular. I wasn't even walking in the direction we usually took out of the small valley we lived in because I knew Dad would be coming home from that way, and I didn't want to run into him.

I was gone less than an hour and might have walked a couple of miles when my dad came tearing around a corner in our blue 1963 pickup truck.

He stomped on the brake so hard it fishtailed and nearly hit me.

He shouted, "Get in the truck!" as he reached over and flung open the passenger door.

There was no way I was getting in the truck when he was that angry.

I defiantly replied, "No. Not when you're so mad."

He glared. "Fine. Ride in the back."

I assessed the situation for a moment, then slammed the door closed and jumped into the bed of the truck. He spun the truck around and drove home.

Nothing was ever said about it. But my mom never hit me again.

****

The last time my dad hit me, I was closer to sixteen than fourteen. The story isn't nearly as dramatic, and I don't remember most of the details.

Dad and I were arguing in the living room in front of the wood stove, the only source of heat in the house.

There wasn't a fire in it, and the window air-conditioning unit behind him wasn't running, so it might have been early spring or late fall.

What I had done or not done that started the problem? I have no idea.

What did I say that resulted in him hitting me? Again, no clue.

But Dad backhanded me across the face.

It was the only time I ever remember him hitting me in the face.

He wore a large class ring on his right hand, and it caught me just right, smashing into my teeth and bloodying my lip.

We both stared at each other, jarred by the violence.

Nothing more was said. I just turned away and went to clean up the blood.

Strangely, I don't remember anyone asking about my bruised mouth. Maybe it didn't bruise that badly.

Maybe I just didn't have anywhere to go for several days.

Whatever the case, that was the last time my father ever lost his temper and hit me.

****

There is something about remembering the last time. It wasn't the worst time or even the most emotionally damaging time.

I didn't have to say *never again* out loud, but there was a very clear moment when we all knew. No more.

The woman I would one day be: clear, self-protective, loud when it mattered, was still deeply buried.

But she flickered in these moments.

Chapter 6
How I Met My First Ex-Husband

trigger warning — sexual assault

The summer I was sixteen, between my sophomore and junior years of high school, my dad decided we would drive to Chicago for his parents' fiftieth wedding anniversary.

We packed the Suburban, hitched up our small camper, loaded up all six kids (and Mom, five months pregnant) and hit the road.

I had gotten my license the day after my sixteenth birthday and could now drive legally. Dad and I traded driving shifts while Mom handled crowd control from the passenger seat.

We stopped in Colorado to visit church friends, where I met a boy who might have been a wonderful partner for the girl I never got the chance to become. If only my dad had been willing to wait for us to grow up just a little bit.

He was almost two years younger than I was and lived on a cattle ranch that was even more rural than where I lived.

He was funny and sweet and I think I was his first kiss. I'm pretty sure I broke his heart when I had to write him just a year later and tell him I was engaged.

I feel sad for those two young souls whose paths crossed so briefly and then were forced apart by circumstance.

****

What I didn't know when we left Colorado was that my destiny had already been set in motion. I was about to meet the man who I would be promised to in marriage less than a year later.

On the second day after arriving in Chicago, we were all at someone's pool: cousins, in-laws, aunts, uncles, pretty much everyone.

I was desperately starved for any kind of attention. Even the wrong kind of attention made me feel better about myself.

I love my mom and know she did the best she could, but nurturing and guiding a teenage girl was something she didn't have the time or tools to do while raising multiple small children.

And my dad? Well, my relationship with him went from me being "Daddy's little girl" to him calling me a "juvenile delinquent" when I started to look more like a woman than a child.

I had been raised to believe that my only value was my body; a woman is only useful as a wife and a mother, and the only way I could get into heaven was to have children. I couldn't do that if I couldn't attract a husband.

The biggest insult my dad could throw was to say that no one was ever going to want to marry me (followed closely by calling me "two eggs sunny side up" because I was athletic and flat chested).

Add in my emotional immaturity and painful naivety, and I was far too friendly, too deferential, too accommodating, and much too handsy for a sixteen-year-old girl.

If I had been ten and wanted grown men to play with me and toss me in the pool, that would be one thing. But I wasn't a child.

I didn't know then that I was already an expert at reading people and reshaping myself to keep them comfortable. Just as a good, godly woman should.

I held eye contact a little too long. Tilted my head just so when I laughed too hard at something that wasn't that funny.

Years later, I would describe it as being able to be the perfect partner for anyone, for about eight months. Until I realized I had lost myself in the process.

All those little pieces added up to something that looked like flirting; even though I never meant to.

Two of my male cousins were at that pool party.

Shadow, who was two years older than me and lived locally. He wasn't paying any attention to me.

The other, Hunter, was twenty-seven. He was eleven years older than me in age, and light-years older in life experience. He had driven in from North Carolina.

He tickled me and snapped my bathing suit straps. Dunked me underwater and suggested I get on his shoulders for a chicken fight with his sister and her husband.

I was special, chosen.

When his fingers lingered when he "accidentally" brushed against my breast, I pretended not to notice. I didn't want to make him feel awkward.

****

Late in the afternoon I was sitting on a picnic blanket helping my youngest sibling eat watermelon when Hunter walked up and loomed over me.

"Do you want to go to the arcade with me and Shadow?"

My breath caught in my throat. No. I did not want to go to the arcade with this grown man.

But my training kicked in and I replied, "I don't know. You'll have to ask my dad."

I figured that would be the end of it. It always had been.

I just went back to eating watermelon.

Less than thirty minutes later I was shocked to see Hunter holding his hand out to me and saying, "Your dad said you could go."

"What? How did that happen?"

"I walked up to him and said, 'Hey Uncle, can Robyn go with us to the arcade?' And he said, 'Sure, if you let me drive your car.'"

Hunter had a gorgeous, candy-apple red '76 Stingray Corvette.

Apparently, the price for taking me on a date was getting to drive a sports car.

I didn't want to go. But what was I supposed to do? My dad said yes, I couldn't very well go back on his decision.

(Note from adult Robyn: Yes, you can and you should. You absolutely have the authority to say no at any time to anyone and you don't even need a good reason.)

I accepted his help getting off the ground and we walked, him still holding my hand, toward his car where Shadow, who looked annoyed, was waiting.

As we got closer, I realized we had a problem. A Corvette is absolutely not designed for three people.

I started to say something about there not being room and that it wasn't a problem; I didn't need to go.

Shadow jumped right on that. He really wanted to go out trolling for girls in that car, and I was bringing down his game.

But Hunter just laughed, "We'll make it work. It'll be fine."

That meant I was going to be sharing a bucket seat with someone.

On the way to the arcade, I sat on Shadow's lap and neither of us was happy about it.

I had never been to an arcade. It was loud, dark, and smelled like stale cigarette smoke. The flashing lights and noise gave me a headache.

But I dutifully cheered and groaned at the appropriate moments as my cousins tried their luck at different games.

They offered to let me play but I hadn't brought any money. No problom, Hunter was happy to pay for me. But I didn't know how to play anything so I just shook my head and awkwardly said I'd rather watch.

It was getting late so I asked Hunter if my dad had told him what time I needed to be back. "Nope," was the only answer I got.

I then remembered my dad bragging to another father at church that I was "such a good kid" I didn't even need a curfew. I had pointed out to him that I didn't have a curfew because I wasn't allowed to leave the house.

But now that was a problem. I was out in an uncomfortable environment and I had no idea how to get out of it.

Finally, the guys decided they wanted to go somewhere else, so we headed outside.

A severe Midwestern thunderstorm was rolling through, and it was *pouring*. Fortunately, the roof of the building extended out and met the building on the other side.

As we walked the guys were talking about sexual conquests. Hunter was bragging that he had just laid some girl near Lake Michigan two days before coming to Chicago.

Shadow laughed and gave him a high five. I wrinkled my nose, pursed my lips and snorted while rolling my eyes.

Hunter pushed me "playfully" and said, "Oh come on. Don't be a prude."

He then noticed that there was an opening in the roof where water was pouring into a storm drain in the middle of the walkway.

Everyone was skirting around it as torrents of water splashed across the sidewalk.

Hunter grabbed my wrist and yelled, "Get her wet!"

Shadow grabbed my other arm and as I said, "No!" they pulled me through the downspout, laughing.

They thought it was hysterical. I was trying not to show that I wanted to cry.

I was completely soaked. Not just a little wet, drenched through to my skin and dripping. I knew I looked like a drowned raccoon with mascara running down my face.

The thunderstorm had dropped the outside temperature and the air-conditioned buildings felt ice cold. It wasn't long before I was shivering and my teeth were chattering.

I tried to bargain with them; they could just drop me off and then go back out without me.

Shadow was excited about going out without me. But when we got to the car, he realized I was still a soggy mess.

"She is soaked. I don't want her sitting on me."

Hunter replied, "Fine. You drive," and tossed Shadow the keys.

Now I was sitting in a bucket seat on the lap of a twenty-seven-year-old man. I could feel his erection pressing into my back, and he was accentuating every bump with a thrust of his hips.

I was mortified, embarrassed, and clearly *not* going to say anything.

I assumed they were going to bring me back to our grandparent's house where my family's camper was parked.

Instead, Hunter said he was ready to be done for the night too and told Shadow to drive to his parents' house; then Hunter would take me home.

When we pulled into Shadow's driveway, I was more than anxious to get out of the car.

The guys said goodnight and made plans to go out again the next night as I, still shivering, got back into the passenger's seat.

We were less than five minutes from our grandparents' house. As far as I was concerned, we couldn't get there soon enough.

But that's not what Hunter had planned.

When we got to the stop sign where I expected him to turn left, he turned right.

Confused, I spun to look at him, "Where are we going?"

He chuckled and said, "I can't take you home soaking wet. Let's just drive around until you dry off a little bit."

I didn't want to drive around. I wanted to go home, get out of my wet clothes, and go to bed.

But I didn't want to risk making him angry. And how was I going to explain being drenched to my dad?

I sat back in the seat and stayed silent, hoping I was just being dramatic. But deep down, I knew better.

****

I had no idea how long we drove around. He was talking, and I was mostly just listening. For once in my life, I really didn't have much to say.

I was too busy trying to keep track of where we were compared to our grandparents' house. But I soon realized I was completely lost and couldn't have found my way back if I had to.

And I was starting to get sleepy.

"Hey, I'm tired. Can we go back now?" I asked innocently.

Instead of replying, he turned into a dark parking lot. "I'm really enjoying your company. Can we please just talk a little longer?"

My sleepiness vanished. My heart pounded, every nerve suddenly on high alert.

He parked so the light from the street was behind him, shadowing his face but illuminating mine.

"You're…" his voice trailed off. "Mature, interesting, different than other girls."

I blushed at the compliment.

(I didn't know then that it was a classic line older men use to flatter little girls who don't know better.)

"I guess we could talk for a little while." Part of me knew it wasn't smart and a quiet voice in my mind was worried that my dad was going to be mad that I was out so long.

But the part of me that was starved for love and attention was basking in feeling seen by someone older and wiser.

He took off his seatbelt and turned his body toward me, reaching over to unclick mine as well. His arm brushed low across my stomach as he guided the buckle of my seatbelt toward the door.

"I love how fit you are. What do you do to stay in such great shape?"

I replied, talking about running track and working around the farm. I thought that was what he was actually asking.

He shifted in his seat, and his shorts gaped away from his leg. It was obvious he wasn't wearing underwear. I'd never seen a man like that before.

He opened his legs wider and smirked, "Do you like what you see?"

I jerked my eyes away and stammered as he continued, "It's okay. You can look."

"I really need to get back. I'm sure my dad is wondering where I am."

"You don't have to worry about your dad. Arcades are open late and you're with your cousins. He's not going to worry."

He set his hand on my leg. "You're safe with me. I promise."

But I wasn't.

Within minutes, his knees were wedged into his seat, one arm supporting his weight against my door, his tongue was in my mouth and I was desperately trying to keep his other hand out of my shorts.

The stubble on his face made my lips burn, and my neck was turned at a painful angle as my shoulder dug into the back of the seat. He smelled like beer and tasted breath mints.

He kept mumbling something about wanting to know how wet I was. In my naivete, I thought he was talking about the rain.

Never before or after did I have to fight so hard for my virginity as I did that night in that car.

I did manage to get home with it intact; but in a sad way, I was a tiny bit wiser.

When he finally brought me back, I felt embarrassed, violated, sinful, and yet somehow special and important.

(Adult Robyn: I know now that this is exactly what happens when a manipulative adult distorts the perception of a naive, young target.)

He came around the car and stood next to me, "You're really incredible. I had a wonderful time. It's really too bad we live so far apart."

He leaned in to kiss me but I stepped back, keenly aware that my dad or any of our relatives could be watching us.

All I said was, "Thanks" as I gave a little smile and walked toward the camper.

Everyone was asleep. As quietly as I could I peeled off my still-damp clothing, put on my nightgown, and climbed into bed beside my younger sibling.

The sting of whisker burn prickled my face. The feel of his hands on my body was forever etched into my memory.

I wouldn't tell anyone the truth about what happened that night for decades. I believed it was my fault, and that the shame was mine to carry.

Chapter 7
Dating a Hunter

The trip home from Chicago was uneventful, except for the wrong turn I made that sent us forty-five minutes in the wrong direction, and the suggestion that I should write Hunter a thank-you note for entertaining me that evening.

I'm not sure why I decided to write it. Maybe I wanted to pretend that night had just been an adult humoring his kid cousin at the arcade.

I wrote something, addressed it and put it in the mailbox one morning after we had stopped to spend the night with another friend of the church.

I thought better of sending it a little while later, and went out to the mailbox to get it. Unfortunately, the mail carrier had already come and the letter was on its way.

I drove the last leg of the trip home, pulling into our driveway in the early morning hours. When the phone rang a few hours later I was still asleep; a rare concession since my dad was usually very strict about it being a sin to sleep if the sun was up.

Dad brought the phone into my room, and held it out to me. "It's for you."

I opened my still sandy eyes and looked at the phone in confusion. Who would be calling me? And even more strange, who would be calling me that Dad will actually let me talk to?

I took the phone, thinking maybe it was my friend from down the street.

Head still on the pillow I groggily said, "Hello?"

A deep male voice with a southern drawl replied, "I have been calling your house twice a day for almost a week waiting for you to get home."

Hunter.

"Oh? Why?"

I couldn't wrap my brain around it. My dad, who always enforced a strict five-minute time limit on phone calls and had hung up on boys who called me, had woken me up to take a phone call, not from a boy, but from a man.

Hunter replied that he had gotten the thank-you card, that he thought it was very sweet, and that he was really happy to hear my voice again.

I was embarrassed and flattered at the same time.

He told me he had been thinking about "that night" and how amazing it was.

I didn't have a reply so I told him we had gotten in really late and that I had been asleep when he called.

His reply: "Do you sleep naked?"

My face went hot.

"I wear a nightgown."

"Hmm," he hummed deep in his throat. "That's too bad."

I giggled nervously. I didn't know what to say. So, I said nothing.

I don't know how the conversation ended but it was the start of him calling and me taking his calls because that was the polite thing to do.

He mostly wanted to talk about sexy things. How did I shave down there? (I didn't.)

Had I ever made out with a boy like we did in the car? (Clearly not.)

And more graphic things I didn't understand but pretended to so he wouldn't feel awkward.

I felt guilty and sinful for enjoying the attention.

A few months later, a boy from school I had a crush on called me. When my dad realized who I was talking to, he took the phone from me, said, "She has a boyfriend," and hung up on him.

Then he turned to me and said, "You're dating Hunter! You can't be talking to other boys."

I had a boyfriend?

I thought Hunter and I were just talking on the phone and writing some letters. This was the first I'd heard that he was my boyfriend, or that we were dating.

How could I be dating someone who lived three thousand miles away?

How did I have a boyfriend when he had never asked me to be his girlfriend?

I tried to explain that I didn't want Hunter to be my boyfriend. But got no support about how to tell him that or what it would look like to ask him to stop calling me.

I didn't want to hurt his feelings. So, I did the easiest thing: buried my discomfort and just went on taking his calls and savoring the attention.

I didn't realize that I was being groomed by everyone involved to be good and submissive.

I wanted to call the boy from school back and explain that I hadn't been the one to hang up on him. Dad didn't allow me to.

When I tried to talk to that boy at his locker the next day, he ignored me.

****

I also started to notice that Hunter didn't have what I considered even basic knowledge about the Bible. I referenced something about Abraham, Isaac and Jacob, who are the founding fathers of the Christian faith, and he was clueless.

He didn't even know anything about Noah and the flood.

This was unfathomable to me. I realize now that I was making the mistake of assuming that he was raised with the same fanatical Christianity that I was because his mother was my father's older sister.

He was not. I'm pretty sure he didn't even go to Sunday School as a child.

When I mentioned this to my dad, he decided that to fill the gap in Hunter's knowledge, we (the three of us) should start doing weekly Bible study together.

But instead of the regular adult Bible study I was already expected to do, we started going through a children's Bible storybook.

On Sunday afternoons I would call Hunter. He would talk about sex until my dad picked up the extension in the study, and then we would switch to talking about Bible stories I had memorized in grade school.

In addition to everything else, I feel like this should have been a red flag for my dad. He wouldn't let me go out with boys who "weren't Christian enough," but was more than willing to adjust for Hunter.

I was too naive to notice the discrepancy and too nice to say I didn't want to do it.

I also wonder how my dad never heard any of the smutty things being said to me as he got on the call.

On top of it all, I was expected to pay for those long-distance calls.

Every month, Dad would sit down with the phone bill, highlight all the calls to Hunter, total them up, and give me a bill. I paid him out of my babysitting and horse training money. After I tithed 10% to the church, of course.

I now know that I was being systematically isolated from anyone who could have been my friend. I wasn't allowed to be friends with any of the "heathens" at school.

The church we went to was an hour and a half away, so I couldn't make friends there (not to mention that I was so hick compared to the people there).

The neighbor girl my age I had been friends with wasn't someone Dad wanted me spending time with because she was Catholic (not a good enough Christian).

So, when a horse kicked me in November and broke my ankle, Hunter was the only person I could call to cry about my track season being ruined.

(It wasn't actually ruined. I healed quickly and was still able to run when the season started.)

When Hunter announced he was coming to visit for my seventeenth birthday in January, I was told that it was pretty special that he wanted to spend money to fly out to see me.

(It wasn't until I was in the process of getting divorced the second time that I finally realized that someone having money and being willing to spend it on you has nothing to do with them loving you.)

Hunter made reservations at the nicest (only) steakhouse in town.

Mom helped me do my hair. I wore my nicest dress. I did my makeup as best I could but realized when I went to the bathroom before dessert that I forgot to put on mascara. I was annoyed at myself about that.

Dad let us borrow the 1964 Ford Galaxie 500. It was a boat of a car with bench seats that you could sleep on.

When we arrived at the restaurant, Hunter told me not to get out, came around the car, opened my door and took my hand. How grown up and fancy.

I was surprised how dark it was inside. It smelled rich; like old wood, earth, and sautéed mushrooms.

They sat us at a small booth in a secluded corner that we had to step up to get into.

Once we were seated and looking at the menu, I realized I didn't know how to order. The only place we ever went out to eat as a family was pizza and I didn't do the ordering.

Hunter chose a bottle of wine and requested two wine glasses. (Legal drinking age in California was twenty-one.)

As the waiter walked away, I looked at Hunter wide eyed. He said, "Just be cool. It'll be fine."

The first sip of wine burned the back of my throat and made me cough. I tried to be discreet, but my eyes watered and I nearly gagged as I covered my mouth with a napkin. (Maybe it was a good thing I hadn't put on mascara.)

I was finally able to recover and drink some water. Hunter just kept looking at the menu and no one said anything.

He ordered for me. An expensive steak, which I was "eh" about, a loaded baked potato (I had never had one of those. Yummy!) and broccoli, which I don't think I ate.

I was trying so hard to act grown up. And I thought I was pulling it off.

However, let there be no mistake: I did not look mature for my age. Looking back at pictures, I looked every bit a child playing dress up.

The server didn't say a word, just turned a blind eye to a grown man buying alcohol for a child.

When I came back from the bathroom before dessert, there was a small, wrapped present sitting on the table.

I was excited because Hunter had told me several times that he liked to buy girls diamond earrings and the box was about that size.

Chapter 8
Pushing the VW Bug Uphill

During my junior year in high school, the baby blue VW bug my dad owned but I often drove started vapor locking.

It would just decide to stop running and you would have coast to the side of the road.

After being stranded a few times, my dad made an appointment at the local shop to have it fixed.

It wasn't really on the way to school, but the only viable option was to drop it off before school and then pick it up at the end of the day.

It seemed simple enough. I would drive the bug to the shop while my dad and my brother followed in another vehicle.

Once I got to the shop, I would fill out the paperwork, slip the keys through the drop-off slot in the door, then get in with Dad and my brother to make the twenty-five-minute drive to school.

I was ready to leave before they were and I remember thinking, "Maybe I should wait so they can follow right behind me."

Yet another instance of my intuition working overtime to protect me and me ignoring her.

I left anyway, figuring it would save time because I could have the paperwork done by the time they got to the shop. Besides, they would only be five minutes behind me.

I got two miles down the road (the same corner where Dad almost hit me with the truck in Chapter Five) when the engine vapor locked.

Annoying but no big deal. I just pulled over, knowing Dad could stop and pick me up and decide what we should do with the car.

Where I was stopped, the road curved to the right and went downhill.

The shoulder was wide and there was room to get the car all the way off the road (which isn't always the case on country roads).

As I sat in the car waiting (safer than standing outside the car), a school bus came from the opposite direction and stopped to pick up some kids on the other side of the road.

I remember being embarrassed that I was sitting there in a broken-down car.

In my rear view mirror I saw my dad coming... Then zoom! He drove right past me.

I thought, "He must not have thought it was safe with the school bus there. He's just going to find a place to turn around and come back."

I sat there considering where the next place to turn around was.

But as seconds, then minutes ticked by, I slowly realized he hadn't seen me.

But surely, when he gets to the repair shop and realizes I'm not there, he'll backtrack toward the house and pick me up.

I waited, not patiently, in a car that wouldn't start.

I was so focused on my responsibility of getting the car to the repair shop, and assuming that if Dad did come looking for me, he would be coming from that direction, that I decided my best course of action was to push the car toward town.

Looking back, that was ridiculous. I should have just left the car where it was and walked toward home.

To make the situation even stranger, I was wearing business clothes. I worked as a bank teller after school, and since there wasn't anywhere for me to change, I often wore my work clothes to school (which regularly got me mistaken for a teacher).

So there I was in a black skirt, button-down top, and dress shoes, pushing a VW bug.

I coasted it down the hills and huffed it up them.

I don't know how long I had been working at it when it occurred to me that if Dad was coming back, he would have been back by now, and that clearly, he had gone on to school without me.

I didn't think in words about what that said about his parenting skills. But it did sit hard on my heart, then and well into the future, that he didn't just call the principal and tell them that he and my brother were going to be late.

Instead, I was thinking about the fact that it was finals week, and it was a good thing my biology teacher had told me I could get a negative seven on her final and still get an A in the class, because it didn't look like I was going to be taking that final.

I was about three-quarters of the way up a very large hill when a pickup truck came flying by in the other direction. He slammed on the brakes, did an aggressive U-turn, and stopped next to me.

"What the hell are you doing?!" He was an older man. I would guess mid-forties. (Yes, that was older then.)

I stopped pushing the car but had to hold it in place so it didn't roll back down the hill. Wondering why he was yelling at me, I said something like, "It vapor locked so I'm pushing it."

He replied, "You're going to get yourself killed! With the sun and the hill, someone is going to hit you."

I didn't think it was really that unsafe, and I was almost to the top anyway.

He then said, "Let it roll down the hill and park it on the side over there." He pointed to a sandy washout next to the road.

I looked at him incredulously and thought, "I almost have it all the way up this hill and you're going to make me lose all that ground!"

But he was an adult and glaring at me, so being a "good girl" who listened to authority, I did what I was told.

Besides, apparently no one was missing me at home, so I had to figure this out myself.

I jumped in the car, no small feat since as soon as I let go it started rolling backward, and expertly maneuvered it onto the shoulder at the bottom of the hill.

He followed me down in his truck and said, "Let me take you to my buddy's house so you can call your parents."

I thought about that for a moment. A guy I don't know. In his truck. This is not a good thing.

I was also concerned that it was going to create all kinds of chaos if I left the bug and someone came back looking for me.

But I didn't see many other options, so I locked the car and got in the truck with him.

He drove me up the hill and into a neighborhood. (Incidentally, I think it was the same one where the babysitting incident in Chapter Four happened.)

We pulled into the driveway of a large house. He jumped out, motioning at me to follow him, saying, "Come on."

Despite my misgivings, I got out and followed him up to the house.

He opened the big front door like he owned the place, and we walked into a huge foyer that opened up into a living room decorated in a very masculine style.

He pointed to a table across the room, "Phone's over there."

I walked across the room, picked up the receiver, listened for a dial tone, and started to dial my home phone number.

Before I got all the way through dialing, I heard a commotion behind me.

I turned around, phone in hand, to see a second man, about the same age, with a beer gut in only tighty-whiteys, holding a shotgun and aggressively talking to the first guy.

I was so embarrassed that he was in his underwear that I turned around and continued dialing the phone.

I remember thinking, "If he's going to shoot me, there's not much I can do about it."

What was wrong with me that a guy with a shotgun didn't scare the hell out of me?

Unfortunately, the line was busy at home. I hung up and tried again while I listened to the two guys talking, first loudly and then more calmly, about the situation.

I tried a couple more times and couldn't get through. I turned around again. Fortunately, the second guy and his shotgun had gone back to the bedroom.

I said, "The line is busy."

I don't remember exactly how the conversation went, but eventually one of the guys decided the best thing to do with me was to just take me home.

I wasn't really a fan of telling them where I lived, but if they meant to hurt me, we wouldn't be standing there trying to figure out what our options were for getting me home.

The first guy drove me back past my broken-down car and let me out at the end of my parents' driveway.

I walked into the house to my mother angrily saying, "Where have you been?!"

I learned that my dad, having not found me at the repair shop where I was supposed to be, did indeed go on to school because he had finals to proctor and my brother had finals to take.

When he got there, he tried to call to let Mom know I was missing.

Unfortunately, my mom had called her mom after we had all left and was in a lengthy catch-up conversation, hence the line being busy.

In addition to all of that, my biology teacher had called my dad's classroom to make an accusation: "Do you know your daughter is *ditching* my final exam?"

I was a straight-A student and had never ditched anything in my life, so that was quite a jump for her to make. I was incensed that she assumed I was ditching rather than wondering if something might be wrong.

My dad told me he replied with something like, "She's not ditching. She's missing."

After some period of time, Dad finally decided to have the operator break into my mom's conversation with my grandmother. They had just hung up when I came through the back door.

(I am thinking about that now. How long could it have been between when Dad got to the repair shop, realized I was missing, and when I walked in the house? An hour? He must have waited at least thirty minutes after he arrived at school to have the operator break into Mom's conversation. That feels like a long time when your teenage daughter is missing.)

Mom brought me to school, in a bit of a huff because I had disrupted her plans for the day and she'd had to unexpectedly take the other children out of the house.

I walked into my biology final two hours late. With only an hour left to take it, I not only finished it, I aced it. My teacher never said anything to me about what happened or why I was late.

I have no idea who those two guys were or what their follow-up conversation looked like. I wonder if they ever tell this story.

Regardless, to this day I'm thankful that this turned out to be just one of my crazy life stories. There were a lot of opportunities where it could have ended very differently.

Chapter 9
I Guess I'm Marrying Hunter

In the spring after the VW Bug situation, I received a letter saying my GPA qualified me to run in our small-town beauty pageant.

I have no idea why Dad and Hunter let me run. The only question Dad asked was if there was a swimsuit section to the competition. When the answer was "no" he said I could enter and Hunter agreed.

I used my own money to buy a gown for the formal section and practiced for weeks until I could get my hair into a French twist by myself.

There were only four of us competing, and we had been given four questions they were going to put into a hat to draw out and ask us.

I had reviewed the questions but hadn't prepared any answers.

When my turn came, they asked, "What do you think is the biggest pressure facing teenagers today?"

I'm guessing they expected to hear something about drugs.

But when I opened my mouth I said, "The pressure to be mediocre. If you don't try, you can't fail. People are mean when you fail. Staying mediocre is safer."

I have no idea where that came from but I still think it's brilliant today.

I think that answer was a big part of why I ended up winning that night.

I was glowing from the emotional high.

Hunter had told me to call him, even though it was the middle of the night in North Carolina.

I did call, excited to share the news that I won. But he wasn't interested in having much of a conversation.

I get it now. It was probably 3 AM for him. But at the time, it hurt. He asked me to call, then barely cared.

My face hurt for days from smiling onstage all night. The picture in the paper that weekend showed me with a grimacing smile, lips pulled back from very crooked teeth. (Wanting braces was vain and vanity was a sin.)

****

I didn't anticipate the problems that winning would create for me with my peers and with Hunter.

The bullies at school were telling everyone that someone as ugly as me must have slept with the judges to win and I now had the responsibility of representing the town at ribbon cuttings, in parades and at various events.

Hunter was not confident enough in himself to be okay with any of that.

I would tell him about something I had to attend.

He would get mad.

I would explain that I wasn't out trolling or looking for boys, I was fulfilling my obligation to the town that I agreed to when he let me enter the competition.

Those calls almost always ended with me feeling beaten down and in tears.

I was now juggling school, work, pageant queen responsibilities and a jealous long-distance boyfriend.

As if my schedule wasn't complicated enough, my parents decided it was a good idea to sponsor a foreign exchange student from Spain.

(Because apparently seven kids and two adults in a three-bedroom one-bath house leaves plenty of room for one more.)

When Juan showed up, it was instantly clear he came from money and expected to get his way. He was a year older than me and because I had my driver's license, I was given the responsibility of showing him around.

I cringed every time he tried to haggle with salespeople, which he did at every single store. I explained over and over that haggling wasn't how shopping worked in the US.

Didn't matter. He kept doing it. I didn't want to hang out with him, but Dad said I had to. So, I did.

One afternoon Juan told my dad he wanted to see the new Batman movie.

I never went to the movies, I had no time and I felt like they were a waste of money. Plus, growing up without a TV in the house, I didn't really enjoy that type of entertainment (still don't).

Dad checked and it was playing at the movie theater in town. He told Juan that if he would pay for me and for gas, we could go (I was not asked).

I barely had time to change. I drove, Juan bought tickets and popcorn, we watched the movie and came home. That's it.

But when I got home, Hunter had called several times and had been told I was at the movies with Juan.

When I called him back, he screamed that going to the movies with another guy was cheating.

I tried to explain.

He wouldn't hear it.

He told me not to call. That he would call me when he was ready to talk and hung up.

He didn't call for two days.

I felt rejected. Misunderstood. Hurt. But at some level, relieved.

Part of me hoped he would break up with me and I would be free.

Sadly, Hunter and my dad had a conversation and I was told I needed to be understanding about how it was for Hunter to learn that *his girl* had gone to the movies with another guy without asking permission or even letting him know I was going.

Dad told me to apologize. I did and the relationship limped on.

It wouldn't be the last time I was expected to apologize when I wasn't wrong just to smooth things over.

****

That summer, as my junior year of high school wrapped up, everything began winding down.

Juan went back to Spain, track meets and 4-H horse shows ended (I competed on a neighbor's old cutting horse named Gentleman Jim and ran barrels on Moriah), and my pageant duties slowed down.

I had just come in from doing my chores and was walking through the kitchen when Dad casually mentioned that Hunter had asked for my hand in marriage and that he had said yes.

It wasn't a heavy conversation. Not a question. Just a matter-of-fact statement, like he was talking about needing to feed the chickens.

I wasn't surprised. I had heard whispers that Hunter wanted to marry me. But I was jarred by how final it sounded, like a prison gate clanging shut.

I knew my dad didn't believe in long engagements, but I assumed I would at least get to complete my senior year of high school. (I did. Barely.)

I had expected to feel something when it became official. Excitement, fear, maybe even anger. But there was just this strange, hollow resignation, like I was watching someone else's life.

I paused, standing between the stove and the sink, and blinked. I might have said, "Okay," then continued on my way.

But as I walked away, I thought, "I guess I'm marrying Hunter," and wondered how I was going to pay for a wedding.

Chapter 10
Officially Engaged

That August, just a few weeks after Dad had agreed to Hunter marrying me, I stood in a dress shop in northern Washington with my mom and her sister. We were visiting family, and my aunt suggested we look for end-of-season wedding sales while we were there.

I had never been the girl who dreamed about my wedding. I had no idea what I wanted my "big day" to look like, what the dress should be or much of anything else.

But I needed a dress and this was a chance to get one on sale.

When we walked into the small dress shop, the sales woman asked me what I was looking for, and I said, "A wedding dress."

She sat me down with a stack of magazines and told me to let her know which styles I liked. I found one that I thought would work and I decided I wanted to wear a hat.

I don't think I tried on very many dresses. There weren't that many in our price range and I wasn't that into it. It just had to be done.

We found one I thought was pretty that was close to my size. With a few alterations, it would fit perfectly.

My dad had agreed to pay for the dress, the minister, and the cake. I think he also paid a little bit to the friends (owners of Moriah), who let us use their yard as the venue.

Everything else, including dress alterations, the fabric for the bridesmaids' dresses, decorations, food, and the tuxedos had to be paid for by me.

(I don't recall Hunter chipping in anything.)

We paid $250 at the store that day. I think that included the hat and veil. But my memory is a little fuzzy.

Either way, I had a dress and we were looking at dates at the end of June, after I graduated, the following year.

****

My senior year of high school started uneventfully. I didn't have to take a full load of classes to graduate.

I had originally planned to take several college prep classes because I had room in my schedule, but now that I was getting married, not going to college, there was no point.

When the topic of college had come up before Hunter came along, I was told I'd need to figure it out on my own, keep living at home, and pay for it myself. I had no idea where to even begin.

Years later, I found it ironic that Dad, who often said, "The world needs ditch diggers," was helping *other* students apply to college. Why was he unwilling to help his own kids?

With no clear path forward and no help figuring it out, marriage felt like the only option I had.

It was just the next thing I was supposed to do as an obedient little girl trying to make her daddy proud of her.

And since I didn't need college prep classes, I had plenty of time to work afternoons as a bank teller and evenings in the back office for a different bank, processing checks. (I am still wicked fast at 10-key because of that job.)

****

The next time I saw Hunter was when he flew out to spend Thanksgiving weekend with us.

On Thanksgiving Day, his mom (my aunt, Dad's sister) called asking if I knew where Hunter was.

She told us that just a week before, he had agreed to join them for Thanksgiving dinner at his sister's house and to bring rolls. They were confused as to why he hadn't shown up yet.

He claimed to have no memory of that conversation. Maybe they called when he had been sleeping?

At the time I thought it was funny. How can you have a full conversation about something like that and not remember it?

Now I realize he was likely either drunk or high when they called and that's why he didn't remember.

But I was still blissfully unaware of that when he laughingly hung up the phone after telling his mom they would just have to enjoy Thanksgiving without rolls.

Since he came to me for Thanksgiving, Hunter and Dad decided that I would fly out to visit him in North Carolina the week between Christmas and my birthday on January 2nd. (Budgeted out of the money I was making babysitting and at the bank.)

I was going to stay with his sister because it was inappropriate for me to stay alone with him at his house.

But a few weeks before I was supposed to fly out, his sister and her family decided they were going out of town for that week.

I scrambled to understand what that meant. Would I not go and just lose the money? Did my parents trust me enough to let me go by myself?

They said they did, but it didn't "look good" so that wasn't an option.

It was finally decided that Mom would go with me to chaperone, taking my baby sister, who was still breastfeeding, with us. She celebrated her first birthday on the airplane on December twenty-sixth.

I didn't think much of it. I was used to going everywhere with multiple small children.

But now I think about the upheaval it must have caused for my mom.

Traveling with an infant is hard enough. But before she could go, she had to prep everything to leave my dad in charge of the house and five children with only my middle sister, who was eleven, to help.

They must have *really* wanted me to go to North Carolina because my dad paid for Mom's flight.

And to be fair, I wanted to go. Hunter was my only friend; the validation and attention I got from him made me feel good and I was promised to marry him. I wanted to spend time with him.

Hunter was living in the house he grew up in. His mom had gotten it in the divorce and was now living with her second husband, so renting it to Hunter was a good deal for both of them.

It was a split level. Three bedrooms and a bathroom on the top floor, an eat-in kitchen and living room on the main floor and a bathroom, small utility room and a big open space in the walk-out basement.

Hunter had his waterbed set up in the basement because it was too heavy to be in the bedrooms. That meant that Mom, my baby sister and I could sleep in the rooms upstairs.

At least, that was how it was supposed to work.

I would always start in the bedroom upstairs. But once mom was asleep, Hunter told me I should sneak downstairs and sleep next to him.

We had finally established that intercourse was not an option until after we were married. But I was learning there were other ways to make him happy.

Not surprisingly, there was no talk of "making me happy." It never even occurred to me that female pleasure was a thing and clearly, he didn't care.

I'm guessing that mom knew I was sneaking down at night and back up in the morning. Or maybe she didn't. She was dealing with a one-year-old who was still nursing. So maybe she was just grateful to get a few nights of sleep with only the baby to manage.

Either way, I was never called out for it.

****

Hunter had been invited to a New Year's Eve house party hosted by one of his friends.

I was excited about it. At one day shy of eighteen, I had never been to a house party; mostly because I didn't have any friends and my dad never let me go anywhere.

I remember being completely overwhelmed when we got there. My chest was tight. I knew I was out of my depth before I even left Hunter's truck.

There were *so* many people and it was *so* loud.

The music was blasting and everyone was screaming to talk over it.

Flashing strobe lights pulsed in some rooms, and the whole place was a gray haze of smoke I later learned wasn't just cigarettes

It smelled like sweat and too much cologne mixed together. It was complete insanity to me.

But I put on a brave smile as Hunter introduced me to people, random men and women hugged me and said things like, "Oh it's so nice to finally meet you" or "I was starting to think you didn't actually exist."

About thirty minutes in, I had already turned down multiple glasses and shots of different kinds of alcohol I had never heard of, and was wide-eyed trying to find a way to make sense of it all.

Hunter yelled in my ear over the music, "I'll be right back" leaving me with a drunk girl, whose name he hadn't told me.

She was too drunk to realize how awkward it was as she swayed to the "music" (some pounding beat with screaming lyrics I couldn't understand).

She swirled her drink so hard it spilled on the floor, and then she asked if I had a light for the cigarette she had put in her mouth backwards.

When I didn't, she wandered away.

I meandered from room to room looking for Hunter, periodically flattening myself against the wall to avoid being stumbled into and waving off joints being thrust into my face by glassy-eyed men.

In one room there were a couple of guys screaming at each other. I stood to the side and watched with detached curiosity as it escalated to fists being thrown.

Some other guys yelled at them to take it outside while physically dragging them out. I had never seen anything like it.

I went out to the backyard hoping for fresh air, but the people out there were weird (high on a whole litany of things) and it was cold.

I saw Hunter a few times but he didn't seem particularly interested in hanging out with me so I just tried to stay out of everyone's way.

Just before midnight I was standing near the doorway between the kitchen and the living room with my ears ringing when Hunter stumbled toward me with a goofy smile on his face.

He was drunk and likely high.

His body crashed into me; I stumbled into the wall as he forced his tongue into my mouth in a possessive kiss.

I stopped myself from pulling away and tried not to make a face. He tasted awful, like beer, smoke and something else I couldn't identify but didn't like.

As the countdown to midnight started, he got down on one knee and pulled out a ring box.

Unbelievable. He was going to propose here, in this chaos, while he was drunk.

The absurdity of it highlighted how incompatible we really were. But I didn't think about that until later.

He opened the box. The solitaire he had chosen looked muted in the murky light. It wasn't what I would have chosen had I been asked.

I couldn't hear him over the noise but I read his lips, "Will you marry me?"

My stomach lurched with disappointment. Not because of the ring, but because even as naive as I was, I knew this was not how this moment should happen.

An engagement should have weight. Joy. Be a moment to remember.

This was none of that.

But my dad said yes and I already bought a dress so...

I gave him a big, excited smile that likely didn't reach my eyes and nodded.

I took the "promise ring" off and he put the solitaire in its place.

Then he stood up, planted a kiss on my mouth and disappeared back into the crowd.

The noise, the flashing lights and the people around me disappeared from my consciousness. I stood there staring at my hand in disbelief.

This was real.

I was going to graduate high school and get married in six months.

A girl with mascara running down her face and wild 80's hair bumped into me, spilling whatever was in her Solo cup on my shoes.

She slurred, "Happy New Year!" directly in my face as she swayed to one side.

I replied. "Thank you! I just got engaged!" and tried to show her my ring.

She was too drunk to notice.

I listened to people butcher Auld Lang Syne and watched Hunter across the room, drink held high in one hand and his free arm wrapped around the shoulders of the guy he was trying to toast.

I wanted to feel happy. But it felt more like a box had been checked. I was just an observer of my own life. Detached. Numb. Isolated. Alone in a room packed with too many people.

These weren't my people. They never would be, and neither was Hunter.

I stayed rooted in that spot, twisting the ring on my finger, until Hunter decided he was ready to leave.

Today there is *no* chance I would get in a car with a person in the state he was in.

But that night, I assumed he knew his limit and that he really was fine to drive.

We didn't die on the way home. That's a plus.

I didn't join him in his bed after I showered. I was too disconnected, too adrift.

It didn't matter. He was too drunk to care.

But what could I do? The wheels were in motion. My destiny was set.

Chapter 11
Medical Abuse and Missing Drugs

trigger warning — medical abuse and trauma

When I left North Carolina after our engagement, Hunter was going to come out to California one more time before our wedding at the end of June.

That plan got turned on its head when he lost his driver's license for doing 110 in a 55 zone in late January.

He thought it was hysterical and bragged about driving recklessly, but his job as a pipeline welder required him to drive the welding rig. He couldn't do that without a valid driver's license.

I don't know why they didn't fire him. Instead, they put him on a legal leave of absence until he could get his license reinstated.

He called my dad to discuss options.

They decided he would move out to California and live with us, get a California driver's license and a local welding job.

He moved in with us in early March, about four months before the wedding.

I brought up that I would like to go to prom, since he was in town (he had forbidden it before).

He quickly shut that down. It was too weird for a grown man to go to a high school prom. (But not too weird to marry a high school girl?)

Besides, we needed the money for the wedding.

I was disappointed, but it made the most practical sense so I didn't bring it up again.

An extra bed had been squeezed into the office my brother was using as a bedroom. The foster kid who lived with us on and off usually slept there. Since he was gone, Hunter had a place to sleep.

Hunter was used to living alone in a three-bed two-bath house. Now he was sharing a bathroom with nine other people, several of whom were less than ten-years-old.

I regularly had a toddler join me in my top bunk in the middle of the night.

They would stand next to the bed and whisper, "Robyn. Robyn!" and I would put my hand down over the side to pull them up next to me; sleeping the rest of the night on my side with my arm wrapped around them to keep them from falling out of bed.

Hunter had zero experience with children so I should not have been surprised when I found him sleeping in the car in the driveway.

I knocked on the window. "What are you doing?"

"Your little brother came in and woke me up and would not leave me alone so I came out here to sleep."

I was embarrassed that my brother had bothered him but that wasn't uncommon for the older kids in the house. Hunter was seen as just another person who could help take care of them.

I think that was one of the reasons why Hunter had a conversation with my father about not wanting to have children right away.

They decided, without any input from me, that I should go on birth control.

My mom made the appointment with the doctor for me to get the physical required for the prescription.

I assumed it would be a physical like I had to get every year to run track. Listen to my heart and lungs, test my reflexes, maybe talk to me about what a good diet is, sign the paperwork and send me on my way.

No one told me I had to get a pap smear. (I didn't even know what that was.)

When I got to the little room at the doctor's office, they asked me to give them a urine sample.

That was different, but okay.

I didn't tell anyone I was on my period because nobody asked, and I didn't know it mattered.

The nurse came back a bit later and asked, "Are you on your period?"

I was embarrassed and whispered, "Yes."

Mom's head snapped around to look at me. "Why didn't you tell her?" The accusation that I had somehow failed a test I didn't know I was taking was clear.

Periods had always been something dirty you kept private and didn't complain about in our house. Why she thought I would have said anything is beyond me.

I just mumbled, "No one asked."

I did end up getting a pap smear that day anyway but I had no idea what was going on the whole time.

The nurse tossed a hospital gown on the exam table. As she left the room she said, "Get undressed from the waist down and put this on. Open in the back."

"Why?"

My mom replied with exasperation, "So they can do the exam."

"Oh. Okay."

I did what I thought I was supposed to do but left my underwear on because I didn't want to get blood on the table and I didn't know any better.

When the doctor came in, a woman (thank God) I had never met, she told me to lie back and put my feet in the stirrups.

Now I was both embarrassed and completely confused. I had no idea what was happening and my mom just sat in the chair behind me saying nothing.

Again, I tried to follow the instructions. As the doctor took her position between my knees she said, "You have underwear on."

I heard my mom tsk behind me.

The doctor continued, "We need to take them off." It was so matter-a-fact. Like I should know what was happening.

I was wearing a pad (Dad considered tampons ungodly) and couldn't have been more embarrassed as the doctor told me to drop my feet down and reached up to pull my underwear off.

She told me to slide my butt down and let my knees drop open. I felt her fingers on my most sensitive private skin.

I was ashamed and distraught. My mind was spinning frantically. What was going on?

Then she inserted the speculum without warning. I gasped. It was cold and hurt, badly.

When she was done, she pushed her chair back, pulled off her gloves, handed me a new pad out of the cabinet and said the prescription would be ready for me at the front desk.

She only gave me a prescription for six months. I didn't know it then but I was going to have to do the whole thing again in less than a year with a different doctor.

What an absolute horror show. I left feeling dirty, humiliated, violated and stupid.

Mom said nothing.

****

In addition to getting on birth control, I needed to have my wisdom teeth removed. Well, "needed" is the wrong word.

In my family, there is an ominous tale about my mom's younger sister having a problem with her wisdom teeth right after getting married and it costing her new husband lots of money because they didn't have insurance.

So, my parents and soon-to-be husband thought it was just common sense that I should get my wisdom teeth removed before the wedding; even though they weren't bothering me at all.

I don't understand why I wasn't taken to an oral surgeon to have it done.

Instead, my regular dentist decided he would do it.

I hated dentists (still do, with a passion) and was absolutely terrified.

At the pre-appointment, which I attended alone, I learned the dentist wouldn't remove my top wisdom teeth. He was concerned that the roots might be in my sinuses.

But he was happy to remove the lower two, even though they weren't erupted.

The extraction was scheduled about three weeks before graduation and six weeks before the wedding.

Hunter drove me to the appointment, promising to hold my hand the whole time.

I was so anxious that I was shivering and had to clamp my teeth together to keep them from chattering.

Hunter introduced himself to the dentist, and they brought in a chair so he could sit next to me.

He held my hand as they started the nitrous oxide and then the injections to numb my mouth.

They talked about souping up cars and doing bodywork on Corvettes as the dentist cut, pried and broke my teeth.

I felt them breaking and the torque as my head twisted to the side with the leverage of trying to get the teeth out. I groaned in pain, my eyes clenched tightly shut in panic.

Hunter told me days later, when I asked why the inside of my arm was completely purple, that the dentist kept turning the nitrous oxide up until I passed out.

When my hand slipped out of Hunter's and my arm banged against the chair, the dentist would turn it back down until I came back to.

They did that over and over.

Turn the nitrous oxide up.

My arm would slam against the chair as I let go of Hunter's hand.

Turn the nitrous oxide down until I started groaning again.

Unfortunately, passing out from too much nitrous oxide means a lack of oxygen. So, every time I came to, I would have a splitting headache and turn my head, trying to get away from the pain.

The dentist got frustrated and started jerking my mouth back toward himself.

I only remember fragments of the procedure. Them talking about cars. The searing pain in my head. My teeth breaking.

I know now that the dentist never should have attempted that extraction. My teeth were *very* badly impacted. He should have realized that from the X-rays or, at the very least, as soon as he opened up my gums

But he went ahead with it anyway.

We left the office with my mouth packed full of gauze and two prescriptions. One that he said to take during the day and the other at night so I could sleep.

Those were the only instructions I was given.

If Hunter was given anything more, he never shared it with me.

We drove to the pharmacy, and I remember standing there in a haze, waiting for my prescriptions to be filled. The fluorescent lights buzzed too loud and were too bright. I felt like I was looking at the world from underwater.

I have no idea why I didn't wait in the car.

The pharmacist finally handed over two small, paper bags, explaining that the bottle with more pills was for during the day and the narcotics were for at night, reiterating that I would need them to sleep.

He emphasized that being able to sleep would be crucial for healing.

I was just glad to be going home.

That was the start of the most miserable six weeks of my life.

Hunter decided he was going to control my medication.

I asked my mom years later why she let that happen, and she told me, "He was going to be your husband. You were his responsibility and I assumed he could take care of you."

It didn't occur to me then that he might not be capable of taking care of me or that he might have competing interests to what was best for me.

During the day, he refused to give me medication until I was in pain. Never on the four-hour schedule listed in the instructions.

And at night I was in agony. White-hot, throbbing pain searing through my face.

I would drag myself on my hands and knees from my bedroom to the side of his bed, sobbing and begging him for pain medication.

He refused; telling me the medication that had been prescribed was addictive and he was not going to marry a drug addict.

I can't tell you how many nights I quietly sobbed, curled in a fetal position on the floor next to his bed, believing that taking the medication would make me a drug addict and praying for the sun to rise so he would give me the daytime pills to make the misery just a little bit tolerable.

Many years later, long after we were divorced, he emailed me a picture of his then-girlfriend, twenty staples running through what had been a beautiful tattoo on her stomach. She had been in a car accident and had emergency surgery to remove her spleen.

The email said, "She keeps begging for drugs. She's such an addict. I can't wait to break up with her."

Only then, as I aggressively typed that withholding prescribed pain medication was abuse, did I realize how bad the situation with my wisdom teeth had been.

I still wonder what happened to that second prescription.

Maybe he took the pills himself. Knowing what I know now about his drug use, that is very possible.

Or maybe he sold them. I have no idea.

But I am 100%, swear-on-the-Bible sure we filled it, and I was not allowed to take them.

In addition to that insanity, none of us knew you shouldn't use a straw after dental surgery.

I ended up with infected dry socket on both sides.

I would not wish that torment on a mortal enemy. It was absolutely hell and I had temporary lockjaw from it.

Two weeks later, between final exams, I had to drive myself to the dentist for what seemed like the hundredth time to have the gauze removed and repacked.

The stench of rotting blood. The bitterness of the yellow antiseptic. The tugging feeling of them trying to get the gauze out and the shoving and pinching of trying to cram fresh gauze down into the holes in my jaw.

It was as foul and painful as it sounds.

When I arrived, the dental assistant asked me, "Why are you in so much pain?"

Through clenched teeth, because I had lockjaw, I replied vehemently, "If I knew that I wouldn't be here!"

My face was still puffy and swollen; my jawline purple from the pooling blood, evidence of the severe physical trauma I had been through. My cheeks were tender to the touch and I was rapidly losing weight.

Nothing the dentist was doing was making it better.

We finally gave up on him being able to solve the problem he created, and Mom sent me to our family doctor.

He took one look at the inside of my mouth and realized I had two nasty puss pockets of infection and was at risk of getting a bone infection.

He lanced the blisters (that is the nastiest taste ever!) and gave me an antibiotic prescription that was, in his words, strong enough for a racehorse.

He told me if the swelling wasn't better in a week he would have to hospitalize me so they could do IV antibiotics instead.

I hoped it wouldn't come to that because I was graduating high school the following week and getting married three weeks after that.

The swelling did go down, I was able to give my valedictorian speech and I don't look too much like a chipmunk in graduation pictures.

After the pomp and circumstance was over and we were all standing around chatting, my grandmother wanted to take a picture of me. Unfortunately, I didn't hear her ask me to look at her, so she grabbed my face and jerked it around toward her.

I gasped and held my breath as pain seared through me, trying desperately to will away the tears as my jaw throbbed.

My grandmother said, "Smile. I'm trying to take a picture."

I did my best to smile, but I'm sure that picture showed the deep hurt of not only the physical pain, but the betrayal of feeling disregarded and devalued.

She didn't apologize.

The good news, if there is any in this story, is that the trauma I experienced meant that all of my siblings got to go to oral surgeons to have their wisdom teeth removed.

The bad news: I still had my two top wisdom teeth and would have to deal with that a few years into the future.

When I went back to the family doctor, he was happy with the progress but wanted me to do another round of antibiotics.

It cleared up the infection in my jaw, but gave me the worst yeast infection of my life. Just in time for my honeymoon and losing my virginity to a man who had already made it clear that my pain didn't matter.

Chapter 12
My First Wedding

Along with the wisdom teeth drama and graduating from high school, I had a wedding to plan.

Since I was paying for a lot of it and I didn't have any big dreams about what my wedding should be, we were doing everything on the cheap.

Dad vetoed the early afternoon start time I wanted. He said I shouldn't ruin everyone's Saturday with my wedding.

We settled on his choice of 7:00 PM, assuming people could spend the day doing weekend chores, eat dinner, and then come to the wedding.

Then there was the whole discussion about who I could and could not invite. Of course, all of the family on both sides was invited.

But I was told I could not invite any kids from school. Dad said they would just "be rowdy, destroy our friends' place, and spike the punch."

I was able to invite a couple of people I considered friends because I gave them jobs, like valeting cars in the horse pasture.

But for the most part, the two hundred and fifty people we invited were my parents' friends.

I was an outsider at my own wedding, and when I looked at the pictures, I barely knew who many of the people were.

The reception, which was held in the backyard after the ceremony in the front by the pond, would consist of wedding cake, homemade candies, and punch.

The logic was that because it was so late, everyone would have eaten dinner before they came and we could "just serve dessert."

It wasn't much but it was what I could do.

Because of the weight loss caused by the fiasco with my wisdom teeth, my dress hung on me, even though I had paid to have it altered to fit me perfectly. We were able to get the seamstress to bring it in a little more at the last minute, so only I knew it didn't fit like it should.

And it still looked nice in the pictures.

Dad had fallen off of a ladder and broken his heel in recent weeks. But it seemed to be healed up well enough that he was going to be able to walk me down the aisle.

The rehearsal was standard, except for the preacher (Dad's second choice. The first had refused because we were first cousins), who said we could sit during the sermon.

Sermon? I was confused. This is a wedding. There shouldn't be a sermon. He claimed it'd be just five minutes.

That damn sermon is five to seven minutes on fast forward on the VHS tape.

He had a captive audience and just wanted to hear himself talk. I should have taken his notes and told him absolutely not.

But I was a good girl not trying to cause a scene.

After running through the processional and such twice, which I thought was unnecessary, it wasn't that hard to figure out, the wedding party and immediate family went to the local pizza place for the rehearsal dinner (I know, super fancy).

I helped make sure my younger siblings got pizza and were taken care of. Hunter and several of the men had beer.

That evening, most people went back to their motel rooms (There were no actual hotels.) while Hunter, his best man, and my family were watching the evening pass, sitting on the porch as the kids played in the yard.

As I walked past my dad's chair, he grabbed my wrist and pulled me toward him. Weird. Except for being spanked, we weren't a physical touch family.

I was forced to stop and turn toward him.

"Come sit with me," he said, gesturing toward his lap.

Okay, that was beyond weird, and moving toward creepy. I hadn't sat on my dad's lap in over a decade and at eighteen years old it seemed inappropriate.

But he insisted, pulling on my arm.

I tried to perch myself on the edge of his knee, but he pulled me into him and held me.

I didn't know where to put my hands, and wanted to crawl out of my skin. I was dumbfounded at what was happening. It felt wrong. Violating. Claustrophobic. But I wasn't sure why.

Then it got worse.

He wanted to talk about sex and my responsibility to "take care" of my husband's needs, that I should never tell him no, and that he and Mom had a good relationship in that way. (I guess so. You already have seven kids and you're not finished yet.)

I don't remember the details of the conversation. I just nodded, agreed and desperately tried to make it end so I could get away.

Looking back, I always wondered why my mom didn't have a conversation with me about something that was actually important. Like, I don't know, having and using lubrication, particularly when losing your virginity when you have a raging yeast infection.

I asked her about it years later. She responded, "Hunter was experienced. I expected him to take care of that."

We already know how horrible he was at caring about my needs.

****

The day of my wedding dawned clear, starting off cool and then getting hot, ninety-five degrees by the late afternoon. Typical for the Central Valley in California in the summertime.

I don't remember how I spent the first part of the day, but by four o'clock I was at our friends' house getting myself ready.

I did my hair and makeup. Mom helped me into the dress and secured my hat.

Of course, there were pictures. All the ones you would expect of the bride, her parents, and the bridesmaids.

I learned later that Hunter's tux had not shown up and, forty-five minutes before the wedding was supposed to start, he was sitting in a lawn chair in the field next to my parents' house drinking beer.

He told me if it didn't arrive, he was just going to come in his cut-off jeans and a tank top.

Thankfully, I did not know any of that was going on.

My grandpa had come by to give me advice about God being a part of a good marriage. (It's on the video, and now that he's gone, I'm glad to have it. Not for the advice itself, but because it shows how much he loved me.)

It was a little chaotic getting everyone seated. The groomsmen had improvised to hold the white runner down with stones. But it still kept trying to blow away in the wind.

But by the time I stood at the top of the aisle with my hand on Dad's arm, Hunter and all the groomsmen were standing at the front wearing tuxes.

As the music started, Dad turned to me and said, "You know you are no longer welcome in my home as a single woman after this, right?"

He said it like it was a throwaway line that didn't mean anything.

There was suddenly a tightness in my body that wasn't there before. I wanted to claw the moment back and ask what he meant. I already knew he had forbidden me to keep his name, "No daughter of mine…" he had said.

And now I wasn't welcome in the house?

But the crowd was rising from their seats, and he was stepping forward, leading me out of the entryway, and just like that, I was moving. Not deciding. Just moving.

I heard the voice in my head: "Smile Robyn." And I did.

Dad's line would come back to haunt me many times over the coming years when it became clear that Hunter had married me for the wrong reasons.

When I asked my dad about it after we were divorced, he told me he had been joking. It didn't feel like a joke that day. It still doesn't.

****

The ceremony was long, way, way too long. The preacher yammered as the light faded. Starting the wedding at seven, I had thought we would be done in about thirty minutes, leaving us time and daylight for the reception. I was wrong.

By the time the preacher pronounced us man and wife, and we had dealt with the reception line (one of my little brothers sobbed into my wedding dress. I think he was more aware of the gravity of the situation than I was), the sun was setting.

There is one picture that stands out in my mind, taken as Hunter was removing my garter for the garter toss.

He is on one knee, my foot on his leg, my dress pushed up past my thigh, and my hand resting on his shoulder, steadying myself. He has one finger hooked around the garter, pulling it away from my leg.

He is looking directly at the camera with his mouth open and his tongue hanging out like a panting dog.

Even as naive as I was, I was disgusted.

When we got the pictures back, he insisted we get a copy of that one. Every time I saw it in our album, I wrinkled my nose in distaste.

It was almost midnight before we left, and we had to drive close to two hours to a cabin near Yosemite National Park that friends were letting us borrow for our honeymoon.

As I sat in the passenger seat next to my new husband, I was exhausted, and had a growing sense of dread I couldn't shake.

Chapter 13
My First Honeymoon

By the time we found the cabin and parked the car, it was close to two AM, and I was delirious with exhaustion.

The day had been long and emotional. I just wanted to take a shower, crawl into bed, and forget all of it for a few hours of sleep.

But before we could even think about that, we had to unload the car.

Hunter went up and unlocked the door as I started to figure out what needed to come in now and what could wait until the morning.

He came back down, frowning.

"There's no electricity," he stated flatly, as if I had any idea what to do about that.

I stared at him. "No electricity?"

"Yes. None of the lights came on."

"Maybe the main breaker is turned off?" I tried to think of reasons a vacation home might have the electricity turned off.

"Maybe. Where is the breaker box?"

I just looked at him. Why would he think I knew? I had never been here. I wasn't part of the conversation deciding this was where we were going to honeymoon, and I wasn't there when he had been given the keys.

I didn't say any of that. I just shrugged. "I don't know. But I'm sure we can find it."

It took some searching, but we did eventually find it. Thankfully, the sky was clear and there was some moonlight.

Hunter flipped the main breaker, and we could hear the hum of the air conditioning.

My shoulders sagged in relief. I wondered why the owners hadn't told us that the breaker would be off. That seemed like something you would think to share when letting someone borrow your vacation home.

No matter. The problem was solved.

I went back to bringing things in from the car.

Hunter took the cooler of food we had packed for the week into the kitchen. I brought the suitcases in and searched for the main bedroom.

I was just heading back out to the car for another load when I heard Hunter from the kitchen: "Hey, come in here."

I pivoted toward his voice.

As soon as I entered the kitchen, he said, "The fridge isn't working."

I sighed. This honeymoon hadn't even started and I was already over it.

"Is there any kind of temperature control on it?"

He rolled his eyes at me. "Yes. I already tried that."

"Then I don't know. We'll have to deal with it in the morning."

"The stuff in the cooler will go bad by then." He stared at me, starting to get annoyed.

I begged my brain to push through the cobwebs of exhaustion and think. Somehow this seemed to be my fault and I should have known it was going to be an issue.

I was the oldest child. I was always expected to anticipate problems and have answers. I should be able to figure this out.

Finally, I said, "Didn't we pass a 24-hour gas station coming in? Maybe they have ice."

He pushed the cooler out of the way and slammed the fridge closed.

"Okay. I'll go get some." He brushed past me before I could get out of the way.

I was thinking I would go take a shower, and then realized there wasn't room in the cooler for ice. We would have to use the fridge as an ice box.

I unpacked most of the food into the bottom of the fridge, leaving room at the top for ice. Since cold air drops, that seemed like the most reasonable thing to do.

I left the milk, sour cream, and butter in the cooler. My logic was it was a smaller space and we would be able to keep those things colder by putting ice directly around them.

Hunter came back with two bags of ice, but didn't like my plan.

He looked at me like he thought I was stupid. "Putting ice on the top will let water drip on everything."

I was too tired to care. "We can move it."

He also didn't like my idea for the dairy products.

"Just put it all in the fridge."

I disagreed, but at that point, I was willing to do whatever would get me into bed the fastest.

Once we had that sorted, he turned to me with a creepy grin and said, "Let's get this honeymoon started!"

I replied, "I am so tired. Can we wait until the morning? It will be more fun then."

He snorted. "I have been waiting for this since Chicago. I'm not waiting any longer."

It was at least three in the morning, and even if I had wanted to, I simply didn't have the energy to fight him.

"Fine. We have to make the bed and I want to take a shower."

But there would be no shower that night because there was no hot water. That happens when the electricity has been turned off.

I washed my makeup off the best I could with cold water and tried to give myself a brief sponge bath with a washcloth.

I then put on the negligee my aunt had given me for my wedding night. I'm glad I didn't realize how see-through it was. I never would have had the confidence to step out of the bathroom if I had.

When I walked in the bedroom, Hunter was already in bed. He wolf whistled and licked his lips.

Fortunately, I don't remember the details of that first time, just that it burned and was very painful.

Looking back, that's not surprising. I had a yeast infection, he hadn't brought any lubrication, and he was in a hurry.

When he finished and rolled off of me, he said, "Sleep naked," and fell asleep almost immediately.

I got up and tried to clean myself with cold water as I wondered if sex would always be this awful.

I shivered as I walked with a towel wrapped around me across the bedroom floor. I dropped it at the bedside and slipped submissively into bed next to him, nude as I was told.

I noticed the sky was gray with the coming dawn before closing my eyes and finally, thankfully, falling asleep.

****

When he woke me up, it was almost noon.

"Are you going to sleep all day?"

Shame and guilt coursed through me for being in bed when the sun was up.

"No. I'm getting up."

I was thankful for the hot water and finally being able to properly wash off my wedding makeup.

We had sex again on the floor in the living room. I stared at the ceiling and tried not to think about my spine against the hardwood floor. Time stretched. Somehow it was even worse than it been the night before in bed.

****

Side note: I didn't know it then, but it would take me almost a year to get Hunter to understand that using lubrication wasn't a failure on my part for "not being excited for my husband," and for me to realize it shouldn't burn or feel like I was tearing every time we did it.

Within that year I also learned that Hunter was complaining to his friends that I didn't know what I was doing in bed.

Obviously, that's a drawback of marrying a virgin. You have to teach them about sex.

One of his buddies had happily offered to "give me lessons" so I could be "better at pleasing my husband."

I told Hunter if he was going to share our sex life with his friends, we should put in bleachers and sell tickets. If he didn't want to do that, he should shut up.

Eventually our sex life became "eh." He wasn't that interested and the few times a month he was, lubrication made it tolerable.

****

We never did figure out what was wrong with the fridge.

Hunter called my dad, who called the owners, who called us back. But they had no idea why it wasn't working.

They also hadn't been the last people to use the cabin, and didn't know the main breaker had been turned off.

Hunter went out to get more ice while I tried to make us something to eat. The kitchen didn't have much in the way of pots, pans, cutlery or even plates. But I was able to make it work.

When he got back, we ate in silence.

As we finished eating, he asked, "What do you want to do today?"

I looked at him, surprised. The honeymoon had been his responsibility. I had been busy planning the ceremony and dealing with family members coming into town.

I wanted to say, "Didn't you plan something?"

But I didn't. That seemed like a good way to get myself in trouble.

(That was long before I realized that, as an adult, I shouldn't "get in trouble." That is how you treat a child, not a partner.)

Instead, I asked as innocently as possible, "I don't know. What did you have in mind?"

We ended up hanging around the house that day, doing nothing. That wasn't a horrible thing, since I was still tired and now sore.

The next day I suggested we go hiking. There is a picture of me sitting on a big rock smiling.

By day three, we were bored. By day four, we decided to just go home. It was too hard to deal with the broken fridge, having nothing to do, and not even really being friends.

Even my middle sister, who was only twelve at the time, knew that coming home from your honeymoon early because you were bored was not a good sign.

Less than a week later, I said goodbye to my parents and my siblings, and boarded a plane with two suitcases of clothing and my dog, Blanquita (a Border Collie mix given to me by my boss at the horse ranch), in an animal carrier in the belly of the plane.

Hunter, oblivious to me as always, drank and joked with the flight attendants, as ominous feelings of resignation, abandonment, and despair washed over me, staying like a rock pressing down on my throat and chest for the whole trip.

Chapter 14
Moving 3000 Miles with a Stranger

Once we landed in North Carolina, I had to unpack my bags and try to get settled. My new reality was that I was living with a stranger, and waking up every morning in his bed.

It was surreal. But it was my life.

Just weeks earlier, I had been living a full and bustling life: school, work, a tiny house filled with too many people, and planning a wedding.

Now I sat in a big, silent house alone. No purpose. No friends. No money to call home.

I realize now I was starting to slip into depression and had some anorexic tendencies that I carried with me for almost ten years.

But Hunter was back in his element. His leave of absence wasn't over at work yet, but somehow, he had somewhere to go every day and was gone most of the day.

At night, he would work in the garage on a car he had promised to repaint for someone before he disappeared to California without telling them.

They had been furious that their car was locked in his garage, partially ready to paint, for the several months he was gone.

I tried to do "wife" things: clean the house (I was horrible at that), do his laundry, make dinner.

He didn't like the way I did laundry, and to be fair, I didn't really know what I was doing. At home I had always just separated out lights from darks from colors, washed them, and then hung them on the line to dry.

He didn't have a clothesline, so I had to use the dryer. I didn't know clothes had to be taken out hot or they would be wrinkled.

And when he finally did go back to work, I didn't know that, at his union job as a welder, they had a uniform service and that he would take his dirty uniforms back to work for them to wash and press.

When I noticed a pile of his work clothes on the floor, I tossed them in the washer.

He yelled at me and told me I was stupid because I had put metal filings in the washing machine and now they would get on all of our other clothes.

He told his buddies at work what an idiot I was and they laughed at my expense.

It felt like buying the wrong sugar as a teenager all over again. I tried to do the right thing and got publicly shamed and berated for it.

Every mistake added to the proof that I was clueless and not good enough.

Cooking for him was even worse.

I had done a lot of cooking at home, but I had never had to plan daily meals. And I didn't realize that my mom's waterless cookware was special.

I tried to make things my mom used to make, and kept burning stuff. I thought it was my fault. Now I know it was the cheap pans Hunter had.

When I was a teenager my family raised beef, chickens, and rabbits, we usually had meat in the freezer.

That wasn't the case now. I couldn't just open the freezer, pull out a pound of hamburger, let it thaw, and make something with it that night.

Some nights, I would go out to the garage to tell him dinner was ready, and he would say, "Okay," but not come in the house to eat.

I would end up eating by myself and putting the leftovers in the fridge.

Other nights, he would come in, take one look at what I made, and say, "I'm not eating that!" Then make himself something else.

Even when I asked him what he wanted for dinner, he would shrug without looking up and say, "I don't know."

It was humiliating and underlined my failings.

I finally stopped cooking and let him do his own laundry. Of course, then I was a "bad" wife. But not trying seemed easier than to keep trying and failing without any direction for how to make it better.

The only attention I ever got from him was during sex, so I would try to initiate that closeness a couple of times a week.

I stopped doing that too when he screamed at me that marriage was about more than sex and that I should leave him alone.

Early in our marriage, if we had sex every ten days, it was a lot. Later on, it was more like once a month.

I'm guessing his drug use contributed to his lack of desire. That, or he was getting it somewhere else and I was too naive to notice.

****

One afternoon, while Hunter was out (he was always out), I decided I didn't like the pile of paper accumulating on the counter and made the decision to go through it to see what needed to be done to clean it up.

There was a booklet that I later learned was his truck loan. I didn't even know you could buy a vehicle on payments. My parents always paid cash for cars, which is likely why we always drove such beaters.

A past due water bill. An electric bill due in two days that hadn't been paid in full the month before. An unopened bank statement.

Then I found his credit card bill with a balance of almost ten thousand dollars and growing. I stared at it as realization dawned.

Every gift, plane flight, long-distance phone call, even my engagement ring and wedding band had been bought on credit. Interest piling up because he only ever paid the minimum payment.

What the hell was this? My dad had chosen him because he was willing to feed me, clothe me, and put a roof over my head. But it looked like he had never actually managed his finances.

I knew where he kept the checkbook and went to find it.

When I opened it, I stared at it in disbelief. He had never written anything in the register. Literally nothing! How was he balancing his checking account? (Spoiler: he wasn't.)

I went back upstairs to open the bank statement but it didn't mean much in the abstract.

That night, when Hunter got home, I confronted him.

And I'll admit, he was not met with a demure, submissive wife with a passive inquiry.

I was fiery, "What the hell is going on with our finances?"

He got defensive but I didn't back down.

The result of that conversation was that I learned two things.

One — the man I was married to wasn't just irresponsible; he wasn't very bright either.

(That would work in my favor because he wasn't able to maintain the grooming put in place by the cult that, as a woman, I was too emotional and dumb to make decisions.)

During the course of the discussion, I told him to stop acting like a martyr, to take accountability for the situation we were in, and that he had failed to disclose it.

He replied by yelling at me for trying to look smart by using words he didn't understand.

I still want to face palm myself about that all these years later.

Two — we were badly in debt and not bringing in enough money to cover the bills.

I took over our family finances from then on.

I went through the envelopes from our wedding. There was a lot of cash because people knew I wasn't going to be able to bring gifts back with me.

Many of the cards said things like, "Don't use this on anything practical. Do something fun. Do something that will make you happy."

But I couldn't abide by those wishes when I was looking at past-due bills.

Our dire financial situation worked in my favor too. It was very clear that I needed to get a job. Married women in my family didn't typically work outside the home. So that was a big deal.

It took me a few more months to learn the third big slap in the face about my new husband. He had a drug problem.

He had told me he *used* to use and deal acid. But I was starting to question the "used to."

And I was learning that he had a regular marijuana habit. As I met his friends, I realized they were living a lifestyle of drugs and alcohol that I didn't understand, but Hunter seemed to fit right into.

****

Back when Dad, Hunter, and I were doing children's Bible study on the phone, Dad had done some research and chosen a Presbyterian church for Hunter to attend.

I thought it was weird that he didn't have a church home already. Did he not grow up in the church? (No, he didn't. But I didn't know that.)

Now that we were back in North Carolina, I expected to meet a church family who knew him and would welcome me with open arms.

Boy was I wrong.

The first time we attended that church, it was very clear they didn't know him. I think he had told my dad he was going, but I don't think he was.

I was an outsider and super country compared to the women I saw.

I also had the weird dilemma of being about the same age as the pastor's twin daughters, who were rising seniors in high school, but being in a completely different place in life, married to an older man.

I did what I thought good Christian wives were supposed to do.

I made casseroles for women when they had babies, even including recipe cards so they could make it again if they wanted to.

I volunteered to work in the nursery and offered to teach Sunday school. Heaven knows I was good with children.

I even joined the choir for a little while.

Nothing worked.

I was too young and too clueless to get into the clique.

I went to that church almost every Sunday for eight and a half years, until Hunter threw me out, and in all that time I was never able to make any friends there.

****

A few months into trying to fit in, I decided to attend the high school girls' volleyball practice held in the church gym. At least I could get some exercise.

I wasn't in as good a shape as the high school girls, but I tried hard and I had fun.

The coach of that team was a woman named Laurie. She wasn't a member of our church, or any church for that matter, and she was nice to me.

That fall, she invited me to be part of the grass volleyball team she was putting together.

I played on that team for several consecutive seasons. We played hard, and dominated the league. We won six or eight championship sweatshirts together.

I had teammates.

I finally had friends.

****

But making friends didn't fill the home shaped hole in my heart.

On a rare phone call from my family, my youngest brother at the time, one of the toddlers whose diapers I had changed and who had whispered my name to climb into bed with me in the middle of the night, got on the phone and said, "You have been visiting Hunter long enough. We need you to come home now."

That night I sobbed into my pillow. The pillow I had forced myself to wash because it was too painful to put my head on it every night when it smelled like home.

I was devastatingly homesick.

Even now, it catches in my throat to look at pictures of their little faces from that time in my life.

I felt like I had abandoned my babies.

And for what? A man who couldn't afford to take care of me, complained to his friends that I was a horrible cook, was bad in bed, and would eventually tell me he had to be high to deal with me because I was such a bitch.

****

I used the cash from our wedding gifts to pay the rent we owed Hunter's mom (we were still living in her house) and to bring the water and electric bills up to date. But the credit card interest kept piling up, and the truck payment loomed. We were drowning.

I needed a job but I had never had to look for a job.

In California, people knew me. I got referred to jobs from teachers and other people who had hired me.

In North Carolina, I didn't know anyone. And Hunter's network was mostly his burnout high school buddies and guys he worked with.

None of them were going to help me get a job with a résumé that consisted of a high school diploma, eighteen months of experience working at two different banks, and training roping horses.

I started looking through the paper.

Working for the airline as a flight attendant was quickly nixed by Hunter. He told me he "didn't get married to have his wife flying all over the country flirting with every guy in an aisle seat."

Rude. But I was learning to accept his insults to avoid fighting.

There were lots of waitressing jobs. My dad had always looked down on those kinds of jobs for some reason. That had been another "No daughter of mine…" speech.

Hunter felt the same way about waitressing as my dad. Too much risk of working nights and flirting with customers to get better tips.

I tried my hand at selling fire extinguishers. That was a disaster.

My next job was as a receptionist for a sleazy "businessman." I'm not even sure what he was selling.

He played rock music so loud I couldn't hear to answer the phone, was constantly yelling at me over the music to bring him coffee, and wanted me to wear shorter and shorter skirts.

I did have great legs, but I wasn't even nineteen and I was just trying to pay the bills. Disgusting.

Then I interviewed for a job working the front desk at a local hotel, followed by an interview to work in the wire transfer room for a small, local bank.

The hotel got back to me first. They offered me the overnight shift, with the possibility of moving to days sometime in the future. Not ideal.

They wanted an answer within a couple of days.

I waited as long as I could, hoping the bank would call me back. I felt pretty good about that interview.

Should I take the front desk job? Should I turn it down even though the bills were piling up?

I was torn and stressed.

Hunter was leaning toward turning it down because he didn't want me gone at night and didn't love that I would be working directly with the public.

(Are you sensing the pattern of insecurity yet?)

I said a prayer and called the hotel to say, "thanks but no thanks."

Two days later, the bank called and offered me the job.

The woman said, "We'd like to offer you the job. Starting salary: $13,500 a year."

I said, "Thank you. I'll take it."

No one had ever taught me to negotiate. I just assumed they would offer me fair pay, and I could take it or not.

She replied, "You'll take it?" She sounded surprised and confused.

"Yes?" I said it like a question because I was confused about why she was confused.

I thought to myself, "*I need a job. I can ride the bus into downtown. It's regular business hours. I'll take it.*"

It had taken me six months, but I had fought off the depression and self-loathing just enough to find a reason to get out of bed in the morning.

Sadly, when I told my dad I got a job, he responded, "Be thankful you were given a job. Work hard. Be respectful, and never quit. You might not be given another one."

****

That was also about the same time my six-month birth control prescription

93

ran out. No doctor was going to just believe me that I'd had a Pap smear in California six months ago and give me a new prescription without seeing me, so Hunter called his doctor, a man, and made an appointment for me.

It was awkward, but at least this time I knew what to expect.

I got a year's prescription and learned two things about my health:

One — Hunter had given me HPV. Knowing what I know now, I shouldn't have been surprised. As my mom said, he was "experienced."

That diagnosis turned into a whole cascade of treatments that medical science now knows are useless and unnecessary. The funny-not-funny thing about that was the doctor's office called Hunter and told him. They didn't call me.

Two — I had hypothyroidism. The doctor hadn't told me he was testing my thyroid function.

I remember that phone call like it happened yesterday. I was in the shower, and that was at the time in my life when I was skipping meals so we could pay bills.

That meant I was so lightheaded all the time that I couldn't wash my hair without the room spinning. I was in the downstairs shower, squatting with my head between my knees, shampoo in my hair, when I heard the phone ring.

I knew better than not to answer it. Hunter got mad when he called if I didn't answer the phone. I stood up too quickly and my eyesight went black.

I knew that was the first step to passing out (I did that a lot back then). I fought it off, grabbed the cordless phone from the counter, and sat on the floor as I answered it.

The nurse was brutal in her delivery. "You have thyroid disease. We've called in a prescription for you."

"Oh... Okay. How long do I have to take it?"

"Forever. This is a lifetime disease."

"Will I die from it?"

"No."

"How did I get it?"

"I have no idea."

"How do people usually get it?"

She huffed and sounded exasperated. "I don't know. I'll have the doctor call you."

She hung up on me.

I crawled back into the shower, too shaken and lightheaded to stand up. I sat on the shower floor trying to rinse the shampoo out of my hair and sobbing.

How was I so sick? I had been healthy my entire life, and now, just barely having turned nineteen, I had an STD and a disease I didn't understand except that I was going to have to take a prescription for the rest of my life.

It didn't occur to me to call my mother; we didn't have that kind of relationship, and I don't think she could have helped me anyway. When I tried to talk to Hunter, he just shrugged and refused to have a conversation about it.

I felt like my body was betraying me and nobody cared.

I learned over the course of the next decade that my thyroid condition was the most bizarre that any medical professional had ever seen.

I didn't have any of the normal symptoms.

But if I didn't take the medication, which I often quit doing for months at a time because doctors were constantly over-medicating me, my blood work would come back with numbers off the charts, and doctors would call me freaking out that I was going to go into a coma.

I have never gone into a coma.

****

I was reeling from my new diagnoses, but life didn't pause to let me catch my breath. I could choose to sit in the corner, rocking in overwhelm, or suck it up and plow forward.

I chose to figure it out and move forward.

I took the city bus to work each morning, arriving downtown in time to hop on the shuttle to the building where I worked on the ninth floor.

In the first month I worked there, I got on the elevator and heard a woman behind me say, "Will one-a all-y'all please mash the fourth floor for me?"

You have to imagine that being said with the deepest Southern drawl, almost like she had a mouth full of marbles.

It was all I could do not to turn around and stare. I had heard of mashing potatoes, but never elevator buttons.

I kept my eyes facing forward and pushed the button for the fourth floor.

Several months later, I got a call from my dad. He said, "It turns out, marrying off your oldest daughter isn't a good form of birth control."

That's how I learned my mom was pregnant again.

I was excited about it, and the next time I saw our pastor's wife, I said to her, "Guess what!"

She deadpanned, "You're pregnant."

I was taken aback. "No. My mom is."

It was a strange interaction but then, my social skills weren't very good.

My lack of social skills was also negatively impacting my ability to make friends at work.

Remember that my dad believed that if something was true, it shouldn't hurt your feelings.

Someone came into our office once and asked, "Where's Jennifer?"

I pointed and said, "She's that bottle blonde over there."

I was a natural blonde. She wasn't. True but unnecessary, socially clueless, and mean to say.

That awkwardness was exacerbated by the fact that I was smart (I didn't realize it yet) and could do the job better than most of my coworkers.

When my boss gave the worst employee a bonus, I said out loud in the team meeting, "Why would you give him a bonus when there are so many of us doing a better job?"

My boss replied, "We are trying to motivate him."

I rolled my eyes and said, "Well, you're demotivating the rest of us."

I was not winning friends and influencing people.

Compound that with my overfriendliness, and things like this happen:

Hunter had a break from work at my lunchtime and came to pick me up in his work truck. When he arrived, he had a single rose for me.

As I took it, I leaned over and kissed him.

I didn't realize that one of my nemeses, Patty, was standing outside the building smoking and saw the whole interaction.

By the time I got back from lunch, the whole office was buzzing with the "fact" that I was having an affair.

I tracked the rumor to Patty, who smugly told me husbands don't bring their wives single roses. Proof in her mind that I was cheating.

I offered to introduce her to him.

She stammered uncomfortably, but the damage to my reputation was done. I had to squash that rumor regularly until I left that department after my boss told me she couldn't promote me because it would be impossible to replace me.

When I left, they hired two full-time employees and one part-time person to take over my job.

****

When Christmastime rolled around, there were a few house parties, and Hunter had friends he wanted to visit. Only one sticks out in my memory.

I don't remember what he told me about how he knew the people we were having dinner with. All of his friends and acquaintances ran together.

I got dressed and was ready to go at the time he had told me to be. As he drove through the deepening twilight, we might have talked about nothing or not at all.

We arrived at the house, and when the door opened, he was greeted with smiles and hugs all around.

I got tight smiles and "Nice to meet you's."

It felt off but I didn't know why.

For most of the evening, Hunter, the married couple who owned the home, and their daughter Stacey, who was about Hunter's age, talked. It sounded like they had a lot of history.

There was also a baby. I think a grandchild of the couple but not Stacey's child.

After dinner, I was sitting on the floor playing with the baby while the adults continued to talk. I know I was technically one of them; it just didn't feel like it.

Suddenly a gift-wrapped package was pressed into my hands. "Merry Christmas," Stacey said.

My cheeks flushed. I hadn't brought a gift for them and certainly wasn't expecting anything.

"Thank you."

I looked at Hunter, unsure if I was supposed to open it now or not.

All the eyes in the room were on me. Someone said, "Open it."

I scooted from the floor onto a chair, not wanting to feel quite so much like a child opening a gift while the grown-ups watched.

I slid my finger under the flap and started to unwrap it.

As soon as I got the wrapping paper off, I felt a little better. It was obviously a regift. Not something that had been purchased for me specifically.

They were wine glasses with tall, black stems. Classic and beautiful.

I smiled. "Thank you. They are very nice. We don't have wine glasses so these will be useful."

Stacey replied, looking at Hunter, with an expression I didn't understand: "Consider them a wedding gift."

The room suddenly had an awkward energy.

It wasn't until we were driving home and I mentioned how weird the whole gift thing had been that Hunter said to me, "That was my ex-fiancée, Stacia."

I whipped my head around, realization crashing through me. "You told me we were going to visit your friends and their daughter Stacey! Why didn't you tell me she was your ex-fiancée? No wonder she was so cold to me!"

I felt like a complete idiot. Everyone there had known the score and I was completely clueless.

I wanted to rail at Hunter about it. Why did he put me in that position? Why did he make a fool out of me? Just... why?

But he cut me off aggressively. "Don't get your panties in a wad. It's not a big deal."

Once again, I was forced to swallow my feelings to keep the peace.

They were nice wine glasses though. I kept them for many years, moving them from house to house, long after I bought crystal and was no longer using them.

I just gave them away to someone who is starting out in their first apartment a few months ago.

Just one more piece of old energy I have let go of, now that I'm finally, thirty-five years later, changing my name to something *I* chose.

Chapter 15
Where the Hell is My Husband?

Roughly two years into our marriage, my mother-in-law (also my aunt) told us she was splitting up with her second husband and would be moving back into her house. The house we were renting from her.

She said we were welcome to stay; she would just live with us. There was no chance I was giving that a try!

Hunter had a horrible relationship with his mother, and more than once, she had belittled me and treated me badly.

One of my proudest moments was when she was berating me over the phone and I told her I wasn't going to listen to it anymore.

She said, "Don't you hang up on me!"

I replied, "I'm not hanging up. I'm saying goodbye." And hung up the phone.

I didn't answer when she called back.

It was very clear that there was no way we were going to be able to all live in the same house.

Fortunately, by that point I had gotten our finances under control. Partly because I told Hunter he wasn't allowed to write checks. He kept bouncing them, even after I put an extra hundred dollars in the account that I didn't record in the register.

I worked for the bank and they could fire me for bouncing checks.

To solve that problem, we agreed that he would deposit his regular pay, and keep his overtime pay in cash.

He always managed to spend every cent of that overtime money. I'm sure a lot of it was on drugs; other times it was on dumb things like the Snap-on tool clocks I found buried in his closet.

He told me they were an "investment." They just looked like mostly naked girls lying across cars, bought with money we could have used for groceries.

All I knew was that his overtime money was always gone by the end of the pay period, and I learned not to ask questions.

But I digress.

By the time his mother decided she wanted to move in with us, the credit cards and the truck were paid off, we had purchased and fixed a wrecked car for me to drive and I had squirreled away a few thousand dollars we could use as a small down payment on a house, if we could find one quickly.

As luck would have it, we found a tiny, old house; three bedrooms, a bathroom, living room, kitchen, an itty-bitty sunroom, and a laundry "room" dug into the dirt cellar on six acres.

The front porch was falling apart and it was right at the VERY top of our budget.

We made them an offer and, after some back and forth, we settled on $87,000.

That was great until the appraisal came back at only $85,000 and the loan company wouldn't loan us any more than that.

I knew that in cases like that, the seller usually had to drop what they were willing to accept.

Without talking to me, Hunter told the realtor he'd just kick in the extra $2,000 in cash.

I had no idea he had a few thousand dollars in cash in his gun safe and of course the loan company wanted to know where this money was coming from.

We couldn't very well tell them "drug sales," although I think that would have been the truth.

We ended up saying Hunter had been saving his overtime pay in cash. Fortunately, we were able to show his pay checks versus the amount he was depositing and they believed us.

And so, shortly before my mother-in-law needed to move in, we were able to move out and into our very own place.

****

Not long after we moved in, Hunter announced that he wanted to build a garage and start his bodywork business.

I tried to point out that our lot wasn't zoned for a business. He told me we were "too far out" for anyone to care and submitted the paperwork for a building permit.

That's when we learned that the graywater from the washing machine just ran through a pipe into the pasture. I don't know if that was missed by the inspector we hired or if Hunter had just glossed over it.

Either way, we had to put in a leach line.

After my 9-5 job and on weekends I learned to use survey equipment, shoveled heavy clay and gravel, helped lay pipe, and then backfilled the whole thing.

It never occurred to us to hire someone to do it. Having grown up the way I did, I knew how to work hard and do physical labor.

And since Hunter worked a blue-collar job, he knew people who could teach us how to do it.

At one point, Hunter took a picture of me in a bikini standing behind the tripod we were using to survey. (I figured I might as well get a tan while I was working.)

He tried to keep a copy of that picture in his work truck, but the guys he worked with kept stealing it. I finally had to tell him to stop putting new ones in there.

Once we got the final sign-off from the inspector that our leach line was acceptable, we could restart the process of getting a building permit for the garage.

It was then that I learned that Hunter was planning to put up a six-car garage with recessed floor anchor pots so he could buy totaled cars and straighten the frames.

I argued that it didn't need to be so big.

He replied, "I wanted to own a body shop long before you came into my life. I will still own it long after you're gone."

That was the first time he hinted out loud that I wasn't part of his forever plan.

****

We did end up building a six-car garage with multiple anchor pots in the floor. It was a metal building with steel trusses. It took some creative engineering for the two of us to get it put up on our own, but we did it.

I don't think he ever painted a car in it for money.

But it was a good place for him to clean deer when he went hunting. (I went with him once; just to spend time with him. I brought a book, thinking I would read, but it was too dark that early in the morning).

I also spent time in there, sitting on a bucket talking to his legs sticking out from under whatever car he was working on.

And because I was always looking for ways to spend time with him, I even learned to wet sand. That's something you do with fine grit sandpaper and water to make the paint on a vehicle really smooth.

But mostly that huge space just became a place for him and his "friends" to hang out, drink beer and get high. Although I didn't realize the getting high part until one of the neighbors came by and tried to give me a joint, saying, "Give this to Hunter for me. I owe him one."

I refused, and when I confronted Hunter, he told me the neighbor was mistaken. I was gullible but not that dumb.

From then on, I always had a little bit of fear that he would get busted and we would lose everything because he was an idiot.

He also decided that it would be good if we could rent out the pasture. But to do that we needed a barn.

We bought and tore down an old building that had previously been a water tower (gorgeous cypress wood).

We spent months breaking that wood down, bought an industrial planer, ran the wood through it to reveal the amazing red color, and then constructed a six-stall barn with a hayloft.

It was impressive!

One Saturday afternoon, I was sitting on a rafter, twenty-six feet in the air, with one knee hooked over another rafter, screwing the tin roof in place with a screw gun, when one of Hunter's buddies came out and started yelling for Mitch (who was built like an NFL lineman).

I ignored him and continued working.

He kept yelling until Hunter came out of the barn and said, "Mitch isn't here."

The guy pointed up at me and said, "He's right there."

I pushed my hood off and looked down at him like he was crazy.

He was shocked that Hunter "let" his wife up on the roof with power tools.

It was winter, and I had on a heavy coat, but even dangling twenty-six feet in the air, I have a hard time believing I was mistaken for a 6'5" mountain of a man.

We were able to rent the barn and pasture out for a few years. Although that came with its own issues. More than once, I had to tell teenage girls they could not use the barn to hook up with boys.

Not long after the barn project wrapped up, I got a notice in the mail that it was time to renew our auto insurance.

Weirdly, the rate had jumped a lot.

I asked Hunter if he had any idea why that would have happened. He told me he had no clue but that it likely wasn't worth digging into.

Just paying higher bills for no reason wasn't my thing, so I called the insurance company.

They explained that they had raised our rate because of a speeding ticket.

I didn't know anything about a speeding ticket.

They proceeded to give me Hunter's name, the tag number and description of his truck, the time, date, and location of the ticket (less than a mile from our house), and the court date where he paid the fine.

Angry isn't the right word. I felt cold, pent-up rage at his complete disregard for me as a human being.

Why would he have not told me to begin with and then lie about it when I asked about the insurance bill?

He told me he "forgot" to tell me when he got the ticket (In the five minutes it took you to get home after being pulled over, you forgot?), that he didn't think it was important enough to mention the court date, and that when I asked about the insurance bill, it "didn't occur" to him that the ticket was the reason.

At that point what was I supposed to do? The disrespect and lying were blatant. I could have gotten angry and yelled but that wouldn't have changed anything.

I just walked away, paid the higher car insurance bill and never brought the ticket up again.

****

Living in Charlotte, North Carolina, meant dealing with hurricanes and tropical storm winds every year.

Because of that, I had been bugging Hunter about taking down a tree that was leaning over our house.

It was one of those super-tall pine trees that goes up what seems like a hundred feet before it has any branches.

The bristle-brush top of it would have crashed directly into our roof if it had broken off.

He told me several times that he would "get to it," but it never seemed to happen.

Finally, there was a storm heading our way, and I reiterated, again, that the tree was going to be a problem.

He told me to stop nagging him about it.

I left for work, and just had to hope that the wind wouldn't be a problem.

When I got home, the tree had been cut down. It was on the ground away from the house with the rope still tied to the hitch on Hunter's truck.

Hunter was sitting on our tiny back deck drinking a beer.

There were several smaller trees that had been damaged, including a dogwood that I really loved. But I decided to just be thankful that we no longer had a tree hanging over our house.

That weekend we were going somewhere with my best friend Carmen in the backseat, and he was telling her about using tree spikes to climb up the tree, tying a rope to the top of it, using the truck hitch to put pressure on the rope, cutting the tree, and watching it crash to the ground, barely missing his truck.

He looked at Carmen in the rear view mirror, laughing, and said, "It's a good thing I had a few beers before I decided to do that!"

I gasped, "You had been drinking before you climbed that tree?"

He looked at me incredulously, "You don't think I did that sober, do you?"

I was flabbergasted at his increasing ability to demonstrate how stupid he was and be proud of it. But it turned out okay this time, so I just rolled my eyes.

To this day, when someone does something really, really dumb, Carmen and I will still say, "You don't think I did that sober, do you?" and laugh hysterically.

In fact, I just had to text her and tell her that I am writing this story. She is an amazing friend!

****

It wasn't uncommon for Hunter to disappear on Saturdays and be gone all day. Sometimes he claimed to be working overtime. Other times he was just gone, and I had no idea where he was.

He claimed he "needed" a beeper, and later a bag phone, when they first came out. It made no sense to me because I could never get ahold of him using them.

I assume now it was drug-related, or maybe cheating.

But this particular Saturday was beyond his usual level of strange.

He came home really late that night.

When I asked him where he had been, this is the story he told me:

He had stopped to help a young woman whose car had broken down on the side of the highway. Upon learning she and her son had been on their way to Carowinds, a local amusement park, he took them there himself.

Then he went back, figured out what was wrong with her car, bought the part, and fixed the car.

Later that afternoon, he picked them up at Carowinds, brought them back to their car, and then followed them home (two hours away) to make sure they made it safely.

The story seemed over-the-top and crazy. Why would he do all that for a stranger he just met on the side of the road?

But Hunter was the kind of clueless guy who would give someone the shirt off his back. So it wasn't completely out of character for him to disregard me and spend his whole day helping someone else.

But the icing on that cake came about two weeks later.

I was home by myself when the phone rang.

When I answered, a young woman's voice asked if Hunter was there.

I said he wasn't, and asked if I could take a message.

She hesitated, then said, "I'm looking for the guy named Hunter who is about six feet tall, with sandy brown hair and a mustache. He drives a dark red Corvette with flames on the side."

She had just described my husband and his custom-painted sports car to a T.

I replied, "Yes, that is Hunter and his car."

She said, "Who are you?"

"I'm his wife."

She sputtered, "I must have the wrong number," and hung up.

Clearly, she didn't have the wrong number. I couldn't help but assume he had failed to let the woman he claimed to have helped on the side of the road know he was married.

Maybe she called his beeper or his car phone after that.

When I brought it up to Hunter that night, he just shrugged and told me he had no idea.

Yet another example of things not adding up. But getting angry would have been pointless, so I let it slide, just like I had so many times before, and like I would so many times in the future.

****

There was one event where things started strange and then turned scary in a way I couldn't just roll my eyes and ignore.

It was a Friday evening. Hunter and I had talked earlier in the day while I was at work, and made plans to go out to dinner when I got home.

As far as I knew, there wasn't a project in the garage, so there was no reason for him to blow off our plans.

I had spent many evenings sitting on our couch ready to go without him ever coming in to shower and take me out.

But tonight, I thought it would be different.

He had told me he was really looking forward to trying a new place he had heard about from a friend.

When I got home, Hunter was on the back deck with a man I didn't know. That wasn't unusual. There seemed to be a steady stream of "new friends" I would never see again coming and going from our house.

It had started happening more often since we moved to our own place. They always seemed to know Muscle Mike, the son of the guy who owned the property next to ours.

(He had made a point to tell us not to eat the opossum because they had a virus. I thought it was a joke. It was not.)

I dropped my bag on the couch before I stuck my head out the back door.

Hunter said, "Robyn, this is Tiny. He's a friend of Muscle's."

Tiny was a huge man. (Aren't they always?) I noticed they were both holding beers, and there were a few empty cans sitting on the railing.

I simply nodded in response to the introduction and asked, "Are we still going out to dinner tonight?"

He smiled and said, "For sure."

"Great. I'm going to shower and change. I should be ready in about forty-five minutes."

Less than an hour later, I was back. There were more empties, some on the bench now, and they were both still holding a beer that looked pretty full.

Confused, I asked, "Are we going soon?"

When Hunter turned to look at me, I knew he wasn't sober, but he replied, "Yeah. In a little bit."

I went in, sat on the couch, and waited.

And waited.

And waited.

I heard Hunter come in and open the fridge, looking for more beer.

I got up and confronted him before he went back outside.

"What are you doing? It's getting late and I'm hungry. Let's go!"

He looked at me and walked away.

I caught the back door before it closed behind him.

"So, are we not going out like you promised?" My voice was sharp and angry.

"We are talking business. You can wait!"

I don't remember exactly what I said. Something about how I always had to wait and he had promised.

He flew into a rage.

He had never hit me before, but I could see it in his eyes that he was coming for me this time.

I darted through the kitchen.

I was hoping to make it to our bedroom, but felt him grab for me as I turned the corner into the hall, so I whipped into the spare bedroom, trying to get the door closed behind me.

He stopped it with his body.

I wedged my foot against the door and leaned into it, trying to keep him out and hoping it wouldn't break my foot.

We stood like that, his drunken breath ragged and reeking.

Me praying I was strong enough to hold him off, because he was so drunk.

He gave one final shove at the door and said, "You're lucky this time. The next time you embarrass me in front of my friends, you'll be sorry."

He stumbled away. The door latched closed as I sank to the floor, heart pounding. I had never been so scared in my life.

I sat there for a long time. Afraid to move. Scared to go look for something to eat in my own kitchen.

Then I heard Hunter's truck start.

I peeked out the window and saw him drive away with Tiny in the passenger seat.

He was way too drunk to be driving.

I stood up, shaking. Walking to our bedroom, I picked up the phone, and called my mom.

I sobbed as I told her what had happened, tried to explain how scared I was, and that I had no idea what to do.

"He's *so* drunk, Mom, and he's driving!"

I was panicked that he would kill someone.

Her advice: "Go to bed and pretend you are asleep when he gets home. Hopefully he won't be so angry in the morning."

With no other option, that's what I did.

I heard him stumble in around three in the morning.

When his alarm blared a few hours later, he grumbled about having to work overtime. I remember holding my breath when he kissed me goodbye, thinking I was still asleep.

I had plans that day with a friend, so as soon as I heard his truck leave the driveway, I jumped out of bed, got myself ready, and left.

When he came home that afternoon, he thought I had left him. And perhaps I should have.

One of his buddies was there when I got home and saw me flinch away when Hunter reached for me. But he didn't say anything.

After his friend left, Hunter apologized for his behavior the night before.

Although he added, "But I was really drunk, and you were rude to me in front of my friend. Don't do that again."

I never saw Tiny again. I also learned not to speak up about anything when Hunter was drinking.

****

It was a running joke among my friends from work and volleyball how different the people I chose to spend time with were from Hunter's friends.

At our parties, his friends showed up in pickup trucks and on motorcycles. They drank beer, smoked cigarettes and weed, cussed like sailors, and hung out in the garage or around the grill.

In contrast, my friends drove sedans and the occasional Jeep. They were college-educated, worked white-collar jobs, drank wine or blended drinks, and didn't smoke or do drugs.

I had nothing against Hunter's friends. They were just different than mine.

When we went to parties at his friends' houses, there would be lines of cocaine on the table and music so loud it could almost make your ears bleed.

My friends had parties where we played board games and spent the night laughing.

That obvious contrast should have been a clue not to bring Hunter to a New Year's Eve party hosted by a couple I played volleyball with. But I wanted to go, and he wouldn't let me go alone, so he came along.

He got ridiculously drunk that night. I think he was doing shots, which I've always thought was stupid.

On the way home, he threw up in my car. The next day, he tried to clean it, then drenched the carpet in cheap cologne. My car reeked of vomit and drugstore musk. It made my eyes water for weeks.

Two days later, he bought me flowers for my birthday and told me I should forgive him because he bought me flowers.

The next time I saw my friends, they told me he had peed in their cat litter.

I was so mortified I couldn't even apologize. I just stammered, "Oh my God…" and stared at them in shock.

When I tried to talk to Hunter about it, he just laughed it off like it was the most hysterical thing he had ever heard.

There was nothing about him that made him a good partner for me, and I knew that I couldn't see myself growing old with him.

But I was resilient to the point of being stubborn. My dad had given me to Hunter, and I had made a promise before God and witnesses to make it work.

Besides, I had no idea how to make it on my own, and I still had enough programming from my childhood to believe I wasn't smart enough to figure it out.

Several nights later, as we bickered about how he treated me, I asked him, "Why did you even marry me?"

His response sliced through me. "Because you're good stock."

I was common chattel to be traded and bred. Not someone to be loved and cherished.

I had already decided I wasn't having children, even if I couldn't find a doctor who was willing to tie my tubes.

How little I mattered to him was cemented even further a couple of months later, when we went to play putt-putt golf and he spelled my name wrong on the scorecard.

I had been married to him for years, and he spelled my name with an "i" instead of a "y."

When I pointed it out, he just laughed and told me, "You know what I meant," but he didn't fix it.

His dismissal hurt me, deep in my core, in a place I couldn't yet name.

It wasn't the end, but the energy was starting to shift.

Chapter 16
The House is For Sale. At a Price

My relationship with my husband was so chaotic I used to joke that nobody would believe it if they read it in a book. But there was also another layer of upheaval.

Within months of purchasing our house, we started getting calls from realtors wanting to buy it, either as an investment property or for developers.

We knew that the people who owned it before us had tried to sell it to a church congregation, but that fell through and allowed us to buy it instead.

Most of the time, we just ignored the realtors' calls. They weren't serious, and I wasn't looking to move again anytime soon.

Especially after we finally had the garage and barn finished.

One realtor actually showed up at our house and was sitting in our driveway when I came home one Saturday.

She asked if she could come inside because she had a proposal for us.

I was willing to hear her out, but I told her I had done some research. I knew what it would cost for us to replace what we had, and I *really* didn't want to move.

She came in and gave me some sob story about how her boss was pressuring her and she really needed us to sell to them.

Her offer was laughable, about $100,000. That wouldn't even cover what we had put into the place.

I was annoyed that she wasn't even being serious, so I thought quickly and decided to say a number so ludicrous that she would just go away.

I said, "I was thinking $350,000."

Her face got hard.

"You'll never get that."

"Then I guess we'll just be happy living here."

Her reply was a threat.

"I'm going to sell the property around you to low-income housing. You'll never be safe. People will be breaking in every week. You'll never be happy here."

Considering I was only twenty-five, my reply still shocks me.

I narrowed my eyes and said, "I will put up a big fence, buy a big dog, and carry a big gun. Get out of my house!"

She slammed her car door and then spun her tires in the gravel getting out of our driveway.

I thought that would be the last of her.

It wasn't.

****

We shared our driveway with the house behind us. We owned the section near the road, but just beyond our house, near the garage, it crossed onto the neighbors' property and continued about a quarter mile back to their house.

We had a friendly relationship with them. They were older and seemed kind enough.

We talked about buying the property from them at some point to give ourselves more room. They had about four acres, and we thought adding that to our six would be just about perfect.

But when they were ready to sell, we were not in a financial position to take on more debt. So we watched it go up for sale and after it closed, went back to meet the new neighbors.

Again, nice enough people. Older than we were and kept to themselves.

They did call us for help when their well stopped working, and again when their roof had a leak. I went up and helped him split a cord of wood once.

Just neighborly stuff.

So it was a little surprising when I came home from work and found they had put in their own driveway without ever mentioning it to us.

I walked down to the garage to ask Hunter about it. He shrugged, and I suggested he ask them what was going on.

He rolled his eyes but got in his truck and drove back to their place.

A short while later he was back. "They said it was better for their property value." He dismissed it matter-of-factly, like that explained everything.

I started asking questions like, "Are they looking to sell?" "Are they in conversation with someone to sell?" "Why didn't they mention it to us?"

Hunter got annoyed. "I don't know, and I don't care. If you're so nosy, go ask them yourself."

And with that, he turned on his air compressor, and the noise made it clear I was dismissed from the garage.

Two days later I came home to find the neighbor had dug a deep trench along the property line, effectively blocking us from getting to our garage. I could just barely get my car into the parking space next to the house without driving off the edge.

Now Hunter was pissed. He stormed back to the neighbors' house and demanded to know what he was thinking by carving out the shared driveway so we couldn't use it.

The neighbor just shrugged and said it was his property, and he could do what he wanted.

I think Hunter threatened to sue.

When the neighbor checked with his lawyer, he learned that because the shared driveway had been there and in constant use for decades, he would likely lose in court for cutting off our access to the garage.

By the weekend, he had put the dirt back in place, but only just far enough that we could get around the tree at the edge of our property and into the garage.

There was no longer room to get big vehicles down there, but at least it was something.

We were disappointed, but not shocked, when rezoning signs went up and we learned our "nice" neighbor had been working with the landowners behind him to sell his property to a developer.

That sale did go through. Instead of an open field in front of my house, I now had to look at an ugly construction fence. And every morning when I left for work, there were leering catcalls from construction workers building a neighborhood of boring cookie cutter homes.

****

Shortly after the last house was built and people moved in claiming to "like living in the country," my great-grandmother died.

I got ready to fly out to Southern California for her funeral and weirdly, Hunter wanted to come. I saw no reason for him to join me, but he insisted.

When we returned less than a week later, there was a message on the answering machine from the realtor I had thrown out of our house months ago.

"We are willing to meet your price with a few stipulations. Please call me."

My stomach tightened into a hard ball.

I looked at Hunter.

He asked, "What price did you give them?"

"$350,000."

"Wow. Okay, I guess we'll call them back."

When we talked to her, I thought the buyer's stipulations were strange, but I have since learned they are pretty normal for developers.

They wanted to put a contract on our house for the price I asked, but they also wanted to pay us a monthly fee to *not* close for up to a year.

That fee was more than our mortgage.

There was a clause that said the property had to pass rezoning or they could back out without penalty.

They were trying to buy our land and Muscle Mike's place across the creek to build an apartment complex.

I asked to add a clause allowing us to take the garage, the barn, and the brand-new furnace we had just installed.

They agreed. None of it mattered to them. They were planning to demolish everything anyway.

After we signed the contract, I felt weirdly cold. Something in my universe had tilted aggressively, and I didn't understand what.

Little did I know that this was the very edge of the very beginning of the end.

Chapter 17
Living on a Catfish Farm

For the first six months or so after we signed the contract to sell the house, nothing happened.

We got monthly checks from the development company, and I put all of it directly on our mortgage.

Hunter and I continued to live our separate-but-together lives.

We didn't fight that much. We just coexisted.

I helped Carmen move into a two-bedroom apartment, and we used her sewing machine to make clothing and Halloween costumes for ourselves.

It became a running joke that we were trying on creations so often as we sewed that, when we ordered pizza, neither of us would be wearing pants.

Those memories still make my heart swell with love.

Carmen introduced me to Amanda because she needed help moving.

I was up for that.

I only went to Amanda's apartment twice. One weekend to help her move, and then the following weekend to hang out at the pool.

I was surprised when Carmen told me Amanda had been gushing about how "masculine" and "manly" Hunter was.

As far as I knew, they had only seen each other when he came to pick me up after I spent the day helping her move. He hadn't gotten out of the car and I didn't introduce them.

It was even more bizarre when I learned she had Hunter's beeper number. I barely knew this girl.

Why the hell did she have my husband's beeper number?

Carmen agreed. Something about it was shady.

I tried to talk to him, but he brushed me off: "Sometimes she just needs to talk."

"Right. But why you? You don't even like to talk to me."

He never gave me an answer.

I'm guessing something inappropriate was going on, but I didn't care enough to fight about it.

What would have been the point?

Another time, at one of the cocaine-on-the-table parties, a random girl came up to me and said, "I'm going to steal your husband."

She was disheveled and strung out.

I looked down at her and replied, "If you can get him, you can have him. If he'll leave, he's not worth keeping."

(I still firmly believe this about relationships. If someone doesn't want to be with you, you're better off without them.)

She opened and closed her mouth a couple of times and then walked away to bum a cigarette from someone.

****

About halfway through our yearlong contract with the developer, we received notice of a public zoning board meeting that the developer wanted us to attend.

Several neighbors from the cookie-cutter subdivision next door also showed up. They argued that they liked looking at the open space and it should not be allowed to be "spoiled" by putting apartments on it.

I pointed out that I used to like looking at the open space where their house now sat and if they wanted to look at pasture they should buy some rather than blocking my ability to sell my land.

Sadly, the zoning board decided that Muscle Mike's land could be zoned for apartments, but ours could not. Supposedly because we were on the other side of the creek. (I have no idea why that mattered.)

I was furious and the people who owned the houses in front of ours were gloating.

I thought the deal was going to fall through.

Fortunately, the developer came back a few weeks later with a new plan. They wanted to put a pitch and putt golf course on our land instead.

The zoning board approved that and we were back on track to close on the sale in May.

That meant we needed to find a place to live.

I didn't want to be too far from downtown because I had to commute to work. Hunter was less concerned about that and just wanted lots of land.

I was working on packing up the house. We had to take down the barn, marking each piece so we could reassemble it wherever we ended up.

We sold the garage structure. Because it was a steel building it was relatively easy to take apart and put on a big truck with a crane.

The fancy cement floor, with the anchor pots for pulling frames that were never used, stood out starkly against the growing grass of a pasture we were no longer mowing.

Hunter found a property forty-five minutes from where I worked.

He really talked it up.

Fifty-five acres, ten ponds, a small house. Some cleared pasture land. Some trees

He talked about putting up fencing and raising cattle. I told him over and over I had zero desire to raise cattle. I grew up doing that and wanted no part of that lifestyle again.

But he was insistent that it was perfect and I should just give it a chance.

So, one windy Saturday in the spring, Hunter, Carmen and I piled into his pickup truck and made the trek out to the property to meet the brother of the owner.

I used to joke that the directions to the place were: *drive to the middle of nowhere. Turn left off the paved road. Keep going until you dead-end into a catfish pond.*

But Hunter encouraged me, saying we could call it the *Rockin' Hat Ranch* (his nickname used to be "Hat Man" because he stole a cowboy hat in high school, and I had been called "Rockin' Robyn").

I tried to keep an open mind as we got farther and farther from town.

When we turned onto the driveway, I saw my first red flag. It was a shared driveway. There were three other houses, all owned by family, that we had to drive past to get to the land.

A mile later, we came to an old, decrepit gate hanging from one hinge. I could see where it scraped an arch into the driveway when I pushed it open.

As we came around the hill and out of the trees, I saw the "house" and a bigger garage-like building.

I grew up poor, and I've lived in some cramped places, but this house was sketchy.

I learned later that the main house on the property had burned down and what was trying to be passed off as a house was actually a fishing shack.

It was a slab of concrete with plywood walls, a tin roof, a fireplace for heat, and two of the smallest water heaters I had ever seen, one under the kitchen sink, the other in the bathroom next to the shower.

They were so tiny that there was only enough hot water to either wash my hair or shave one leg. I ended up on a three-day rotation.

There were two exterior doors, both on the same side of the building: a regular wooden door near the driveway, and a glass screen door, with no curtain, that led into the bathroom.

There was no insulation to keep grass and weeds from growing under the walls, and I regularly had to cut the grass in the bedroom.

The electricity was a temporary junction box hanging directly on a telephone pole.

The "house" was so close to a pond I could have fished out of the bedroom window.

And the mice! There were so many mice. The grossest thing I have ever done was step on a dead mouse with my bare feet in the middle of the night in that house.

But I didn't know any of that yet.

Carmen and I walked around the property, taking in how much trash had been randomly thrown into the woods. There was an old, rusted car with a tree growing through it, cinder blocks, other broken building materials and so much trash.

We found what looked like piping and tubing from a still (used to make moonshine). Carmen asked me if I thought that's what it was. I rolled my eyes and said I wouldn't be surprised.

When we got back to the "house," we found the guys, and Carmen jokingly asked, "Where's the still? We saw the pieces, but the still is missing."

The owner's brother answered flatly, "He took it with him to Tennessee. Why would you think he would leave that here?"

Carmen and I just looked at each other.

I wasn't keen on living way out in the middle of nowhere in a shack. But Hunter was adamant that we could pay cash for the land and have enough left over to build a really nice house.

We would only have to rough it for about six months.

I should have realized there was no way we could get a house built in six months. But I didn't think about that.

I did the "good wife" thing and just trusted him, and believed we wouldn't be living in that shack when it started to get cold.

Part of me remembered how hard it had been for my mom when I was six, my brother was four and my middle sister was an infant, and we were living in a house on blocks with a garden hose in the window for water.

If Mom could do that, I could do this.

I didn't feel like I had the right to say, "I don't want to live like this," when my husband, the man of the house, wanted it.

I fell back on old patterns of giving parts of myself away for someone else's happiness.

Before we left, Hunter and the owner's brother shook hands on the purchase once our place sold.

We would never even start building a house there, and I would be gone before the end of October.

****

With closing day for the sale of our first house approaching rapidly, Hunter made a handshake agreement with the owner of the catfish farm allowing us to start moving things to the property and fix some of the biggest issues before we legally owned it.

We tore down our beautiful barn and hauled the lumber out there, stacking it near where we thought we might one day put it back up.

(I learned years later that Hunter poured gasoline on that wood and burned it before he sold the land. It breaks my heart to even think about that.)

There was a culvert going under the driveway that was caving in on itself. We needed to dig it up and replace it before we moved out there.

The week before we had scheduled to do that, I broke my arm playing volleyball.

My health insurance wouldn't let me go to the emergency room so I ended up splinting it myself with an Ace bandage and some cardboard.

I slept better on the couch with a broken arm than I did next to Hunter on that stupid waterbed.

Fortunately, I was able to get in to see my regular doctor. She took an X-ray and confirmed it was broken (I knew that) and sent me to get a cast put on it.

I finally got the letter from the insurance company approving me to go to the doctor, two days after my cast came off.

On the weekend the cement was coming for the culvert, I put a bread bag around my cast with rubber bands to keep it dry and worked all weekend standing in the creek in my irrigation boots moving rocks by supporting them on my cast with my other hand.

It was hard, dirty work. But in the end, we had a safe, functioning culvert that didn't look half bad.

****

Two weeks before closing day I got a call from our contact at the development company. She wanted to know how the move was coming and asked if we wanted to rent the house back from them for a few months.

I told her we were making progress and should be out by the closing date.

We just had to disconnect and remove the furnace. (Remember I added that to the contract?)

Hunter had told me he didn't know if he was going to have time to get the furnace out or not. But I was dead-set on taking it. It was brand new and we were going to need one for the house we were building.

The woman on the other end of the line said, "You can't take the furnace! That's part of the house!"

I simply replied with the page and paragraph of the contract that said I could.

She paused, I could tell she was reading, and then said, "I'll call you back."

About two hours later she called back to tell me that they were planning on renting the house and could I please leave the furnace.

I told her I was open to selling it for the price it cost me to purchase it and have it installed, and gave her a number.

Two days later I had a signed contract for them to purchase the furnace in a house I no longer owned.

That little moment of strategy still makes me proud.

****

Then it was a mad dash to the end.

Hunter's friends "helped" us move, gouging the top of our beautiful dining room table by throwing rough lumber on top of it.

I had purposefully left that table for a second load so it wouldn't get damaged and was livid when I realized how careless they had been.

I was dismissively told, "If you don't want your shit damaged, don't ask friends to help you move."

Hunter just shrugged, told his friend he should have been more careful, and told me there was nothing that could be done about it now, and to "get over it."

Under my breath I fumed about his useless, drug addled friends. Out loud, I bitched at one of the guys for throwing his cigarette butts on the ground in my yard.

Happily, the waterbed had to go to storage because it was too heavy for the thin slab in our new "house." The last thing we needed was to slide into a catfish pond in the middle of the night.

Instead, Hunter and I took the two bunk beds that had been in our spare bedroom and pushed them together to make a king-size bed with a split down the middle.

No more dealing with his wiggling keeping me awake at night. Amazing.

****

Once we moved in, it didn't take long for us to start bickering.

I was assigned the responsibility of going to the feed store every weekend to buy catfish food and then feeding the fish in all ten ponds every day.

I told Hunter we were throwing away money. The fish were too big to sell, we had no idea how to farm catfish, and I had no desire to learn. But he insisted I keep doing it.

It finally came to a head when I fell going across what I called "Wobbly Rock Creek" to feed the fish in the pond on the other side. It was pouring rain, and the rock I had to step on to get across was slippery, and of course, wobbly.

Soaked to the skin, juggling two five-gallon buckets full of feed, I stepped onto the rock, tried to balance, and pushed off. My boot slid off the rock, and my other boot stuck in the muddy creek bank. I crashed into the water as fish food went everywhere; on me, in the mud, floating downstream.

I sat there for a moment trying to determine how hurt I was and realized I was more angry than hurt. I stormed back to the house, bruised and fed up.

"This is stupid!" I raged. "There is not another woman on the planet that would do this. Why am I feeding the catfish? We aren't making any money on them and there is no hope of making any money!"

Hunter looked up at me, dry and unbothered. "You're not supposed to make money on a hobby."

I blinked. This was his idea of a hobby? Who said anything about wanting a catfish hobby?

I found my voice, "A hobby is supposed to be fun! I am not having fun. I'm not buying catfish food or feeding catfish anymore!"

I stormed the ten feet from the living room to the bathroom to strip out of my wet, filthy clothes and take a disappointingly short shower to get the mud, catfish food and grime off of me.

****

Interestingly, once I stopped feeding the catfish, no one fed them. Not even once. I guess it wasn't a "hobby" Hunter wanted after all.

(A funny side note: someone came and stole all the catfish a few months after I left. I don't have any idea how that works but I think it's hilarious.)

Just because I wasn't feeding catfish anymore didn't mean there weren't obnoxious amounts of work to be done.

Every Saturday, Hunter disappeared for "work" (maybe he was really working overtime, maybe not). But he left me a list of chores to finish before he got back, like he thought I was some kind of farmhand.

On this particular day the list had maybe half a dozen things on it.

I only remember the top two:

1. Move rocks from hillside to creekbank
2. Plant rose bushes

Moving the rocks from the hill to the creek to stop erosion was going to be a massive job.

I got dressed and put my .38 revolver on my hip. It was loaded with refills I had made myself, filled with birdshot. It was perfect for the snakes that lived in and around the ponds and creeks.

I put on my hiking boots and took my irrigation boots down to the edge of the creek.

For hours I pushed a wheelbarrow uphill, loaded rocks, brought them down the hill, dumped them in the creek, changed into irrigation boots to wade in, sorted and placed the rocks, then changed back to start again. Over and over and over.

Like some kind of muddy, snake-dodging Sisyphus.

Around three o'clock in the afternoon I decided to take a break and have a sandwich.

I was in the house eating when I heard Hunter's truck coming up the driveway.

My gut clenched. I knew I was going to be in trouble for being in the house rather than outside working, heaven forbid I stop to eat.

To try to avoid him "catching" me in the house, I met him in the driveway, sandwich in hand.

"Come see the work I did on the creek," I said proudly.

He walked down to the creek bank with me and looked at my efforts.

It looked great and I had worked really hard on it.

He turned to walk away and said gruffly, "You didn't plant the roses."

I was deflated and demoralized. I had just spent all day doing backbreaking work and all he could see was what I hadn't done.

He got in his truck, telling me he was going to go work on the fence at the back of the property.

I had no idea when he planned to be back so I just finished my sandwich standing in the driveway and then started working on planting the roses.

****

That June, we had been living on the catfish farm for about six weeks and it was a few days before our eighth wedding anniversary.

Hunter needed some help with the fence he was working on and told me to jump in the truck.

I grabbed my work gloves and opened the passenger door.

There, sitting on the seat, were the unmistakable pink and white stripes of a Victoria's Secret box.

I smiled, assuming it was an anniversary gift. "Ooo what is this?"

Hunter got in, looked at me for a moment, and then simply took the box out of my hands and shoved it behind his seat.

I was a little bit hurt, but I thought maybe he was embarrassed that he had ruined the surprise for me by leaving it on his seat.

I was wrong.

He started the truck and said, "That's a gag gift for the secretary at work."

The delight I had felt moments before drained out of me with aching dread. Did he really think I believed that? Fighting about it seemed pointless so I said nothing as we drove up to work on the fence.

A few days later I told him I thought we needed couples counseling.

He disagreed that we had a problem but said he would go a few times if I scheduled it when it worked best for him and if I promised to stop acting so "miserable" around the house and be "easier to be around."

It was an insulting trade, but I took it because it was my only hope.

Chapter 18
The Last Fight

It took real effort to find a couples counselor whose schedule aligned with what Hunter was willing to do. Even then, he warned me: if he was offered overtime, he wouldn't show up.

Our first and only session started as you would expect. I explained that I worked a full-time job, had a list of chores as long as my arm at home and barely saw him.

Hunter talked about how I was a nag.

I didn't think that was fair.

I was just trying to discuss how our lives worked and what the plan was for not living in a literal shack.

At the end of the session, the counselor gave Hunter an assignment: "You need to spend fifteen minutes a day talking to her."

Hunter's reply floored me, "I don't have that kind of time to waste."

I sucked in a breath and held it. Fifteen minutes was too much time for him to give me?

I thought the counselor would at least defend me, say something about talking to your wife not being a waste of time. But that's not at all where he went.

Instead, he just said, "It doesn't have to be all at once. You can split it up into four or five conversations of less than five minutes."

Hunter snorted, "Yeah. I don't have time for that."

We made an appointment to go back but it got rescheduled a few times and finally canceled because Hunter was never available.

Weeks later, while we were working on clearing some brush, I tried to talk to Hunter about if we were going to continue working with the counselor or not.

He wasn't saying much.

Then he fired up the chainsaw, and as he walked away, he yelled over his shoulder, "Keep talking. I'm listening."

Obviously, I didn't bother continuing and he didn't notice.

That night, he told me that I was the problem because he had "given me time to talk" and I hadn't used it.

****

One Saturday morning, not long after that, I woke up alone, as usual. I assumed he'd gone to work, though honestly, he could've been anywhere.

I decided I wanted to take a quick shower before starting on the to-do list that I was sure was sitting on the counter.

Remember how I mentioned that our bathroom had a glass door leading to the outside? I hadn't covered it yet because it was a metal door, impossible to put a curtain rod on, and since it looked out over rolling hills of empty fields and trees, I assumed the catfish and deer didn't care if they could see into our bathroom.

But that morning, as I stood there drying off, I happened to glance up to see a man I didn't recognize standing in our driveway.

He was facing away from the house, deliberately looking at the sky with his hands in his pockets.

Clearly, he had seen me and was trying to be gentlemanly.

That was polite; but who was he and what was he doing standing in my yard in the middle of nowhere?

I didn't even bother to feel embarrassed that a stranger had seen me naked.

I just threw my wet hair into a bun, pulled on a pair of jeans and a shirt, switched out the birdshot for regular slugs in my revolver, checked to make sure the safety was on and tucked it into the waistband of my pants at the small of my back.

I took the time to put on my work boots. They were easier to move in than my slip-on irrigation boots if things went sideways.

I walked toward the guy, deliberately scuffing my feet in the gravel on the driveway to make noise.

When I got about twenty yards away, I spoke in a super friendly and casual tone, "Hey."

He turned around. "Oh hi."

I asked the obvious question. "Who are you?"

He told me his name like I should know who he was. But it meant nothing to me.

"What are you doing here?"

He explained, "I dropped off gravel for your driveway. Hunter is spreading it now." He pointed toward the tree line where our driveway disappeared.

I looked around for a truck or trailer. Something that would indicate someone had hauled in gravel.

I didn't see anything but I did remember Hunter saying he wanted to add gravel to a low spot, so the story could be true.

I made some small talk about how he knew Hunter and if he had been paid for the gravel yet. They were doing a barter of some kind.

I didn't actually care. I was just buying time, assuming Hunter would come back for the guy pretty quickly if his story was true.

It didn't take long for me to hear the familiar sound of our tractor. When I looked up, Hunter was coming around the trees and up the driveway.

I closed the conversation, saying something like, "Okay great. It was nice to meet you. I'm going to get back to work."

I backed away as I spoke. When I felt like I had enough distance to hear him coming and be able to react if I needed to, I turned toward the house.

I wasn't about to turn my back and risk him grabbing my gun.

When I finally did turn, the guy yelled at me, shock evident in his voice, "Hey! Do you have a gun in your pants?"

I turned back to face him and tilted my head in confusion. "We are in the middle of nowhere. Did you really think I would confront a random man unarmed?"

He started freaking out. "Holy shit! Hunter needs to tell you next time I'm coming! He almost got me shot!"

I calmly explained that he was nowhere near "almost shot." I never even took the gun out of my pants.

Hunter never said a word about the whole thing, but the story must have spread. After that, his friends always made sure I knew they were coming, sometimes even calling me themselves, just to be safe.

****

August was especially brutal that year. Working outside under the sun tanned my skin a deep, golden brown and bleached my naturally blonde hair nearly white.

When Carmen asked me to go with her as moral support for her audition for a local theater production of *Brigadoon*, I was happy for the break from sweating outside.

For her audition she did a great job of singing *"Wouldn't It Be Loverly"* from *My Fair Lady*.

As we were getting ready to leave, the person running the auditions stopped us and asked if I wanted to audition too.

I hadn't even thought about it. I don't consider myself a singer, and I told them I didn't have anything prepared.

Carmen piped up, "You know my song!"

That was true but it was in a key that was too high for me to sing well. The judges didn't seem to care and told me I should just go for it.

I thought, "Why not? I can mostly hold a tune."

When they called a week later to offer me a part, my first thought was panic. What if they cast me but not Carmen? But as it turned out, we were both offered nonspeaking roles.

I realized later that they just needed townspeople in the chorus and were taking anyone with a heartbeat. Didn't matter. Carmen and I were both excited to be part of it.

It also meant I was away from home nights and weekends for rehearsals and shows.

I don't remember if Hunter even noticed. He was rarely home, and we were living such separate lives by then, he might've actually been relieved I wasn't around.

I met some amazing friends and was reminded that, in high school, I had really enjoyed theater.

There is a picture of Carmen and me after opening night, dressed up for the "gala" in fancy dresses we made sitting on the floor in her apartment. Hers was red sequins and black lace. Mine was royal blue.

We both look incredibly happy.

I was beginning to realize how different I was when I had to put on a mask to be with Hunter versus the person I was when I was out on my own.

****

One Monday in mid-September, my coworker and friend Hank pulled me aside at work, a serious look on his face.

He had always made it clear he would have dated me if I weren't married. In fact, when he switched jobs, he hired me away from the bank to work in tech with him because I had "nice legs."

His boss choked when he heard him say that. I thought it was funny.

But Hank had always been respectful of my marriage. He'd met Hunter a few times and we had recently been at his house for a party.

So, when he pulled me aside and dropped his voice to say, "I'm not sure why I didn't tell you this sooner" I was curious.

I tilted my head and frowned, "Okay...?" inviting him to continue.

"When you, Hunter and Carmen came over a couple of weeks ago..." He trailed off.

"Yes?"

"Hunter asked to buy drugs from me." He said it quickly, in all one breath.

I knew Hank was into that lifestyle.

But Hunter had told me he had stopped all of that when we bought the catfish farm. He insisted it was "too risky to keep it on the property."

I wasn't shocked, just disappointed. And honestly, how dumb did he have to be to try to buy from one of *my* friends?

Hank continued, "I asked Hunter how he was getting away with it. I know you're not cool about drugs. He told me he keeps it in the back of the top drawer in his toolbox. Said you have no reason to look there."

I inhaled deeply and blew it out through my nose while gritting my teeth.

"I'm sorry I didn't tell you sooner. I realized I was keeping a secret for someone I didn't like from someone I really do. I respect you, Robyn. You deserve a man who doesn't lie to you."

That last bit was a play but he was also right.

I told him I appreciated him telling me and just went back to work.

A couple of weekends later, I found myself standing in the garage. I'd come out to grab a tool for a project on my to-do list.

I had what I needed in my hand when I stopped and looked at Hunter's tall, red, Snap-On rolling toolbox.

I stood there for a long moment. Did I really want to know?

If I looked and there were drugs, what would I even do?

I set down the tool I was holding and walked over to the toolbox, almost hoping it was locked. If I couldn't open it, I could stay in denial and pretend my life really wasn't this crazy.

I looped my fingers under the top-drawer handle and pulled. It slid smoothly open and my stomach tightened.

I stepped back to pull it all the way out and, even though I'm 5'9", had to stand on my tiptoes to see into the very back compartment.

And there, in the middle, tucked tightly between two dividers, was an unmistakable baggie of drugs.

I thought about flushing it. Or burying it.

But I didn't want my fingerprints on it and the real issue wasn't the drugs. It was the lies. The purposeful deception. The way Hunter had looked me in the eye and pretended to be someone he wasn't.

He wasn't a partner to me. I was more of an adult at eighteen than he was now.

I had continued to grow, develop and learn. He hadn't changed at all; stuck in the same phase of life he had been in when I met him almost ten years ago.

I was living in a shack trying to make the best of a horrible situation.

He thought about the risks. Talked to me about it. And then decided that it — that I — didn't matter.

I closed the drawer and held my palm flat against it for a moment. Then I took a deep breath, turned, picked up the tool I had come into the garage to get, and walked back out into the sunshine.

Nothing in the outside world had changed, but inside, everything had shifted.

****

That night, the house was cool with the coming fall. My skin prickled with dread like it was much colder.

I knew I needed to have the conversation but also really wanted to avoid it.

How do you even start a conversation like that? I didn't want to fight. There was no reason to cry. I didn't even know what I wanted the outcome to be. I just knew I couldn't keep going like we were.

Hunter came home late and went straight to the shower without even acknowledging me.

I sat on the floor next to the fireplace, enjoying the heat from the small fire I had built.

He came out of the bathroom with a towel wrapped around his waist; as he walked through the living room toward the bedroom, I spoke.

"Hank told me you tried to buy drugs from him." My voice sounded flat. Resigned.

He replied sharply, "Yeah. So?" then turned the corner and disappeared into the bedroom.

I didn't want to yell from the other room so I got up and followed him.

His towel lay damp and discarded on the floor on my side of the bed. He was already settling under the covers.

I needed a shower, and there probably wasn't any hot water left. Maybe it would be warmish by the time we finished talking.

I started to undress, waiting for him to say something.

The silence stretched.

I folded my shirt and set it on the tiny table to wear again tomorrow.

As I slid my pants off, I said, "I saw the drugs in the toolbox."

His eyes were closed, but I knew he was awake.

I folded my pants and put them on top of my shirt, then reached back to unhook my bra and set it on the pile.

"We need to talk about this."

He opened his eyes as I took off my socks. The disdain, and maybe even hatred, was unmistakable.

"What is there to talk about?" He spat the words at me in a way that seemed disproportionate to my calm tone.

I sighed, stepping out of my underwear and picking it up with my socks and his towel to toss in the laundry basket.

"You told me you weren't going to have drugs here. We talked about the risks if you get caught. Not just for you, but for me. It would ruin my life to be associated with that. You know I'd lose my job."

He shoved himself into a sitting position, his eyes flashing with anger.

That's when I realized he might actually be high.

He barked, "Fine. You want to talk. I'll talk."

The energy in the room turned dangerous. But somehow, I didn't feel exposed, even though I was completely naked.

"I have to be high to even stand being around you. You're such a bitch!"

The words hit me like he'd struck my chest with his fist. I didn't respond. I couldn't. It felt like I had to remind myself to even breathe.

His face contorted into a sneer.

"I don't love you.

"I don't want to be married to you.

"And I don't want you living in my house!"

Each sentence, a punctuated staccato. Sharp. Definitive. Final.

By the end he was yelling.

I stood there, blinking. It seemed like a long time, but I don't think it was.

Then I replied simply, "Oh," before turning and walking out of the bedroom.

I got about five steps, then I stopped and turned around to walk back into the bedroom.

He was still sitting up in bed.

I looked at him feeling both empty and adamant. "You realize this means you no longer have access to my body. Right?"

I didn't wait for an answer. It wasn't actually a question.

I left him sitting there and went to take a lukewarm shower.

He would never see me naked again.

Chapter 19
You Just Don't Steal a Girl's Gun

I don't remember the exact conversation with Carmen, but she basically told me that she had seen the writing on the wall that my marriage was going to implode and that is why she had rented a two-bedroom apartment.

She even had an old bedroom set from her mom's house for me to use. We joked that it was the bed Carmen had been conceived on. But I think it really was.

Without a lot of fanfare or discussion, it was decided that I would move out of the shack on the catfish farm and into the apartment with Carmen.

Two weeks after the "I don't love you" speech, Hunter took my car to work and left the one-ton dually pickup he usually drove at home so I could use it to move my stuff.

He kept the dining room set that his buddy had scratched in the move, the bedroom furniture, most of our kitchen stuff, the TV and his stereo.

I took the washer and dryer and my clothes.

I wanted my revolver and he had told me it was mine. I just had to get a gun permit from the state to legally transfer it to my name.

I jumped through all those hoops. But when I met him to exchange the paperwork and get it from him, he casually told me that he would sell it to me.

That was the lie that made me take off my wedding ring.

I didn't yell, carry on or throw it at him.

I told him to keep the gun, slipped the ring off of my finger, and tucked it into my pocket as I walked away.

You just don't steal a girl's gun.

As far as I know, he still has that gun with the beautiful rosewood grips carved in the shape of a bearded man.

But I think he bent the cylinder putting hot loads through it.

Sorry, I digress.

The day I moved out, Carmen made the drive out to the shack to help me.

We quickly realized getting a washer and dryer up into that tall pickup was going to be a challenge.

Hunter had already told me not to expect his help in any way.

But Carmen and I were smart.

I backed the truck up to a spot where the hillside had been cutaway at a sharp angle. Once we put the tailgate down, we would only have to lift the machines about a foot.

I got the hand truck out of the garage, attached it to the washing machine, drug it through the grass and then, with me pulling from in the bed of the truck and Carmen pushing from the bottom, we were able to lever it into the truck. We did the same with the dryer.

I was pretty impressed with us.

I don't remember how we got them off the truck when we got to the apartment. But together we were able to get them both moved over, hooked up and working.

We had all my stuff moved, and I was back at the shack when Hunter came back with my car.

He didn't speak.

He just tossed my keys on the counter, and disappeared into the garage.

Before I left, I wrote him a note:

"If you'd like to try counseling again, call and make an appointment. Just let me know when it is and I will be there.

"If you don't, the phone book is open to a page of divorce mediators. I have circled one that I think will work.

"Give them a call and have them call me to let me know what the next steps are for us to get legally separated."

(In North Carolina a couple has to be legally and financially separated, living in different places for a year before they can file for divorce.)

I signed it with just my first name (spelled correctly).

Then I picked up my keys, walked to my car, and drove into the next chapter of my life.

****

I cried into my pillow for so many nights.

Because I felt like a failure.

Because I felt shame for not being able to make it work.

Because I was alone.

Because Hunter called my dad and told him he had thrown me out for being "lazy."

Because my dad called me and told me I "would have been able to make it work" if I had been "appropriately submissive." And that I was, "bringing shame on the family."

He also said he didn't want me to take back his name.

I did anyway.

Though now, I have a name that's just mine.

It doesn't belong to anyone else.

Within a month of my moving in, Carmen met the man who would become her husband and the father of her children. In short order she was spending nights with him.

I liked him. He was (and is) a great guy.

I used to joke that I was doing her laundry at our place and he was doing her laundry at his.

A pretty good deal for her for sure.

Carmen, unlike me, could sleep through anything. I used to have to ask her if she was awake enough for me to talk to when she was standing in the kitchen eating cereal. (That still makes me laugh.)

She had the worst screeching alarm clock I have ever heard.

When she was home, it was fine because she might hit snooze once or twice but then she would get up and turn it off.

When she stayed with her boyfriend that damn alarm would start blaring and I would have to stumble from my bedroom to hers to shut it up.

I could never figure out how to turn it off so it stayed off. The first couple of times I would think I turned it off but had only snoozed it. I would be just going back to sleep and it was screaming again.

So, it became common for her to come home and find her alarm clock unplugged and the batteries out of it laying on her bed.

I asked her to turn the alarm completely off before she left, but then she would forget to turn it back on and end up oversleeping.

Neither of us was mad about it. We just got into a rhythm. If the alarm went off when she wasn't home, I took the clock apart; she would put it back together and reset it when she came back.

It was almost shocking how easy it was to coexist with her after the chaos of living with Hunter.

Chapter 20
The Church Always Blames the Woman

As I settled into my new life, I wondered which path Hunter would choose: more counseling or legal separation.

It took less than a month for me to receive a call from the divorce mediation group I had circled in the phone book for him.

They told me my husband wanted to create a legal separation agreement and asked if I was willing to work with them or if I wanted to hire lawyers and go through the courts.

I was happy to work with them and asked what they needed to get started.

There was lots of required documentation and some back and forth, but in the end, it wasn't too bad.

We made roughly the same amount of verifiable income (obviously his drug income didn't count), so no alimony in either direction.

Hunter wanted to keep the catfish farm, which was totally fine by me, and the mediator helped us negotiate a fair trade.

I got most of the cash we had in the bank, Hunter signed over a large chunk of his retirement account, and I gave him a personal loan at the going 30-year mortgage rate for the balance he owed me.

I think it was for seven years.

The mediator suggested I put a lien on the property as collateral. I thought that was good advice and they helped me do it.

Hunter kept his truck.

I kept my car, although we had to move the title over to me and he made me pay for that myself.

My only heartbreak was my dog, Blanquita.

She was getting old and had always been an outside dog (I wasn't a very good dog owner back then).

There was no way I could move her into the apartment with me, so Hunter agreed to keep her.

I drove out to the catfish farm a few times to see her. But it was so far and I hated the risk of bumping into Hunter.

I don't know what happened to her or how she died. I'm guessing she was buried on the catfish farm.

She was a good dog, and I could have done so much better by her, even though that was a crazy time in my life.

The little dog I have now, Nebula, is also a medium-sized black-and-white dog.

I hope the love and care I show her makes up for my failings with Blanquita.

****

Six months after Hunter told me to leave, I received a letter in the mail addressed to me in Hunter's handwriting.

Inside was another envelope, with just my first name written in handwriting I didn't recognize.

It contained a letter, with the name, address and phone number of the church we had been attending, typed in large, bold font across the top.

I kept that letter in the folder with the paperwork from our divorce.

I have retyped exactly, typos and all:

Dear Robyn,

Greetings to you in the name of our Lord and Savior. I trust you are in good health these days, and it would be good to see you, since I have noted your absence from worship services since December, particularly as your husband has continued in regular attendance. When I asked about your well being, Hunter discreetly informed me that you are no longer living at home.

Quite naturally, news of this separation came as somewhat of a shock to me, as Hunter and I had shared only one conversation last summer, in which I suggested some biblical principles for strengthening his relationship with you. I also offered to meet with both of you for further prayer and counsel, but I heard nothing more until your absence became obvious, when I asked Hunter about the situation. He indicated that there appeared to be willingness (on both sides) to reconcile differences up until October, when legal separation was instituted. As you know, I asked Hunter around Christmastime if I could speak with you, an offer you apparently declined.

I wanted you to have the opportunity to (the next part is highlighted) *defend yourself from any false rumors and also to answer any accusations concerning your actions. That offer is still open.*

Without attempting to fix blame, may I remind you of the wedding vows you made before God and to your husband, to "live together in the bonds of holy matrimony...until death do you part." Hunter seems to be willing to honor these vows, assuming there is sincere response from your side, but each passing day makes reconciliation more difficult. At this point, in is not a matter of who is mostly in the wrong, but whether both of you are willing to do what is right according to God's Word. I am a firm believer that the God of all peace can resolve our conflicts when we follow the directions of Scripture, and I see no reason to doubt the same in the situation at hand.

While no person is without sin, it is the duty of the elders to inquire into the spiritual well being of those under our care, for you promised in your membership vow, to "live as becomes a follower of Christ, to support the church in its worship, and to submit yourself to the discipline of the Church." So, I have enclosed a self addressed, stamped envelop and ask that you make a brief response concerning your intentions with regard to both your marriage and your membership. Do you intend to be reconciled with your husband? Do you desire to remain a member of Christ's church? If you prefer, you may meet with the elders to answer these questions and to share any other concerns you have. Our purpose is to be helpful, not to be condemning.

I look forward to hearing from you soon. Please reply within two weeks and be assured of my continued prayers for you!

Yours in Christ's Love

[Pastor's first name]

This is what was on the second sheet of paper:

To: The Session of the Church

Date: (left blank)

I do not/ do intend to be reconciled with my husband in the bonds of Christian matrimony, as I have vowed before God.

I do not/ do intend to resume regular worship and fellowship with the Church, as I have vowed before God.

I would like to meet with the elders of the church to discuss my situation on this date (please give us several options):

Sincerely in Christ,

(Feel free to add any other comments)

Reading that letter, my body went cold and shame coursed through me.

It screamed: *Failure. Loser. Evil. Bad.*

I sat on the edge of my bed, closed my eyes, and focused on my breath. Just for a moment.

I had several problems:

1. It was more than two weeks since the date on the letter. I had already missed their response window.

2. I had no idea Hunter had spoken with him over the summer, and the "biblical principles" were never shared with me.

3. I knew nothing about the pastor asking to speak in December. That message had not been passed along to me.

4. Hunter kicked me out in early October. The pastor didn't notice I was missing until December? This letter was dated mid-April. That's when he finally decided to start asking questions?

5. Obviously, Hunter had failed to mention that I wasn't living at home because he had told me to leave.

6. I had not been attending church because how weird would it be to continue to attend the same church as my estranged husband? Was I just supposed to sit in a different pew and act like everything was fine?

I thought about trying to write back, explaining what actually happened. But how could I possibly explain eight years of hurt, confusion, and neglect in a letter?

And I wasn't confident they actually wanted to understand. My experience with churches was that they didn't care about the woman's point of view.

Besides, writing and sending a letter would delay my response even further.

Instead, I decided to call and talk to the pastor. He knew me. Surely, we could have a reasonable conversation.

I called several times the next day but I just got the church office voicemail.

Eventually, I left a message saying I had received their letter, and that I *was* living in submission to my husband. He told me to leave, so I did.

I also told them that if they could get Hunter to agree to a meeting with the pastor or an elder, to let me know where and when and I would be there. I even offered to take time off from work.

I never heard back from them. Literally, no response. And I didn't try to chase them down.

Over the next couple of years, I saw the pastor at various volleyball tournaments. He went out of his way to avoid me, pretending not to know who I was.

That was fine with me. I didn't want to deal with him looking down his nose at me in the way only condescending, holier-than-thou Christians do.

I don't know if they ever officially excommunicated me.

And quite frankly, I stopped caring a long time ago. I never mattered to anyone in that church beyond my commitment to tithing, and I no longer believe I need their permission to worship as I see fit.

Reading that letter now, all these years later, I still feel the judgment from the system that invalidated and condemned me. It's so paternalistic.

And the multiple-choice confession form. As if the decision to end my marriage could be summed up in a checkbox. It's like a scrawled fifth grade "Do you like me? Check yes or no," note but with my eternal damnation on the line.

My parents' church was on the same crusade.

I happened to be home visiting my parents on a communion Sunday.

My mom quietly pulled me aside, and told me that because I wasn't living in "submission to my husband," and didn't have a letter of good standing from the men of my church, I wasn't allowed to take communion.

I thought about pointing out that Hunter had thrown me out and I was in submission by leaving. But I bit my tongue. I didn't care enough to bother.

I was only attending church because it was important to my parents. I didn't need to eat a little cracker and have a sip of wine.

But then my dad announced loudly in the crowded church vestibule between Sunday School and the service: "You know you can't take communion, right?"

My face burned with humiliation.

I don't know what I said to him but it was along the lines of, "Just because I don't have a letter from a bunch of old men saying I'm in good standing with their god does not mean a bunch of old men in this church get to tell me how I can and cannot worship!"

I stormed out of the church insulted and furious.

I was pacing the old, cracked sidewalk in front of the church when I heard the music start. I had zero interest in going back in there.

My youngest sister, a teenager, came out to check on me.

"Are you okay?"

"No!" I whisper-yelled. "I am most certainly *not* okay."

I ranted about the double standard and how stupid the whole thing was.

When we heard the second hymn start, my mom came out.

She said, "Robyn, I understand why you're mad. But this is my church and I have to attend here. Please stop embarrassing me and come back inside."

Out of respect for my mother, I went back in. But I sat scowling in the very back pew.

When they started the communion service I only lasted until the pastor got to the part where he said,

"But let a man examine himself, and so let him eat of this bread, and drink of this cup. For he that eateth and drinketh unworthily, eateth and drinketh damnation to himself, not discerning the Lord's body."

I couldn't just sit there and listen to that hypocrisy. They didn't care about my relationship with God. They only cared what some men they didn't even know thought about my relationship with God.

146

I wanted to yell that they were hypocrites.

Instead, I silently got up and walked out.

I told my mom I would never set foot in that church again.

And to this day, I haven't.

I struggle with what I will do when my parents pass away if they decide to hold their funerals there.

I hope that by then, I'll have let go of the bitterness and disrespect.

If it were to happen today, I'm not sure what I would do.

Chapter 21
Who Am I?

Outside the craziness of the church, I was trying to figure out who I was as an adult.

I was twenty-seven years old and I had never made a decision by myself in my life.

I had also never dated.

The first person I went out with was a coworker.

Right after we were seated, he went to the bathroom, and while he was gone, the waitress came by to take our drink order.

He always got unsweet tea and put half a packet of "the pink stuff" in it.

When he came back, I was stirring his tea.

He blinked. "You ordered me tea?"

"Yes, and I added sweetener."

As he sat down, he looked at the half-empty sweetener packet I had folded closed and set on the table, then up at me.

When he spoke, it was almost like he was talking to a child. "Robyn, you treat everyone like you love them. It's confusing."

I tilted my head and frowned. "What do you mean?"

"I mean, you know I drink unsweet tea with half a pack of sweetener in it."

"Yeah, so?"

"Most people only notice that kind of thing when they're around someone a lot, and they only act on it if they love them."

I didn't understand. "It bothers you that I ordered you tea?"

"No. It doesn't bother me. I'm just trying to tell you that guys are going to get the wrong idea because you're way more observant than most girls, and you're too nice."

This wasn't the first time I had been told I was "too nice." But I had no idea what he meant.

He spent a lot of time that night over dinner trying to explain how dating worked and that I needed to be more stand-offish.

I didn't get it.

Now I know it was a trauma response. I had been so conditioned to fill the caregiver role that I did it for all men.

I had spent so much time with emotionally volatile men that I became hyper-observant, constantly scanning for what made them happy, what set them off, what made their life easier.

Once I recognized those things, I acted on those observations automatically. I was running a script that said, *if the man is happy, I am safe.*

But I didn't know all that then.

I also learned while out with that coworker that I had anxiety about eating in public. He once commented that I must like the bread. I ended up in tears and refused to eat anymore that night.

For some reason, my brain translated, "You must really like the bread" into "You're a selfish fat cow."

There was so much trauma I didn't yet know I needed to unpack.

What I did know was that I didn't want to date anyone seriously and I made that very clear.

I told guys up front:

I was in a bad marriage for a long time.

I am not dating anyone exclusively.

I will not lie to you.

Do not ask questions you don't want to know the answers to.

Over time I started adding a snarkier message:

"Welcome to Robyn's world. Here are the rules:

Rule one: Do not fall in love.

Rule two: See rule number one."

Clearly, I had the dating maturity of a teenager.

But I was stumbling my way through, trying to figure it out.

I did know enough to realize I needed to pay for my own meals if I wanted to keep things casual. I wasn't having sex with anyone, either.

Don't get me wrong, I did sleep next to some of them. I did travel with some of them. But I was not having intercourse with any of them.

I learned I could date anyone for about eight months because I would contort myself into whatever worked best for them.

Around eight months they would think they had found their perfect match and I would realize that I was no longer me.

I would end things and they would be heartbroken, saying I had changed.

I would try to explain that the girl they fell in love with didn't exist. She was just a version I created to keep them happy.

Over time I added this to my introduction:

"I don't cook. I don't clean. And I don't have babies."

There are a few dating stories I want to share: Aaron, Marcus, Dale and three different guys named Sean.

But before we get to that, I have to tell you about The Apple Strudel Heist.

I started calling it that the very first time I told this story.

The whole thing was so bumbling, I had to give a nod to the 1975 Don Knotts comedy-western, *The Apple Dumpling Gang.*

Even funnier, one of the guys involved had a name that sounded like strudel.

Chapter 22
The Apple Strudel Heist

As I mentioned, North Carolina law requires a couple to be legally separated, living in different places and financially independent from one another, for a full year before either party can file for divorce.

Once our legal separation was in place, I just lived my life; not really keeping track of when the year would be up or even thinking about the fact that one of us would eventually need to actually file for divorce.

Plus, I didn't think it was fair that I would have to pay 100% of it if I filed. So, I just didn't.

When Carmen's lease was up, she and her boyfriend (future husband) decided to move in together.

Which meant I was suddenly without a place to live.

Since I had the cash from my separation just sitting in the bank, I decided it would be smart to buy a house.

It took me a while, and almost having to fire my realtor, to find one.

I had made it clear to her that I didn't like houses with stairs in the entryway, and that I wanted to spend about $30,000 less than what the bank wanted to loan me (that was back when banks were giving out money all willy-nilly).

The final straw was when I used my lunch break to meet her at a house that she insisted was "perfect" for me.

When I arrived, the paperwork showed the house was well over my price point; and when I opened the front door, it practically banged into the stairs.

I didn't even step into the house.

I turned around and said, "If you show me one more house with stairs in the foyer, I will fire you."

I then walked back to my car and left.

The next house she showed me didn't have stairs in the foyer, was within my budget and I bought it.

I rented out the extra bedroom and put every cent of that rent money toward the principal on my mortgage.

Most of the money Hunter was repaying me from the property loan I had given him on the catfish farm was also going toward my principal.

By the time I sold that house, when I made the mistake of getting married a second time, I was just two years from having it paid off.

Outside of work, I was playing volleyball, swimming, lifting weights and had a very active dating life.

Hunter, his crazy friends, and the nonsense that was his life, weren't even on my radar.

Until one day when I picked up my work phone and it was him.

He didn't say hello or make small talk. Just: "Hey."

I frowned. I was always skeptical when I heard from him. "What's up?"

What he said next was so far out of left field, I just blinked.

"There was a break-in at Stone Muller's Lake Wylie place. The Pineville sheriff is gonna call you. But you don't know anything about it."

My first thought was, *"Dumbass! If you hadn't called me, I wouldn't know anything about it!"*

What I actually said was, "Stop talking. I don't want to know. I'm hanging up."

I hung up the phone and stared at it, stunned. Why would he be stupid enough to call me, *tell* me something I didn't know, and then add that I didn't know anything about it?

I shook it off and went back to work.

I forgot about it until several days later when, once again, my office phone rang; an outside number and the name "Pineville" showed on the display.

I tapped the button to answer the call on my headset and using my most professional voice, identified the bank and gave my first name.

What I heard next made me squinch my face. It was the deepest drawl you can imagine. Much like the woman in the elevator years ago who had asked me to "mash the fourth floor."

But not only did this guy sound like his mouth was full of marbles, all of the vowels were extra-long, like he thought they were pulled-taffy.

I'm not going to try to write it the way it sounded, but if you ever get a chance to ask me about it, I can do the accent really well and it makes the story even funnier.

This is how the conversation went:

"Is this Mrs. Hunter Weebler?"

I cringed. "Yes. Technically."

"Mrs. Weebler, this is Sheriff so-and-so from the Pineville Sheriff's department."

"Good afternoon, sir. What can I do for you?" I already knew he was calling about the break-in Hunter had tipped me off about. But I was keeping that to myself.

"Ma'am, do you know one, Stone Muller?"

"Stone Muller — of the South Carolina Mullers? Made their money in illegal gambling machines. Owns a house on Lake Wylie. *That* Stone Muller?

"Yes ma'am. That's Stone Muller. Do you know one, Joe Strudel?"

"Joe Strudel — Short. Fat. Redneck. Drives a red diesel pickup truck. Cusses a lot. *That* Joe Strudel?"

Yes ma'am. That's Joe Strudel."

He paused. I'm not sure if it was for dramatic effect or if he forgot the details of why he called.

I waited in silence.

Then he continued, "Ma'am, are you aware, that on such-and-such a date, there was a break-in at Stone Muller's Lake Wylie address where $250,000 in cash and several guns were taken from his gun safe?"

"No sir. I was unaware."

"Ma'am, are you aware that your husband, Mr. Hunter Weebler, has a handgun in his gun safe, given to him by Joe Strudel, that was hot?" (hot meaning stolen)

"No sir. I was unaware."

153

"Ma'am, are you aware that your husband, Mr. Hunter Weebler, recently purchased a piece of earth moving equipment for cash, and it was hot?"

"No sir. I was unaware."

I waited a beat and then continued, "Sir, if I had known my husband had that kind of cash, I would have been going after it because he owes me about $43,000. I have a lien against the property he's living on; you can look it up.

"Also, he and I have been legally separated for almost two years. I can supply the paperwork for that as well. I try very hard to not involve myself with him or any of his lowlife, redneck friends.

"I'm sorry I can't be of more help to you, but I really have no idea what is going on in his life.

"But feel free to call me back if you have questions I *can* answer."

Silence stretched while I waited for him to process what I had just said.

His reply was simple. "Thank you, ma'am. I understand. I will be calling you back if I have any other questions. You have a good afternoon, ma'am."

I pushed the button on my phone to disconnect the call thinking, *"Holy shit, what kind of mess has Hunter dragged me into now?"*

I immediately dialed to get an outside line and called our lawyer.

As soon as his paralegal picked up, I introduced myself and said, "You need to file my divorce paperwork, *immediately* if not sooner. My husband has gotten himself into something involving the police and I don't want my name attached to it."

She asked if I thought Hunter would sign it or if we were going to have to go to court.

It didn't even occur to me that he might fight the divorce.

Ten days later Hunter called me again. This time he was ranting about how I clearly didn't value our marriage vows and that he couldn't believe I was filing for divorce.

I waited for him to finish and then replied, "I don't know what you've been doing for the last two years, but I've been dating. There is zero chance we are getting back together, especially after whatever you've gotten yourself involved in that has the sheriff calling me. Sign the paperwork or I'm going to have to bring that all up in court."

He huffed. He sputtered. But he signed it.

A few weeks later I was legally divorced. Oof. Bullet dodged.

It wouldn't be the last I would hear from Hunter though. He still shows up in my life for the weirdest reasons.

Chapter 23
I Have No Clue How to Date

Over the next few years, I went on a lot of first dates, some with people I knew, some with complete strangers. Like the guy who approached me while I was waiting for my car to be "washed" at a high school marching band fundraiser.

He made a bit of small talk, and just as my car was getting finished, asked to take me to dinner that night, I had nothing else going on. So, sure, why not?

He made a reservation for 7:00, and asked for my address, so he could pick me up.

I told him I would meet him there.

He said, "Make it 6:30. We'll get a drink first."

I explained that I didn't drink because I was a competitive volleyball player. So 7:00.

He tried to argue further but I shut it down: "7:00 or not at all."

That night I barely said two words.

Have you ever been in a conversation where you became so interested in how they transitioned from one topic to the next that you almost stopped listening to what they were actually saying?

It was like that.

He told me on repeat how beautiful I was. That he was looking for a wife. That he wanted to move me to Paris and take care of me for the rest of my life.

He was talking like it was a done deal, even giving me dates for the move.

I made it through dinner. When I offered to pay half, he got offended, saying something about me "insulting his manhood" and slapped down his credit card to cover the full check.

He insisted on walking me to my car, when I unlocked it and turned to say goodnight, he leaned in aggressively to kiss me.

I put my hand, fingers spread wide, on his chest, leaned away and said,

"No, thank you. I'm not looking to get married, move to Paris, or be taken care of."

He was ranting about gold-digger women using him for free meals as I drove away.

I'm so glad I never gave him my number or address.

****

The first guy I went out with regularly, was Aaron. He worked on the same floor I did, doing some kind of coding.

I never called it "dating," because that's something you do when you're looking for a partner.

I wasn't looking for a partner, but I was happy to do interesting things with fun guys, and I tried to make that clear.

Although, they usually didn't listen.

I had very few requirements for saying yes to doing something.

1. Was this someone I could enjoy spending time with? (Most people are.)

2. Was my schedule open?

3. Was whatever they were proposing fun, interesting or necessary?

When Aaron asked if I wanted to go to lunch and I didn't have anything else planned, I said, "Sure."

I can talk to a fence post and make it interesting. So guys got the impression we were "hitting it off."

I never thought it was anything special.

Later, when Aaron asked me to dinner, I realized he wanted more than just coworkers grabbing lunch, so I explained my Welcome to Robyn's World rules.

He laughed.

I probably should have been more forceful about the fact that I wasn't kidding. I hung out with him because it was better than doing nothing, but we weren't connecting on some special level.

We started spending time together about once a week, but he often had to work around other things I had going on.

One night, when he was dropping me off, he said he was too tired to drive home. My clueless self completely missed what was really going on.

(I was 28 but my dating IQ was about 15.)

I explained to him that I had plans the next morning (with a different guy) and that I was being picked up at 8:00. But if he wanted to sleep next to me, that was fine.

Looking back, it's no wonder guys got confused. I genuinely thought I was just being nice, letting a guy sleep over when he was too tired to drive.

Nothing else happened. We literally just slept.

It didn't occur to me that letting him sleep in my bed might make him think the relationship was 'moving forward' somehow.

****

At around the same time, I met three guys named Sean.

One was a temp that the bank brought in to help finish a project that was behind schedule.

He and I "played" tennis a few times a month. Meaning we mostly just whacked the ball around and talked about office gossip or philosophy.

We actually had a guy interrupt us once to ask if we were talking about real people and events or writing a sitcom.

That's just how crazy my life was at the time.

I met the second Sean out dancing.

I gave him my business card with my personal number written on the back. He never called. But I thought it was him when one of the other Seans called, and that added unnecessary confusion to my life.

The third guy lived in the same apartment complex as Carmen and me.

I met him briefly the day I moved in and didn't remember his name.

I didn't know he was the one scraping frost off my windshield before I got up.

And I didn't realize it was him when he called asking if I wanted to meet for dinner.

(Thinking about it now, I'm not sure how he got my number.)

I said I couldn't; I already had plans. He changed it on the fly to bagels and coffee Saturday morning instead.

I was available then, and because I thought it was the guy I met dancing, I said yes.

Imagine my shock when I walked up to the bagel place and saw my neighbor, not someone I would have agreed to meet, sitting at the table smiling at me!

I wasn't willing to deal with the awkwardness of explaining the mistake, so I just went with it.

We sat outside on wire seats that leave crisscross marks that look like cellulite on your skin.

After I finished my bagel, I leaned back in my chair, stretched out my legs, and put my feet up on the chair next to me.

I chilled in that devil-may-care pose while we chatted about anything and everything; including that I enjoyed swing dancing (which I promptly forgot I told him).

The next week, I got flowers at work with a card that said, "When are we going dancing? — Sean" Again, I thought they were from the guy I had met dancing.

It wasn't until neighbor-Sean called to ask if I'd gotten them that I realized who had actually sent them.

I didn't know it then, but that was the beginning of a complicated, but long and wonderful, friendship.

We were never romantic. He would have married me in a second, but that just wasn't where I was in my life.

We are still friends. In fact, I let him pick his alias for this book. Going forward, anytime I mention Sean, it's him. He's the only one who has stayed a part of my life.

Every card, every call, every email and now every text from him always ends the same way, "Be safe."

****

When the fall volleyball season ended, I went in search of places I could play indoors for the winter. Indoor games never kept me in the shape playing on the beach or in the grass did, but it was better than nothing.

I played some pick-up ball at the local Y but it wasn't as competitive as I had hoped it would be.

So, I walked into a huge, new sports facility to see if they were running a winter league.

It turned out they had a few teams in the coed division looking for female players.

I told the guy at the desk what level I played and gave him my contact information, saying he was welcome to pass it along to the captain of whichever team he thought would be the best fit.

Less than a week later I got a call and I was playing on a team by that Friday.

I was playing in that league when I met Steve and Marcus.

Steve was a really nice guy who I'm still friends with. I would have dated him if we had ever been single at the same time.

As Marcus and I got to know each other and he learned the "rules" I had, he once said, "I don't understand why anyone would date you."

I just shrugged and responded, "I don't know, but lots of them do."

Eventually, Marcus became my regular coed two's partner, and we hung out whenever he wasn't dating someone else, including going on vacation together.

We likely would have been a great couple, except he wanted children and I knew I didn't.

Sean and Marcus once stood in my driveway chatting while I changed clothes; Marcus was late dropping me off, and Sean was early to pick me up for the next thing.

Neither of them seemed to have a problem with it, partly because I was very open with everyone that there were other men in my life.

Marcus and I were at a volleyball tournament when a guy on another team started giving me lip. I smirked and replied, "I didn't come to hear your mouth. I came to see your game. I hope you brought it."

I heard Marcus laugh behind me. He just got me and we enjoyed each other's company in a comfortable, easy way.

I lost contact with him when he got engaged and his fiancée told him, "It's either her or me."

He told me about her ultimatum when I was sitting between sets on the pull-down machine in the gym where he and I had worked out together for years.

I understood why she saw me as a threat. She was what he wanted his life to become. I was just a fun place-filler. I cared about him deeply and wanted him to be happy.

With tears in my eyes, I said, "If you ever need a pint of blood, you know where to find me."

We had a running joke about having the same blood type.

He did have kids (three, I think) and I truly hope his life turned out exactly the way he wanted.

****

One of the "dates" that Sean planned for me was to go sailing on his tiny sailboat.

It was very sweet. He packed a picnic lunch, including ice cream that he kept cold with dry ice. It was so frozen that I couldn't even take a bite out of it.

That made us laugh.

We were cruising around the lake, chatting toward the end of the afternoon, when we looked up and saw a speedboat bearing down on us at full throttle.

They were pulling a skier behind them, and everyone in the boat, including the driver, was turned around looking at him.

Sean tried to angle our boat so if the speedboat hit us, it would go over the bow and we might at least have a fighting chance to survive.

At the last second, I summoned my loudest, scream-across-the-pasture voice, and bellowed, "HELLO!"

161

The driver whipped his head around and I saw panic in his eyes as he threw the boat into neutral and turned the steering wheel hard to the right.

I saw the bottom of the boat as it continued to plow sideways toward us.

Fortunately, the wake it created pushed our smaller, lighter boat just far enough to avoid a crash.

But that same wake was a towering wall of water that soaked us.

The speedboat driver mumbled "sorry" and quickly drove away to pick up the skier.

The sun was setting. My cute summer dress clung to me, drenched and heavy. The cool air prickled my skin, and my hair hung in limp, dripping strands.

But we were alive. I was going to take that as a win.

I never wanted to go sailing again. Not even when I started dating Dale, who raced sailboats and thought I'd make "great crew."

Sean made it up to me though. Not with more sailing, thank God.

He took me to Jamaica, where I spent a week playing beach volleyball on sand as fine as sugar, surrounded by absolutely gorgeous men while Sean went diving.

It started out in a funny way though.

I was lying on the beach when I saw three guys near the volleyball net peppering the ball around.

I got up and walked over to see if they wanted a fourth.

One of the guys said, "Have you ever played volleyball?"

I was coy. What was I going to say, *yes, I've won money playing*?

Instead, I just said, "Yeah, I've played some."

Two of them laughed and ducked under the net, clearly thinking they'd stuck their buddy with the cute but useless tourist.

I turned to the guy they had left standing next to me, (He was one of the best-looking men I had ever seen in person) and said, "Where do you like your sets?"

He blinked, "What?"

I clarified: "Are you right-handed or left? Do you hit outside? On the net or off? High or quick?"

He smirked, "You've played more than some," then told me he was right-handed and where he wanted his sets.

We wiped the court with the other two guys.

When the game ended in their embarrassing defeat, they wanted to switch up the teams.

My partner said, "You didn't want her. Now you can't have her."

He and I ran that court the entire week I was there.

Fun volleyball memories.

Sean and I made the most of the rest of the trip too. Sunset dinners, warm ocean water, and dancing in the sand. He practiced his photography with me as the subject.

I have some amazing photos of my younger self on those beaches.

Years later, Sean told me he was grateful I had said yes to Jamaica. He wouldn't have gone if I hadn't.

Chapter 24
My First Stalker

trigger warning — suicidal themes

While I was trying to live my best life and figure out who I was, Carmen and her boyfriend got engaged.

Of course I was her maid of honor. The only attendant she decided to have.

She made me a custom ice-blue dress that clung in all the right places.

I had planned to take Aaron as my plus one, but on the night before the trashy-lingerie bachelorette party I had planned for her, the whole situation with him went sideways.

I will admit, right here at the top, I did not handle it with the kindness and compassion I should have. I had not done enough work on myself at that point to have those things to give.

So as you read this, I ask that you extend some grace to the version of me who had swung too far in the opposite direction of being a people pleaser.

****

It was a Friday night. Aaron and I had gone out to dinner and were heading back to my place for him to drop me off.

He was supposed to go home that night because I had a busy day planned starting early the next morning.

All through dinner he had been dangerously circling my "don't ask questions you don't want answers to" rule.

When we got to my place, he asked me if he could come in for a little while.

I told him we could continue talking while I got ready for bed, but that I was not going to stay up having a drawn-out conversation with him.

Just as I was about to show him out and lock the door so I could get to sleep, he asked the fateful question:

"Have you kissed any other guys while we've been dating?"

I had made it very clear to him and everyone else; I won't lie to protect your feelings.

I didn't get into the semantics of what dating meant. I just replied, "Yes."

I didn't expand on it. He knew full-well we were not exclusive. I had reminded him of that on several occasions.

He started to tear up. "How many times?"

"Really? You don't actually want to know and I don't even have an answer. I'm not doing this with you."

I waited to see if he would realize he was headed down a path of no return.

He didn't backtrack.

I almost shrugged as I said, "I need to get to bed," and started walking toward the door.

In a weepy voice he said, "Please let me stay."

I probably rolled my eyes. I didn't have the patience to deal with this, and getting a good night's sleep was a priority for me.

"Fine. But I don't have time to deal with this tomorrow. You know my plate is full."

"I know. I just want to stay."

And so, we went to bed.

I knew it wasn't over. I knew I had just stuck a lid on a pot that was going to boil over. I simply wasn't willing to deal with it and wanted him to manage his own big feelings right then.

Very early the next morning, like 4:30 early, he got up to go to the bathroom.

I half consciously heard the toilet flush followed by running water in the sink.

But then I heard what sounded like marbles clinking together.

My foggy brain couldn't make sense of it. What was he doing? Where did he get marbles? Why was he running the water for so long?

He came back to bed and I asked, "What were you doing?"

"Nothing. Just go back to sleep."

But his voice sounded weird. Something wasn't right.

I reached over and turned the switch on the lamp next to my bed so I could see him.

He wouldn't look at me.

I wondered if he had somehow vandalized my sink or damaged something in the bathroom because he was still butthurt about last night.

I got up and walked into the bathroom and saw my Tylenol PM bottle sitting on the counter. I knew damn well I hadn't left it there.

I picked it up. It was empty.

I tried to remember, had I just bought a new bottle, or had I been thinking I needed to?

Had this bottle been full or almost empty?

I wasn't sure.

I took the bottle with me and walked back into the bedroom.

"How many of these did you take?"

"I don't know."

"You don't know? Three or four? Or you don't know the whole bottle?"

"Let's just say I'm going to be really sleepy in a little while and I shouldn't drive home."

Son of a freakin' bitch! He was purposefully trying to sabotage my plans so I would have to babysit him all day.

I lowered my voice to a growl and spoke deliberately. "How many did you take?"

He just closed his eyes and turned his head to the side on the pillow.

My blood was boiling. There is no way I'm allowing this man-child to ruin my plans because he asked a question he knew better than to ask.

"Get up. I'm taking you to the hospital."

He didn't budge.

"You know that Tylenol will damage your liver and that is a slow and painful death, right?"

Silence.

I walked into the hall and knocked on my roommate's door. She answered, still mostly asleep.

"Hey. Aaron just took a bunch of Tylenol PM. Do you have any idea how much is too much?"

She stared at me, blinked, frowned, and then replied, "We can call poison control."

We walked downstairs together to look for a number.

Poison control must not have been staffed around the clock because no one was picking up the phone.

I decided to call the emergency mental health number for the bank I had just quit working for the week before.

They answered, but told me they really couldn't help me because I was no longer an employee.

I pleaded, "I understand that. But can you please just tell me how dangerous Tylenol PM is in high doses?"

"How high a dose?"

"I'm not sure. Somewhere between five and the whole bottle."

(At the time, I didn't realize the "marbles" I heard were actually him dumping most of the bottle down the drain.)

The woman at poison control replied matter-of-factly, "He needs to have his stomach pumped. If he won't go willingly, call 911 and have the paramedics take him by force."

I thanked her and hung up the phone.

I clenched my teeth and looked at my roommate.

She raised an eyebrow. "What are you going to do?"

"I'm going to give him the option. He can either let me take him to the emergency room or I'm going to take her advice and call 911."

I was thinking that if I did nothing and something serious happened to him, that would be on me.

When I walked back into the bedroom, he was still in bed with his eyes closed.

"You need to get your stomach pumped. This is serious."

No response.

"Look, Aaron. I know you can hear me. Tylenol doesn't work that fast. You can either allow me to take you to the emergency room or I'm going to call an ambulance."

He opened his eyes. "I'm not going to the emergency room. I'm just going to stay here and sleep it off."

"Nope, that is not what we're doing. You are going to the ER. Either voluntarily or involuntarily. It's your choice."

"You can't force me to go."

"You're right. I can't. But I can call 911 and tell them to come get you."

Silence.

"Okay. Fine."

I dialed 911, explained the situation to the operator, and asked her to please send the EMTs.

Fifteen minutes later, there was an ambulance and two cop cars parked outside my house. And it was barely five AM.

I was sure my neighbors were wondering what kind of circus I was running.

I met everyone at the door, filled them in on what had happened, and led them to the bedroom.

I then went back downstairs.

I don't know how much force they had to use to get him from the bed to the gurney, but a bit later they carried him down the stairs and out the door.

One of the EMTs came back and asked what hospital I wanted them to take him to.

And this is where my anger got the best of me. My reply was cold and bitter: "I don't care. Just don't let him die in my house."

She said, "You should be worried. Not angry."

I wasn't having it. "Just tell me where you're taking him so I can drop off his car later."

She gave me the name of a nearby hospital and left.

I asked my roommate if she could go with me to drop off Aaron's car at the hospital, but she had plans.

It was too early to call Carmen, so I took a shower and tried to sort out how the rest of the day was going to play out.

A few hours later, I got ahold of Carmen and explained the situation to her, asking if she would meet me at the hospital and then drive me home after I dropped off Aaron's car.

It was a thirty-five-minute drive for her and not how she planned to spend her Saturday before we were to meet up for her bachelorette party. But she was a great friend.

(Do you know the difference between a good friend and a great friend?

A good friend will help you move.

A great friend will help you move a body, and the only question she'll ask is, "What'd he do?"

The only answer she needs: "He needed killin'."

I kid of course. Do not ask your friends to help you move bodies.)

She told me she would meet me at the hospital at 11:30.

Before I left, I called Aaron's mom, told her what happened, and gave her the name of the hospital the EMT had given me.

"He's going to need someone to talk to, and I'm not the right person," I informed her flatly.

I don't remember her saying anything. She just took down the information and thanked me for calling.

I arrived at the emergency room parking lot at 11:20, walked in, and asked the nurse behind the desk if Aaron was there.

She said yes, pointing and telling me how to get to his room.

I cut her off, holding his keys out to her. "Please give these to him and tell him not to call me."

She looked stunned but took the keys.

I turned on my heel and walked out.

I was beyond angry. The manipulation and attention-seeking both infuriated and disgusted me.

How dare he pull a stunt like this when he knew I was swamped with Carmen's wedding plans for the next two weeks?

I never for a moment believed his life was actually in danger.

The next day he called me to ask if I would drive him home because the hospital had told him he wasn't allowed to drive for 24 hours after having his stomach pumped (which apparently is not a fun thing to have done) and took away his keys.

He told me he had only taken a handful of the pills and washed the rest down the sink (that's when the marbles suddenly clicked for me).

But he had refused to tell the doctors anything, so they pumped his stomach out of an abundance of caution.

I listened to his story, becoming more annoyed by the minute.

Just as I had thought. It had been a conscious attempt to sabotage my plans and put the focus directly on him.

I refused to drive him home.

When he asked what he was supposed to do, I suggested he take a cab home and then back the next day to get his car.

That was the last interaction I had with him for several weeks.

A few days after Carmen's wedding, he left a bottle of wine in her mailbox with a note that said, "I'm sorry I wasn't allowed to come to your big day. I had been excited about attending. I look forward to congratulating you in person soon."

He no longer worked in the same building I did, so I thought that would be the end of it.

I was wrong.

Less than a month later, I started to receive gifts.

First, an obnoxiously large bouquet of flowers, almost as tall as I was, which probably cost several hundred dollars.

Then, two professionally framed prints by an artist I liked. Aaron had written personalized notes on the back in Sharpie.

One said: *If you play with firecrackers, you're going to get your fingers burned — Love Aaron*. (He had called me Firecracker before.)

The other said, *To the woman of my dreams, Robyn. From the man who will always love you — Aaron*

I didn't respond. I simply wasn't interested in playing this game.

The gifts kept coming, smaller in scale but steady.

Then I started hearing whispers from shared acquaintances at work.

He was talking about how materialistic and shallow I was, how I would never return the gifts because I was all about what I could get out of a guy without giving anything in return.

I also learned he had called my father and spun some sob story about how I should "belong" to him now, just because we had shared a bed.

He insinuated that we had sex. We had not.

My father has never mentioned that phone call to me, but it must have been the talk of the family at the time because I've heard a few variations of it from different siblings.

In the middle of Aaron acting the fool, I had a trip planned to visit my family.

While I was there, my mom and I bumped into a friend of hers. I was appalled when this woman I didn't know told me she was praying for me, while sharing very private and specific personal details about my life.

I asked her how she knew those things, and she said, "Your mother shares them on the prayer chain so we can pray for you." Like it was normal and perfectly acceptable behavior.

I later told my mother in no uncertain terms that she needed to stop sharing my personal life on the church gossip chain under the guise that I needed prayers for divine intervention.

That incident also caused me to stop sharing the details of my life with my family.

****

A few weeks into the steady stream of "gifts," I was on the phone ranting to Carmen about the complete insanity of it all when her new husband chimed in, "You know, we could just go drop off all of his stuff at his apartment."

It had not occurred to me to ask my friends for help dealing with this mess.

We made a plan.

I knew Aaron was a late to bed, late to rise guy so if we dropped everything off early in the morning, he wouldn't be awake to fight about it.

The following Saturday, Carmen, her husband, and one of their other friends (who happened to be pregnant) arrived at my place around 7 AM.

We loaded up all the stuff and drove it over to Aaron's, stacking it quietly on his front stoop.

I rang his doorbell.

When he answered, in his underwear and clearly still asleep, I handed him an envelope and said, "Here's the key to your place, and all the gifts. Please stop telling people I am materialistic and greedy. We are done."

As I walked briskly away, he shouted after me, "This is not it! Do you hear me? This is not it!"

As I jumped back in the van and Carmen's husband drove the four of us to breakfast, I assumed he meant it wasn't over. Little did I know how soon that would be clear.

After enjoying a leisurely meal with my friends, they were going bring me home and then the three of them had things they were going to do together.

But as we pulled into my neighborhood and got close to my house, we all realized at the same time that Aaron's car was in my driveway and he was sitting in it.

There was no way I wanted to deal with that confrontation so I told Carmen's husband to keep driving.

Unfortunately, Aaron recognized the car and aggressively backed out of the driveway to follow us.

I started to panic. I didn't know the back of my neighborhood very well. I knew there was one turn that led to a dead end and the other took you around the block and back out past my house.

I wasn't sure which was which and I didn't want to get trapped in a dead end with Aaron chasing us.

I guessed right and we were able to get out of the neighborhood and back onto the main road.

That's when things went from weird to menacing.

Aaron started trying to bump us and run us off the road.

My heart was hammering in my chest. My blood pressure pounded in my ears so loud I could barely hear anything else.

What had I gotten my friends involved in? This was so dangerous and they had nothing to do with my relationship with Aaron.

That's when Carmen and I learned something about her new husband that neither of us knew.

His previous job had sent him to Colombia on several occasions. And because of the risk of Americans being kidnapped and held for ransom there, he had taken a full course of evasive driving lessons.

I have never been so impressed with someone's ability to drive a minivan as I was that day.

He would let Aaron get super close and then make a sudden left turn, forcing Aaron to go through the median to follow us.

Or change lanes to put a semi-truck between us.

I pulled out the cell phone I carried for work and dialed 911.

My adrenaline was so high that everything seemed to be happening in slow motion.

The 911 operator was trying to relay where we were to a police cruiser so they could help us.

But because we were driving erratically to try to keep Aaron from running us off the road, they couldn't catch up to us.

I suddenly realized we could just drive to the police station.

We were on the verge of running the last red light to make a left turn into the station when the blue lights lit up behind Aaron.

We pulled into the median and my hands started to shake.

Carmen's husband had his gun sitting on the dashboard (North Carolina is an open carry state), so when the cop came up to his window, it had to be declared.

The cop asked to see it, took it, unloaded it, and said he would give it back after the stop.

Then I opened the back door to tell the cop my side of the story.

I could see they had roughly pulled Aaron out of his car, and he was now sitting on the ground in handcuffs. And of course he was wearing a dirty wife-beater T-shirt. Why wouldn't he be?

I was living in a melodramatic TV show.

The cop told me I had to officially ban Aaron from my life and from the lives of my friends.

He wrote out exactly what I had to say and brought me back to where Aaron was sitting.

I read the statement as calmly as I could, even though I was vibrating with anxiety.

The cop then asked Aaron if he understood my request and told him there would be criminal charges if he bothered me or my friends again.

The second cop then took the paper from me, signed it with his name and badge number, and handed it back to me.

I wish I had kept it. But it got lost somewhere along the way.

That was the last I heard from Aaron for almost a year.

And then one morning, I walked downstairs on the phone with Marcus and saw all the stuff I had returned to Aaron sitting on my front porch.

My stomach dropped, and my blood ran cold. Was he back? What was going on?

I cautiously walked to the window and looked out.

No one was in my driveway, and I couldn't see any cars parked on the street.

I opened the front door.

That's when I saw a note taped to the frame of one of the prints.

It was a piece of notebook paper, folded in half with my name on the outside.

I unfolded it.

It said that he had accepted a job several states away, and that he and his cat were moving, that the stuff had always been meant for me, and it seemed silly to move it when it would just be a painful reminder that he loved me.

He signed it with something like, "*I hope you have a nice life.*"

That was my very last interaction with Aaron.

I wish him no harm. I hope he found a woman who could love him back in the way he needed to be happy.

Chapter 25
Hunter Resurfaces

After the insanity of the Apple Strudel Heist and the finalization of our divorce, I had no reason to interact with Hunter.

One Christmas, a basket of gourmet coffee showed up on my porch with a less-than-helpful card that read, "Love Me."

Of all the people who might get me a gift, who would be oblivious to the fact that I didn't drink coffee, leave it on my porch rather than hand it to me directly, and not sign their name?

I looked at the scrawled handwriting while I thought about that and came to the correct conclusion that it had to be Hunter.

Being too curious for my own good, I called him.

"Did you leave a basket of coffee on my porch?"

"Yeah. Merry Christmas."

"Thank you. Why did you choose coffee?"

Then he did that butthurt thing men do when they think they've done something charming and you're not properly fawning over them in gratitude.

"I didn't have to get you anything."

"That is true. I'm just wondering why coffee when I never, in all the years we were together, drank coffee and I still don't."

I don't know why it mattered. I could have not called or just said thanks and let it go. Maybe I was trying to rub in the fact that he never really bothered to get to know me.

I was too subtle apparently because his retort was, "Fine. I won't bother to try to be nice to you ever again."

I was surprised when I got a call from his bank several months later, asking me to make an appointment to come in so he could repay the loan he owed me.

I wasn't sure where he was getting the money. But since it was the bank giving me a check, not him handing me a bag of cash, I assumed it was legit.

The day of the appointment, I printed out the loan schedule I had created in Excel, including the payoff amount, took an early lunch, and walked over to the downtown branch.

When I was shown into the bank office, I was surprised to see Hunter there.

He stood up and tried to hug me but I turned my shoulder into him and did the awkward side-hug-thing.

The woman behind the desk introduced herself and said, "Thank you for coming in. We are prepared to pay the remaining balance on the personal loan Mr. Weebler has with you. In return, we're assuming you're willing to release the lien on the property he owns?"

I nodded. "Yes. Of course. Assuming our payoff amounts are the same. I am happy to do that."

It didn't take very long for us to compare numbers and reach an agreement.

The bank employee walked away to get a check cut for me, leaving Hunter and me sitting by ourselves.

He turned toward me "How are you?"

"I'm fine. You?"

I expected him to say "fine" as well. But instead, I got a whole explanation as to why he was paying me back now.

It turned out he had taken what little money was left in his retirement account and bought himself a new truck.

He knew he was going to have to pay taxes on it but had not realized there was also a penalty for early withdrawal.

Somehow, he hadn't filed his taxes properly and now he owed a large chunk of change to the government.

His plan was to get a loan from the bank to pay it off, using the catfish farm as collateral.

However, when the bank did the title search, they found the lien that our lawyer had filed against the property for me.

(I am so very thankful they did that. I would have just given him the loan on his word. Sometimes I worry about how clueless I was.)

The bank informed him that they could not loan him the money unless he cleared the debt with me because they were not willing to do a second lien.

So, he was borrowing enough money to pay me and to pay the back taxes plus penalties he owed.

At least that was the story he told me at the time.

Looking back, I wonder if the debacle with his taxes was a ripple from the financial problems the cartel was creating for him.

But we were both completely unaware of that at the time, and I was happy to be able to cut one more string connecting me to his life.

The bank person walked back in and handed me an envelope containing cashier's check, drawn on the bank, made out to me for the correct amount.

I looked at it and nodded as she slid the paperwork for me to sign across the desk.

I signed it, pushed it back toward her and stood up to gather my things.

She stood and reached across the desk, extending her hand and saying thank you.

I shook it and replied, "Thank you."

Hunter stood and moved toward me like he was going to try to hug me again, but I had already opened the door and was heading out.

I turned slightly, "Take care of yourself and good luck."

I don't know what I was wishing him luck on. It just seemed like the thing to say.

He stopped awkwardly and said, "You too," before flopping back into the chair.

I walked straight to my bank and deposited the check. As the teller handed me the receipt, I exhaled, releasing anxiety I hadn't realized I had been holding.

Once the check cleared, I applied the whole amount to the principal of my mortgage.

The next time I heard anything about Hunter it was my father telling me Hunter had "stopped by" my parent's house because he was in Montana working and was "close by."

I don't know in what world Montana is close to central California, but sure.

After that, I wouldn't see or hear from Hunter again until we both attended our grandfather's funeral, years later.

Chapter 26
Meeting My Second Stalker

Carmen and her husband owned an older home in a small town on the outskirts of Charlotte. She lived a little farther away than I might have liked, but we made a point to have lunch together during the week when we were both working downtown (or "uptown," as Charlotte insists on calling it).

When she told me they were planning on having friends come over to help put a new roof on the house, I was happy to show up to help.

I had done plenty of roofing in my life. It's not hard work, just tedious. So on the designated Saturday, I showed up in work jeans and work boots.

We had to remove two layers of old shingles first. That required flat shovels to get under the shingles to pry them off.

Sometimes you get lucky and get a run where a whole section comes off at once. Sometimes it's slow going and feels like you're only getting one shingle at a time.

When there are enough people, you can have some working on prying shingles while others pull up the nails that are left behind. The goal is to create a smooth surface so the tar paper goes down cleanly, making it easy to lay straight, flat rows of new shingles.

My job was to use a crowbar and hammer to remove old nails. The ones I couldn't pull, I pounded flat against the roof.

I was sitting on the roof, sliding myself from nail to nail without a problem until the butt of my jeans caught on a nail head. I heard it tear and knew that was going to be an issue.

I was wearing my oldest pair of work jeans. The fabric had been worn thin from years of weeding flower beds, hauling rocks, feeding catfish and now working on roofs.

But there was nothing to be done about it, so I just kept working. As the day wore on, those pants split from seam to seam across my butt on both sides.

I was the only woman working on the roof, and apparently the guys had a bet going about whether or not I was wearing underwear. (For the record: I absolutely was.)

Fortunately, I wasn't particularly shy and aside from my skin being in direct contact with the roof, the issue was more annoying than concerning.

Weeks later Carmen patched those jeans for me, and I kept wearing them for several more years.

One of the guys working on the roof project happened to be Dale. He was the roommate of a friend of Carmen's husband. (Did you follow that?)

I vaguely remember meeting him, mostly because he was tall; about 6'3". But overall, I have no interesting memories about him.

Unlike one of the other guys, who couldn't lay a straight row of shingles to save his life.

Come on, dude! There's literally a guide right on them. All you have to do is line it up before you nail it down. We ended up sending him off the roof after we had to remove several sections he had put down because they were crooked.

Him I remember because I couldn't fathom how someone could do something so simple so wrong after being shown several times how to do it right.

****

Months later, Carmen and her husband hosted a good old-fashioned barn raising. They wanted to put up a pole barn and needed help putting it together.

Naturally I was going to help. That's what best friends do. And this time Marcus came with me.

By then, he had gone out a few times with the woman who would eventually become his wife. They weren't serious yet, so he and I were still doing stuff together off the volleyball court. We even had plans to go to Key West that December.

We talked about the new girl on the drive to Carmen's. I thought she sounded nice. I didn't know then she would be the reason Marcus would end our friendship.

Dale also showed up for the build. I learned that day that he was an architect. (Not technically. He hadn't taken the licensure exam, but conveniently left that detail out.)

He was chatting me up most of the day, even though I had introduced him to Marcus.

181

Dale told me later that he had looked at Marcus and thought, "I'm going to steal your girl."

I pointed out that I wasn't "with" Marcus. We were just really good friends. More importantly, I wasn't property you could steal. That's not how it works.

A few days after the barn was up, Carmen called to say Dale had asked for my number.

If I'd had the good sense God gave a goose, I would have asked Carmen or her husband, "What do you think of him? Would he be fun for me to hang out with?"

Or maybe, I could have given two seconds of thought to the fact that Dale's roommate was weird, like really weird and not at all someone I would want to spend purposeful time with.

But I didn't think about those things.

Instead, I thought about how awkward it would be to see Dale at events at Carmen's house if I said no.

I wish I could reach back in time and give myself a Gibbs. (You know, the slap on the back of the head that Mark Harmon's character in NCIS gives Tony DiNozzo when he does dumb things.)

And so, I said yes.

When Dale called to ask me to dinner that Friday, I was already booked (likely with Sean), so he picked a different night. We decided he was going to pick me up, and I added it on my calendar.

I had a rule when I had plans with guys: if they were more than fifteen minutes late and I hadn't heard from them, I would be gone when they got there. I was always dressed and ready to walk out the door at the time we had decided.

None of that ridiculous thing where the guy shows up and the woman's still 45 minutes from being ready.

In that vein, on the night Dale and I were going out, I had the shoes I was going to wear, a fashionable pair of high heel boots, sitting by the front door.

I was dressed nicely, as one does for a first date. Hair and makeup done.

Not dressed like the farmhand I had been when he met me roofing a house and raising a barn.

When the doorbell rang at five minutes after he was supposed to arrive, I brushed it off. Five minutes isn't too bad.

Then I opened the door.

He stood there in a sloppy t-shirt, cut-off cargo pants and Birkenstock-like sandals.

I stared, trying to process how overdressed I was.

And again, if I'd had the good sense God gave a goose, I would have said right then, "This isn't going to work" and called someone else to go out with.

But I hadn't done enough therapy yet to have that kind of self-confidence.

So instead, I said, "Why don't you come in? I'm just going to run upstairs and grab my shoes."

He told me later that when he came in, he noticed my formal living room had no furniture, and assumed it was because I was too poor to furnish it.

The truth was, I didn't use that room and saw no point in spending the time or money to fill it with stuff I didn't need.

While he was busy judging my lack of home decor, I ran upstairs and grabbed my tennis shoes (or as my current husband calls them "sneakers").

It was the best I could do on short notice to not feel completely overdressed.

(As I write this, I notice I'm framing it like I was overdressed when, in reality, he was embarrassingly underdressed and too clueless to realize it.)

When we got in the car, he broke another cardinal rule I had that I didn't think needed to be said out loud. Whoever initiates the "date" is required to plan it.

As I clicked my seatbelt, he said, "So... where do you want to go?"

Geez!

I must have looked dumbfounded because he added, "I don't live in this area so I don't really know what's around."

I wracked my brain for a place that wasn't fast food where he wouldn't be underdressed. I couldn't come up with a great option but there was a little pizzeria that I thought would work.

I gave him directions to the University Area.

We had barely gotten settled in our seats when he opened the menu and said, "This place is more expensive than I had planned."

More expensive? It's a freakin' pizzeria. But I felt like I had done something wrong. I could have picked the nice steakhouse just down the road.

Overcoming my churning thoughts, I replied, "I was planning on splitting the bill."

Dinner went exactly how you'd expect: me bending over backward to make him comfortable, and him thinking we were hitting it off *amazingly* well.

I did tell him my "Rules for going out with Robyn."

He laughed like he didn't believe me.

I tried to make it clear that I was serious, but he brushed it off.

(Side note: if you're trying to have a serious conversation with someone about something that matters to you and they act like it's a joke, run like your hair's on fire.)

There is a part of my brain that can't fathom what possessed me to continue to spend time with Dale after that disaster.

But in reality, I know why I did.

I had time.

Marcus was dating the woman who would become his wife. And years later, I found out why I was seeing less of Sean. He had someone in his ear, telling him he deserved better than a woman who wouldn't commit to him.

I know there is at least a part of him that regrets listening to them.

With free time to fill, Dale became someone to do things with.

I didn't realize he was falling in love until it was too late.

****

It was doing things with Dale that finally made me realize that just because I *could* do something didn't mean I *should*.

He took me fishing.

I spent an afternoon in a tiny, flat-bottom boat in a spot completely hidden by reeds, swatting bugs and wishing I was anywhere else.

He seemed to be having fun though.

He begged me to crew his sailboat. His parents owned a yacht club, and he grew up racing motorless sailboats. He would try to regale me with tales of sailing.

I told him about almost being run over by a speedboat while sailing with Sean.

His response was to take me to the club where his boat was stored, and we spent most of a day listening to guys tell stories about "turtling" their boats (that means it turned upside down in the water).

Why he thought hearing stories about almost sinking would make me *want* to sail is beyond me.

He would say, "You're tall, light and strong. That makes you perfect crew!"

I cannot articulate in words how much I did *not* want to be crew. Period. Full stop.

We visited some of his friends for New Year's Eve, and he drank until I finally slid a shot glass away and replaced it with water.

The next day, he thanked me for "policing" his drinking because he didn't know when to stop.

I also learned that he liked to smoke pot "sometimes."

Yeah, because my history with men who drink and do drugs has gone so well.

(Red flags, Robyn. Please. Notice the damn red flags.)

He also wanted me to help him work on his fixer-upper house.

I guess because he met me doing handiwork, he thought that was something I enjoyed.

I explained, every time he asked, that I did that stuff for Carmen because I love her. It was not something I would do for fun and I was not interested in working on his house.

He started spending more time at my place. I learned later that he liked my house better because it was newer, cleaner, and bigger.

Well, yeah. I liked my house better for those reasons too.

Then he started to fuss about having to wait for me to get home from the gym at night.

More than once he said, "I'm tired of sitting in my car in your driveway waiting for you to get home."

My reply was always the same: "Then stop doing it. Go home. I can call you when I'm done working out."

He didn't. He just kept complaining about it.

He was also annoyed that I was lifting so often.

"Your body thinks you're building a pyramid. You're going to be fat and sloppy when you get older because all that unnecessary muscle is going to turn to fat."

I knew that wasn't how muscle worked. But arguing with him was pointless. Besides, working out made me happy. I wasn't going to stop just because he wanted me to be home earlier.

The real cracks started to appear when he asked me to come to his place to work on his car.

I told him I didn't want to work on his car, but I would come over and lay in the sun nearby to keep him company.

While I was there, Brent (my boss's boss) called me.

I had a company issued cell phone for my job doing production support and project implementation for a division of General Motors.

I was always on call.

I didn't realize then that Brent was trying to weasel his way into my life.

Back to not having the good sense God gave a goose. There was no reason my boss's boss should be calling me on the weekend to have a personal conversation.

But I had no idea how to tell him I didn't want to talk to him and not to call me.

Dale didn't like me talking to Brent (rightly so I suppose) but he didn't have any suggestions on what I should do. I couldn't not answer my phone. I was on call and my boss's boss might have a legitimate reason for calling me.

I certainly wasn't going to hang up on him. That's a good way to get yourself fired.

The final *this-is-just-stupid* moment happened a few days later.

It was late in the evening and I was getting ready for bed when Dale asked me why I had a broken pair of sunglasses in my nightstand drawer.

I felt immediately violated. I had left the house first that morning because I had an early meeting. I just told him to make sure the door was locked when he went to work.

"Why were you going through my nightstand?"

"I was looking for a picture of you I could use to masturbate." He said it like it was normal. Like it was something I should be happy about.

Instead, I was completely skeeved. He had invaded my privacy.

I didn't even try to explain it. I just said, "I think you need to sleep at your place tonight."

Anger flashed across his face. He raised his voice, "Do you realize I haven't slept at my house in almost six weeks?"

I stood there, alarmed and dumbfounded at the same time.

I looked around the room. He had brought over a TV that now sat in the nook in my bedroom. His licensure exam books were piled on my couch, untouched since he had dumped them there.

I had let him move in without a conversation and completely by accident.

I snapped, probably more aggressively than necessary, "Then I think you *really* need to go home tonight!"

I expected him to just storm out. Instead, he started gathering his things. I think he was trying to make some kind of dramatic statement by gathering everything up, but I just let him do it.

By the time he sped out of my driveway, there was nothing of his left in my house. And I was a little surprised how relieved I felt. I wasn't sure the relationship was over. I thought he was just being dramatic and we would talk about it in the morning.

But when it took him several days to call, and then he acted like nothing was wrong, I knew I was over it.

What I didn't expect was that Dale wasn't just disappointed and sad when I told him I was done. He was angry. Like, *really* angry. Way out of proportion for what I thought was just a light-hearted, hanging-out kind of relationship.

Chapter 27
Out with Dale. In with Brent.

The situation with Dale escalated quickly over the next couple of months.

He told our friend group how awful I was. They reminded him that I had made it very clear, over and over, that I was not looking for an exclusive, long-term thing. They were surprised that he was surprised that I had ended it.

Then he started calling me at work during the day and at home in the evenings.

At first, I answered, thinking he just needed closure. I didn't realize that "closure" is often just a way for someone to try to change your mind and berate you when you won't.

When I stopped answering his calls, he started leaving messages. Some begged me to take him back and try again. Others called me an awful, horrible, useless human being.

When I didn't respond, he started calling my home phone in the middle of the night just to wake me up.

I turned my ringer off.

Then the messages started getting dark, threatening me or threatening to harm himself.

Of course, the police told me they couldn't do anything because "no crime was being committed."

(It is a perpetual frustration for women everywhere that it seems like we have to be killed before law enforcement is willing to help us.)

I turned off my voicemail at home.

He then started leaving messages for me at work. Every morning, I would come in to escalating messages that veered wildly from "I love you" to "I hate you" and back.

While I was carrying that emotional weight in my personal life, I had office politics threatening my livelihood.

There were about a dozen of us working in the building who were employed directly by General Motors. Together, we were managing two vendors.

One vendor staffed the call center, while their competitor handled all the tech installation and ongoing management.

(What executive thought that was a good idea?)

My role was to be a communication liaison between GM management in Detroit and both Charlotte based vendors.

Tina, my counterpart and manager of the "tech guys," and I got along well at first. But over time, our relationship had started to deteriorate.

Ian, GM's site director, kept reminding me (privately and in team meetings) that I was the client and had to hold Tina accountable to their contract and support standards.

What I didn't know was that Ian was dating one of his employees, and in an effort to keep the spotlight off of them, he was telling Tina that she shouldn't let me boss her around, that she and I were equals, and that I was power hungry.

Ian tried to look like a hero to Detroit leadership by bragging about how well he was managing two "high-intensity" women.

On top of that, another manager once brought a sobbing employee into my office. He said, "Her boyfriend just held a gun to her head for two hours. Can you talk to her?" And walked out.

I was a tech liaison! I had zero training in dealing with those kinds of situations.

I was able to get her calmed down and then took a long lunch to go with her to their apartment to get some of her things (we hid the guns first). I told her she could stay with me for a few days until she figured out what to do.

She stayed one night before going back to him. (That was before I understood the cycle of abuse, and how hard it is for a woman to leave.)

Enter my boss's boss, Brent. He seemed calm, understanding, and truly interested in doing what was best for me (ha!).

He flew down from Detroit shortly after he was hired to try to figure out what was going on in the Charlotte office and who was at fault.

Days before Brent arrived, Ian kicked me out of my office. He claimed it was because they were going to tear it down to put in more call center seats (which we didn't need).

So, instead of an office with walls and a door, I was now in a cubicle on the second floor. No one else worked on that floor, and I was a five-minute walk from the people I was supposed to be supporting.

That floor was so deserted, employees were stealing memory from the unused computer towers.

Since I was no longer near the production floor, I wasn't getting real-time updates when we experienced outages, and my direct boss in Detroit started complaining that I didn't know what was going on.

Without an office, I had to watch who might overhear every sensitive call, which was basically my whole job.

When Brent arrived, he sat in the cubicle next to me and talked to me all afternoon. Some about work, a lot about other things.

I don't think I got any work done that day.

That night, he asked me to join him for dinner. That seemed like the right thing to do when management came to town, so I went.

But we didn't talk about work. Much like the times he would call me, we talked about pretty much everything except work.

The next morning when I got to my desk to take the daily 7:30 status call, Brent was already there.

I was surprised because I thought he would need to talk to other people in the building, but there he was.

Before I even got my purse put away, he said, "Your voicemail light is blinking."

I rolled my eyes and sighed, "Yeah, the guy I broke up with a while back always leaves me messages overnight."

"What does he say?"

I didn't bother to try to explain. I just dialed my voicemail, put it on speaker and played it.

After listening, Brent didn't say much. He just got up and walked away.

Had a conference call to dial into so, I didn't think much of it.

But a couple of hours later, I got a call from the head of security for the whole division, the big guy in Detroit.

He said, "Brent called and said you were being harassed and that I needed to get involved to make sure you're safe."

What?

I really didn't think it was that big of a deal. It was just voicemails. Dale had stopped being threatening and was mostly just complaining about what an awful human I was.

I realize now that Brent was trying to swoop in like a superhero to "save" me.

Before he left to go back to Detroit, he shared with me "in confidence" (Watch out for men who do that. It's a ploy.) that he had been sent to Charlotte to fire me, but that after spending a few days with me, he didn't think I was the problem.

At the time, I had no reason not to believe him.

Knowing what I know now, I am 98% sure he was lying. It was just a way for him to stir the chaos so he could act like he was my savior.

He even made me promise to record Dale's voicemails onto cassette tapes (yes, it was that long ago), in case I ever had to go to court.

I thought that was overkill. But I did it.

I found one of those tapes in a box that had been moved multiple times without being opened.

This message was left by Dale on my office voicemail on November 6, 2002, at 4:44 AM:

"I am so completely overwhelmed with how much you have ruined me. My hatred for you runs so deep that you have permanently changed me. It has been impossible for me to overcome. I have new people in my life; I have elements of you that remind me of you and it's unbelievable the hatred I have toward you and the way that you played me. You used me as a person. You destroyed me. Never have I ever met or heard of anything that is so wretched as the feelings I have for you. I cannot believe the selfishness of you. And you need to know that you ruined a good thing and somewhere there will always be an energy that is me. It's fucking unbelievable. And you know what. I really hope that you're suffering as a product of this. You're

unbelievable. You fucking ruined me. I was a beautiful thing when you met me. I was beautiful. I was beautiful Robyn. And I'm not anymore. It's gone. My summer is over."

****

It never occurred to me to try to find a therapist. I grew up in a family where you just powered through. I didn't even realize I wasn't okay.

I had always used exercise to manage stress, so I drove myself harder at the gym and on the volleyball court.

One night I came home exhausted from a late volleyball game. All I wanted to do was shower and crawl into bed.

Brent called as I was pulling into my driveway. Of course, I answered. It was my work phone, and he was my skip-level boss. I couldn't not pick up. But I told him I was just getting home and needed to get to bed.

He replied, "Call me when you get out of the shower so I can say goodnight."

I didn't want to call him. I wanted to go directly to sleep. But I didn't want to piss him off either. I just said, "Okay" to get off the phone.

I turned on the shower and stripped out of my sweaty volleyball gear.

If I could have fallen asleep under the warm water, I would have. But eventually, I washed my hair and scrubbed away the gym smell with flowery scented body wash.

As I wrapped the towel around my wet hair, turban style, I flipped off the bathroom light and opened the door to walk into my bedroom.

I got two steps in and my heart plummeted.

Dale was standing at the foot of my bed, staring at me.

I stood frozen, looking back at him in shock. A few seconds stretched into forever before I could move.

I carefully took the towel off my head, wrapped it around my naked body, and asked as calmly as I could, "What are you doing here? How did you get in my house?"

He answered the second question first, "I've always known your sliding door didn't lock right."

The reality that he knew my house was vulnerable and never bothered to mention it made me wonder later how he could ever have claimed to love me. You don't leave people you care about exposed like that.

But in the moment, I couldn't think about that.

He held out a folded piece of paper.

"Take it!" he demanded, waving it at me.

I stepped forward, holding my towel in place with my left hand, and extended my right hand to take it from him. Then I stepped back to put more distance between us.

"Open it!" It wasn't a request.

I unfolded it while trying to make sure my towel didn't come dislodged.

I skimmed the writing. It was the same obsessive ranting he had been leaving in the voicemails.

But my eyes got stuck on the drawing. There was a house on a cliff with a stick figure human with x's for eyes that looked like it had jumped off the cliff and was falling toward the rocks.

I looked up at him. I had no idea what to say.

My company cell phone started to buzz on the bed. I knew it was Brent wondering why I hadn't called him back like I promised. But I certainly wasn't going to try to get past Dale to answer it.

Instead, we just stood there in silence until it stopped vibrating.

Dale's face was hard, "That was Brent, wasn't it?"

I didn't respond.

"You know what I realized about you this weekend?" He didn't pause for me to respond.

"I was driving my motorcycle really fast Saturday night... Sunday morning. The road was wet. I was a little drunk.

"For just a second, I lost control. I thought I was going to hit the cement barrier.

"And I was kinda sorry I didn't, because then I wouldn't have to feel how

194

you've destroyed me, made me a shell of the amazing person I was."

My phone started buzzing again. Brent was not a patient man.

Dale ignored it.

"But then I realized something about you. You'd be happy if I died. You'd count that as victory. That you ruined me so badly that I committed suicide over you."

I opened my mouth to protest but he raised his hand and hissed at me.

"Don't even bother to deny it! I know you better than you know yourself. I'm not going to give you the satisfaction.

"I'm going to live. And you are going to have to just suffer with the knowledge that you failed!"

I wasn't sure if he was done so I waited.

"Well? What do you have to say? You always have some sharp but meaningless comeback!"

"Dale, I'm not a good partner for you."

"You don't get to tell me who is or isn't a good partner for me!" he bellowed angrily.

I tried again, not realizing that rational and logical were the wrong tactics at that moment.

"Look, you've talked a lot about your friend Ann. How she is remodeling her house herself. How she likes to sail. I think she would be a great partner..."

I didn't get to finish.

"I don't love Ann! I love you! You stupid, ungrateful bitch!" Spit flew from his mouth as he raged, his breath ragged and his eyes burning into me.

I stepped back and did the only thing I could think of to protect myself.

"I'm sorry. I'm so sorry I hurt you."

"No, you're not! You don't care about anyone but yourself."

My phone started to vibrate again.

"And fucking Brent. You better hope I never see the two of you in public, Robyn. You better just pray, because it will be ugly..." He trailed off.

Then, for the first time since I walked out of the bathroom, he took an actual breath.

"You know what?" his voice was still dripping with venom. "You aren't worth it. You're worthless and stupid.

"I wish I had never met you. You're unbelievable. I want nothing to do with you ever again. Don't you dare even think about me."

He spun around and stormed out of my bedroom and down the stairs.

I followed him just to make sure he actually left the house.

He went out the way he'd come in, crashing through the vertical blinds, and out the sliding glass door, which he had left standing open.

I was freaked out about having to close it. What if he was standing just on the other side in the dark to grab me?

I strained to hear anything that would tell me he really left. I was met with eerie silence.

I gritted my teeth, pushed the blinds back so I could reach the handle and pull the door closed. I locked it and tested to make sure it was actually secure.

I never closed that door again without verifying that the lock caught correctly.

When I got back upstairs, my phone was buzzing again with Brent's number on the display.

I picked it up, shaking and almost sobbing. All I could get out was "Oh my God."

Brent's energy shifted from anger to what I thought was tenderness. "Robyn, what's wrong?"

"Dale broke into my house."

"You have to call the police!"

"He's gone now."

The adrenaline was wearing off and I was starting to recover from the shock.

"It doesn't matter. You still need to call the police!"

I didn't want to. I didn't feel like dealing with cops. He hadn't hurt me. I was fine.

"I'm not calling them. I'm too tired. I just want to go to sleep."

He kept insisting as I crawled into bed.

"I'm beyond exhausted. I need sleep. Not hours of paperwork."

"If he comes back and hurts you, I'm going to say *I told you so*."

"Yeah. I can't do this right now. Let's talk about it tomorrow. Goodnight, Brent."

I hung up and was asleep almost instantly.

****

I never saw or heard from Dale again.

I learned through the grapevine that he did end up dating and eventually marrying Ann. They took over his family yacht club and won awards racing sailboats. They might have even had children.

I did my best to move forward, wondering why I kept meeting men who created chaos in my life.

A friend said, "Robyn, one stalker is a mistake. Two is a pattern."

She wasn't wrong.

And there was Brent, sliding into my life with gifts and promises that felt like safety and love.

He claimed he was protecting my job, creating security for me, treating me like a princess. But there was always an undercurrent of menace I couldn't quite name.

Because he was my boss's boss, he wanted to keep it a secret.

That's the worst place to be. Emotionally vulnerable, in the crosshairs of a narcissist, and unable to talk to anyone about it.

Chapter 28
When Not-Enough-Therapy Meets a Narcissist

The first four times I went to dinner with Brent, I assumed they were business dinners. I said yes not because I was interested in him, but because he was my boss.

Because of that, it didn't occur to me to tell him my rules: don't fall in love, I didn't date exclusively, I wasn't looking for anything long-term, and to always split the bill.

I don't remember what clued me in. It might have been that he expected us to talk every day. That seemed like a lot for work-related contact.

I finally asked him, "When we've gone out to dinner, have you been expensing it to the company or paying for it yourself?"

He looked hurt (I would learn he was good at that). "I've been paying for it myself. Did you think they were work dinners?"

What was I going to say? The truth? *"Dude, I don't find you attractive. I don't think we have anything in common, and if you weren't my boss's boss, I wouldn't be sitting across the table from you now."*

That seemed like a good way to get myself fast tracked to being fired.

So instead, I laughed and said something like, "I didn't realize you were interested."

Cue him gushing about how amazing he thought I was: smart, beautiful, funny. Perfect for him. Exactly the kind of woman he had been dreaming of meeting.

It's not like he was going to tell me the truth: *"I'm a narcissist in need of a new supply victim. You've clearly got trauma, struggle with boundaries, and are vulnerable to love bombing. That makes you perfect."*

Even though my intuition was screaming, I felt professionally trapped, and I let his tide carry me along.

****

Six weeks after meeting him, he said, "I love you" for the first time.

My stomach lurched like I had just dropped over the edge of a roller coaster.

In my head, I was screaming: *No! No! No! No! He can't. He doesn't know me yet!*

My face must have gone ashen. I didn't want anyone to love me. Love meant control. Love meant losing freedom. Love meant I couldn't be me.

He looked deeply into my eyes and repeated, "I *said* I love you."

In the past, when guys had said that to me, I had replied, "I'm sorry." But the stakes were too high. He had too much power.

I finally found my voice. "What does that mean to you?"

He didn't answer my question. Instead, he gave me the kicked-puppy-dog look and said, "You don't love me?"

I must have waited too long to reply, because he added irritation to the sadness, "After everything I've done for you? Helping you deal with Dale, making sure you didn't lose your job? You don't love me?"

I had no idea what was happening. I didn't know we were in a power negotiation that I was going to lose.

"Of course I am super thankful for everything you've done for me. You've been kind and sweet…" I trailed off, feeling weird, like I was trying to smooth over a problem I didn't really understand.

He smiled. "You love me. You just aren't ready to say it yet."

I returned his smile tightly and looked down at my empty plate.

"I'm going to go to the bathroom. Maybe we can look at the dessert menu when I get back?"

He said, "Sure." But I knew things weren't okay.

I don't know what happened in the few minutes I was gone, but when I came back, two servers were cleaning up ice cubes and shattered glass at our table.

Brent's shirt and pants were soaked, like he had purposefully dumped water on his lap.

I stood to the side so I wouldn't get in the way and asked, "What happened?"

He scowled at me. "The glass slipped out of my hand, obviously."

That didn't make sense. Just dropping a glass wouldn't have shattered it like that or sent ice and shards scattering so far from the table.

I glanced at the nearby tables. They were all purposefully not looking in our direction, like they were embarrassed. The wait staff kept their heads bowed.

I felt like everyone was staring at me, even though no one was actually looking at me.

I couldn't help but think, *"what did I miss?"*

He stood abruptly, banging the table and causing the plates to clatter, threw down his wet napkin, and said, "Let's go."

I grabbed my purse and wrap, scrambling to catch up as he stormed out the door.

At the time, I was baffled by what had happened. With experience, I learned he had likely lost his temper and hurled the glass at his plate when I walked away. It is even likely that he had screamed an expletive.

That was the first of a long line of manipulations designed to force me to say "I love you too."

But it wasn't all blatant and aggressive. Some of it was sticky-sweet.

He would say things like "I love you more than you will ever be able to love me."

Or "We're going to have such a great love affair, people will be jealous."

Over time, the voice in my gut, the one that knew it was a trap, got too quiet to hear. Maybe he was safe. Maybe he actually did love me.

He certainly spent money on me like he loved me.

(That was before I understood that having and spending money has nothing to do with love.)

There were red flags piling up everywhere. But I kept allowing him to explain them away because I didn't realize I was being abused.

The first time I went to his place in Detroit there was a box of stuff sitting on the kitchen counter that belonged to a woman he told me he had "only gone out with a few times."

They had gone to Aruba as friends, and he had "let her down gently" on the plane home saying he wanted to stay "just friends."

That was how he justified it to me, but it didn't make sense. If they had only gone out a few times, why did she have several personal things at his house?

Now I think he had been wooing her. Took her to Aruba. Got her to sleep with him. Then dumped her in favor of his new target: me.

There was also the time he was in the kitchen, and one of his designer cats got underfoot. He pressed his foot into the cat's side and shoved it across the floor, bellowing, "Get the fuck out of the kitchen!"

Later, once he had calmed down, I reminded him that he had purposely chosen Birmans because they were more like dogs than cats.

But he locked them out of the bedroom, and was rarely home. He shouldn't be mad that they wanted to spend time with him.

I added that I would be heartbroken if he ever screamed at me for doing something as minor as being in the kitchen when he didn't want me there.

He pulled me into his arms and said, "Baby, I could never scream at you like that. You're too precious to me."

I foolishly believed him.

In time, he would scream at me like that and worse. Often.

One event that stands out in my memory was the night when Tina, my coworker, and I decided to go out for dinner and drinks.

I told Brent the day we decided to do it and reminded him again before I left the house the day of. He never expressed any concerns, and I thought he was fine.

Since Tina and I lived only ten minutes apart, I swung by to pick her up. We could visit on the drive and would only have to park one car.

That had always been the plan; I just hadn't thought to mention it to Brent. It was a non-thing for me.

On the way to the restaurant, Brent called. I considered letting it go to voicemail, but that had upset him before. So I had Tina answer it.

Brent was instantly angry.

I was as confused as a chameleon in a bag of Skittles. *What had I done to set him off this time?*

When I finally figured it out, I was baffled.

He was mad because I had picked Tina up, and I hadn't told him we were riding together. He said we were "clearly on a date."

I had no comeback. I couldn't understand why he would think that.

Of course, that was before I knew he was bisexual. In hindsight, it was a clue. He was accusing me of something he was actually doing.

We argued a bit before I told him this was a ridiculous conversation, and I was hanging up.

He proceeded to call and text me incessantly. I finally had to turn off my ringer because my phone was buzzing every other minute.

I wish it had made him angry enough to break up with me. But instead, it was just enough to fuel a couple days of screaming, berating, and verbal assault.

You might ask: why didn't I break up with him?

Fear. Fear for my job. Fear that if I got fired, I would never get another job. Fear that I would lose my house.

None of that was true. But I believed it anyway.

And I didn't realize his behavior was actually creating a hostile work environment for me.

I kept trying not to do things that would make him mad, and to appease him when he inevitably was.

****

Some red flags weren't waved directly at me. But I remember them clearly. Like the time he gloated about making someone cry when he fired them.

It was like he enjoyed causing psychological pain.

Or the time he was on a conference call I was managing during an outage and started screaming, literally screaming, that if we didn't get the system fixed, he was going to fire everyone on the call.

I was the only person on the call directly under his authority. Everyone else was a vendor. The only person he could actually fire was me.

I texted him while we were on the call, telling him he was overreacting and that screaming wouldn't make anyone work faster.

That didn't go over well.

He texted back that I was being insubordinate and could be fired for it.

So I'm your girlfriend, unless we are on a business call? In that case, if I message you privately, you're going to threaten my job?

It's no wonder that I felt so off-balance; like my life was in complete chaos. He was keeping me in that state on purpose.

And I don't think there is anyone in the world who is better at playing the victim than he was.

He would hurt my feelings or cross my boundaries, and by the end of the conversation, I would be apologizing to him.

That is a key component of being an energy source for a narcissist. Being willing to apologize just to restore peace, even if you were the one who was harmed.

****

A Pause Before We Continue

My relationship with Brent was so obviously broken and toxic from the very beginning that it's embarrassing to share it with you.

Which is why I want to pause before we go any deeper, because it gets so much worse, and speak to you as the woman I am today.

The woman who has done the work to heal many of my traumas and who can now recognize the ones that still need tending when they pop up.

I can feel it. That tight, frustrated swirl of emotion that rises up when you read about someone tolerating behavior that is so clearly intolerable.

Here's what I know now that I think is important to pass along:

I didn't have the language for what I was experiencing or the tools to handle it. I didn't recognize the red flags because no one had ever taught me what a narcissist was.

I had never even heard the word.

I didn't know I was being manipulated by his charm, that "love" could be wielded like a knife, how skilled he was at weaponizing my empathy, or how subtle and disorienting the erosion of my boundaries became.

I wasn't weak. I wasn't dumb. I was trying to survive a situation I didn't understand. I was trying to be good, to be kind, to not mess up my job, to not lose my house, to be nice.

It wasn't my fault I believed him when he lied to me. I thought if I just tried harder, we could create the Camelot he kept promising.

I was doing what so many people do: trying harder, giving more, even as the ground kept shifting underneath me.

And the most twisted part? When someone like Brent manipulates you into feeling like everything is your fault, you start believing you *are* the problem. That they are the wounded one.

You end up comforting the person who is damaging you. You apologize for your own pain. And in the process, you start to vanish.

If you have ever been in something that looked "fine" or even great from the outside but felt like emotional whiplash behind closed doors, I see you.

If you've ever stayed longer than you now think you "should have,"
I understand.

If you're reading this and feeling shame rise up from your own story, I want you to know: you're not alone. You didn't blow it. You didn't fail. You aren't failing.

You were targeted. You were in survival mode. And that is not your fault.

I know better now. I know the signs. I know how to walk away. I know how to help others walk away too. But back then, I didn't. And if I could go back and whisper one thing to myself in the middle of that chaos, it would be this:

You are not crazy. You are not overreacting. This is not love.

Now, if you'll join me, I would like to get back to the story.

There is so much more I want to share with you.

Chapter 29
Engaged for the Second Time

While I was trying to maintain my emotional and professional balance in the chaos that Brent was creating, Marcus and Sean were both dating women who would eventually become their wives.

Not surprisingly, I wasn't invited to either wedding, nor were they invited to mine.

It is interesting how I considered both of those men dear friends, yet our lives diverged so much that we didn't share something as important as our weddings.

Meanwhile, Brent was rushing our relationship so fast, I couldn't breathe.

He all but demanded that I go with him to his parents' house in Georgia and join their Christmas traditions.

When we arrived, his mother was standoffish. His sisters, who were seventeen and twenty years older than he was, were nice but certainly not warm.

He had a niece a couple of years older than I was and two nephews just younger. They treated me like the flavor of the month.

It didn't make sense to me at the time, but looking back, I totally get it. I was at least the fourth woman Brent had brought home who he introduced as his "soulmate."

When he said that about me, I thought, "We really don't know each other well enough for you to say that." But I smiled politely and went along with it.

I didn't want to cause waves.

Brent's dad was a different story. He was kind, funny, and genuinely interested in getting to know me.

Over the years, we developed a friendly relationship. He especially loved watching me pack boxes when it was time to put everything away. (I have elite-level packing skills that impressed him.)

When I walked into the living room that first Christmas, I was completely overwhelmed by the number of boxes stacked around the tree.

There had to be at least three gifts for every person from every other person, including gifts for me.

On the 23rd, I learned from Brent that he had brought gifts for everyone, but they needed to be wrapped.

That year started the "tradition" of me spending December 23rd wrapping and making bows for the hundred or so gifts he had bought, including the ones I was expected to be surprised about when I opened them.

By the time I was done, my fingers hurt from creasing paper and twisting ribbon.

If I got confused about which gift went to which person and put the wrong name on one of them, there would be hell to pay when it was opened.

Fortunately, that didn't happen the first year.

At least his family was impressed by how good the gifts I wrapped looked. That was a nice feeling compared to the general awkwardness I felt the rest of the time I was there.

Their family tradition was to open gifts the evening of Christmas Eve.

It would start with the youngest person, Brent's great-niece, opening a gift while everyone watched, and proceed in order to the oldest person, his dad, before starting over.

The problem was that it would take hours to get through all the gifts.

By the time we finished, it was the wee hours of Christmas morning. The children were sobbing, and the adults were either actually drunk or so exhausted they looked drunk.

And there were piles of boxes, crumpled wrapping paper and opened gifts everywhere.

It was the most ridiculous "happy" event I had ever seen.

I was used to how my family did it. As a child, I was lucky to get a single Christmas ornament (all of which I cherish now) and some socks for Christmas.

And we opened gifts on my parents' anniversary, December 20th, because we shouldn't get gifts on Jesus' birthday.

The whole process took us less than an hour.

During a break in the gift-opening, Brent pulled me into a bedroom, took a stack of Visa gift cards from his jacket, and told me to fill out the envelopes as if they were from me.

They were for $50 each, at least $500 worth of gifts that he wanted me to pass off as if I had brought them for everyone.

I didn't want to lie.

But he insisted, aggressively whisper-yelling that it would be embarrassing if I didn't give them something.

So, with shaking hands and a pounding heart, I wrote each person's name on an envelope.

He had to tell me their names; I couldn't remember them all under that kind of pressure.

And I couldn't spell Heidi to save my life.

I asked him to spell it, but he said it so fast that my stressed, dyslexic brain couldn't keep track of the letters. I had to ask him to slow down and spell it again three times, which annoyed him even more.

I was on the verge of tears as we walked out of the bedroom, and I handed out the envelopes with a smile and a "Merry Christmas!" to each of them.

If only I had realized that level of fakeness was completely normal for Brent and that I would be expected to play along for as long as we were together.

****

Another tradition I learned about was Brent's insistence on leaving his parents' house on Christmas Day to go on a cruise for the following week.

That first December, it felt novel and fun. We were on a Caribbean cruise for my birthday, and they made a big deal out of it.

What I didn't think about was that this pattern meant I would never get to see my family over the holidays.

Brent told me it didn't matter because: "Your family doesn't have any traditions anyway."

That was true.

But it became tiresome; being expected to attend and participate in his family's dog-and-pony-show Christmas every year, then box up and ship the gifts home, sort through them after the cruise, and take whatever we couldn't use or didn't want to Goodwill.

Eventually, I started putting donations to animal shelters and organizations that support women leaving abusive relationships on my wish list, just so I wouldn't have to bring home quite so many things I would never use.

****

Brent had started talking about engagement rings before the holidays.

I thought it was ridiculous. We had only started "dating" in the early fall, and I hadn't even realized it at first.

But he was adamant: "We love each other. Why wouldn't we get married?"

I think the issue was my rule that I didn't have intercourse outside of marriage. A vestige from my staunch Christian upbringing.

If I had slept with him, he probably would've gotten bored and dropped me, just like the woman he was seeing when we met.

Instead, I was a prized trophy to hunt down and then display on his wall.

I was surprised when, one night while we were on that cruise, he pulled out sketches of a ring he was designing for me.

He didn't hand the drawings to me; he started showing them to the other people at the table.

We always chose group tables on cruises. It gave us people to talk to and was more fun than us sitting alone. (That should've told me something. But alas, I wasn't paying attention.)

By the time the drawings were handed to me, everyone else, eight strangers, had seen the design and commented on it.

One even looked at me and said, "He must really love you! Look at the size of that rock!"

It was a large, two-carat diamond that looked even bigger in the sketch.

What was I supposed to do, tell a table full of impressed strangers, "I'm nowhere near ready to talk about engagement rings?"

I just smiled, nodded, and looked pretty while sipping my wine.

****

When we walked back to our room that night, Brent was mad. Like mad-mad.

Apparently, I had made him look bad by not being "happy enough, involved enough, or complimentary enough" about the engagement ring.

I tried to share that talking about engagement rings when we had been dating long-distance for barely four months seemed rushed to me.

He didn't want to hear it. I realized if I didn't start giving him some feedback, he was going to create a ring I didn't want to wear.

It would have been much more sensible to simply not accept a ring, of any kind, since I did not want to get remarried.

But I didn't make that smart decision.

Instead, in early February, while we were sitting at a ridiculously fancy dinner in Denver, Brent pushed a ring box across the table and said, "Let's get married."

It wasn't a proposal. It was a statement.

I noticed the waiter standing awkwardly off to the side, holding our next course and trying not to interrupt.

I took the ring out of the box and said, "It's beautiful. You did a great job."

(It really is a gorgeous ring. If I have a regret about that marriage ending, it's that a ring that pretty no longer gets worn.)

He replied, "Put it on."

I did what I was told, just so the waiter could set down the plates.

It didn't feel like the right moment to cause a scene.

I don't remember what Brent and I fought about that night. I'm sure I wasn't appreciative enough about something.

But I do remember lying in bed next to him listening to him snore, twisting the ring around my finger, pulling it off and putting it back on, thinking about the mess I had gotten myself into.

I knew marrying him was going to be financially stable. He made *really* good money and was not afraid to spend it.

But I wondered if it would always feel like chaos.

Then I thought about the nuclear war that would happen if I broke up with him.

I was sure I'd get fired, and I knew he was vindictive. He could easily ruin my reputation and make my life miserable.

Somehow, I convinced myself that once we were married and living in the same place, he would be more confident in our relationship and stop blowing up over tiny infractions.

I was wrong. But that was how I justified staying in the relationship.

****

Before long, we picked a date: May 25 of that same year; only nine months after I realized we were dating.

As I type it, I know how crazy it sounds. How did I end up married, *again*, without really wanting to be?

That's the problem with not doing enough therapy: I didn't realize how badly my internal compass was broken.

I still believed the "be a good girl" lie that made me an easy target to be exploited.

I had been told for so long that my intuition was "witchcraft." That feelings weren't logical. That women were too emotional to make important decisions.

I had been conditioned to silence my inner voice, so I just pushed all of it away and moved forward like I was in a trance.

I sobbed when we were trying to pick out wedding invitations. (*Hello, Robyn. This is your intuition speaking. Please pay attention.*)

I was so stressed trying to choose flowers that my hands shook and tears slid down my face. (*Hey, intuition trying again. Are you listening?*)

Carmen offered to make my dress. I chose a beautiful eggplant color that Brent approved, but looking at dress patterns put a rock in my stomach.

Brent got tired of me going back and forth and chose one.

Carmen did a great job. The dress was stunning.

By mid-March, Brent had signed a contract with the officiant and the restaurant he wanted to rent. The ceremony would be on one side and the reception on the other.

(The same place where he broke the glass after he told me he loved me for the first time.)

When I read through the contract for the officiant, I noticed it required us to attend a handful of premarital counseling sessions.

Brent was annoyed, but agreed to do it.

I remember sitting in her office, frustratedly explaining that Brent wouldn't "allow" me to have a trashcan next to the toilet at his place because: "It looked ugly."

I had tried to tell him that when I was on my period, I needed a trashcan nearby, not clear across the room under the sink.

The counselor was really blunt and graphic about it. She said, "Imagine your penis dripping blood and you have to walk across the room to get to the trashcan."

I was mortified.

Brent's "compromise" was to let me have a trashcan next to the toilet in the spare bathroom.

Gee. Thanks.

For one of the sessions, Brent couldn't make it. I think he got stuck in Detroit because of weather or maybe a work thing.

Since it was already paid for, I went by myself.

The counselor didn't say it out loud, but I swear she was trying to tell me telepathically: "This marriage is never going to work. Run!"

I still have a business card she pressed into my hand before I left that day. On the back she wrote:

"I will NOT downplay my needs!

Does everything need a rationale? — NO! Why not?!"

I kept that card in my Day-Timer at work and looked at it often.

Sadly, I was unable to absorb and use her message.

I wonder if she ever thinks about the attractive, emotionally damaged girl I was, and wonders how I'm doing.

Chapter 30

If I Can Just Explain What I Need the Right Way, This Will Work

Brent had me so brainwashed that I honestly believed that if I could just say the right words in the right order, he would understand what I needed and be happy to do it for me.

I thought that if I was open and vulnerable about who I was and what I wanted in our relationship, he would do the same, and we could decide together how to create something that was beautiful and worked for both of us.

I didn't know I was trying to love an illusion; one he created to manipulate me.

It never occurred to me that he would take the most personal and sensitive things I shared, my softest underbelly, and use them against me.

So you can understand how dangerously vulnerable and open I was with him, I need to share some of my parts with you.

****

At some point in my mid-twenties, after I got divorced from Hunter, I started describing myself as having "protector" parts.

I called them "The Bitch," "The Ego," and "The Flirt."

I would say, jokingly and yet deadly serious, "I have a bitch in my back pocket. Don't make me get her out and put her on her soapbox."

That part of me was, and still is, smart enough to be hurtfully mean. She doesn't come out often. But when she decides I or someone else who is vulnerable needs defending, she will don her battle gear and charge into a fray without a second thought.

The Ego is the part of me that looks confident, even if I am completely clueless. I used to get asked for directions in cities I had never visited before. People would say, "You were walking so confidently, I thought you lived here."

Nope. My ego mask is just that good.

The Flirt knows just the right turn of phrase and the right tilt of her head to make a man feel like he is an amazing, powerful protector and she needs saving.

She didn't come out in a manipulative way, although she certainly could have. She was there to protect me when men got scary.

I realized later that there was another part. Her name is Harry-ette.

She is the part of me that hates me. She believes I'm fat, ugly, stupid, and useless. She remembers and uses all of the mean and hurtful things anyone in power has ever said to cut me.

She's not as vocal as she once was, but she is still there, happy to tell me I'm not good enough and will never be worth being proud of.

After those four pieces came The Little Girl. She is six to eight years old. Not confident and easily hurt.

The other four are her staunch protectors.

I learned within the last year that this way of talking about the self is common among trauma survivors, and the process of working with these parts is called "Internal Family Systems."

(If you would like to learn more about it, I highly recommend the book *No Bad Parts: Healing Trauma and Restoring Wholeness with the Internal Family Systems Model* by the founder of the model, Richard Schwartz.)

****

It was *so* important to me that Brent understand who I was, what my fears were, and how I needed him to be gentle, kind, and help me take care of my little girl, that I wrote him a story.

I knew I kept a copy of that story.

But for two decades I haven't been able to find it.

This week, when I was looking for the letter the church sent me after Hunter threw me out, I found a folder with the wedding planning details from when I married Brent.

Tucked inside that folder, I found the story of the little girl who lived in a castle.

I am going to reprint it here, just as I wrote it then, before I had ever gone to college and when I was desperately trying to say, *"Don't just look at me, see me. Love me for who I really am. Not just for the classically attractive woman who looks good on your arm."*

214

****

The Little Girl

Once upon a time there was a little girl who lived in a castle surrounded by a moat with a drawbridge. The little girl had caretakers who made sure all her needs were met. Anything she needed they would provide to her. She would play happily inside the castle walls. When the weather was nice, she would enjoy the sunshine in the courtyard. Every now and then the little girl would venture across the moat to explore the hillsides beyond her castle. But she would always return before nightfall to the security of her caretakers and the warmth of the castle.

Often on her adventures into the countryside she would meet new people. They all thought she was a lovely little girl and would want to spend time with her. But many of them did not know how to treat her. Some did not realize she was a little girl. They would hurt her feelings and laugh when she ran back to the castle to cry. Some wanted to make her their own little girl and would not let her go back to her castle. When she did not come home, her caretakers would come to find her and help her return. Some wanted to be friends with the little girl but didn't like her caretakers. There were even some who threatened to burn down the castle. But many, many more walked by the castle and never knew the little girl who lived inside. All of this made the little girl timid about leaving the safety and security of her castle.

Then one day a boy came to the castle gate and asked about the little girl he had heard lived within. The caretakers told him she did not wish to come out to play that day. The boy smiled, said thank you and went away. The next day he returned. After ringing the castle bell, he was again told, "not today." This happened many times. But each day the boy would politely ask and walk away with a smile. One afternoon as the boy was leaving, he turned to look at the castle and saw the little girl in the window. As he waved to her, he thought, she is as lovely as they say. The little girl returned his gesture with a shy smile and a little wave before disappearing from the window. The boy continued down the path with an extra bounce to his step. From then on, he would look up as he walked away and she would be there with a shy smile and a wave of her hand.

On a fall morning when the castle gate swung open and the boy asked his now familiar question, to his delight he saw the little girl behind her caretakers in the shadows. Although the answer was the same, "not today" his heart soared because she was indeed a beautiful little girl. Each day she

215

was a little closer to her caretaker. The boy would ask his question and the caretaker would answer but he would look into the blue eyes of the little girl.

Then the day came that the boy had been waiting for. The caretaker said the little girl would like to come out to play. But you may only go as far as the end of the drawbridge. You must let her come back before nightfall. The boy readily agreed and smiled broadly as the little girl stepped around her caretaker to join him outside the castle gate. They spent the day playing and talking. At the end of the day the boy walked with the little girl to the castle. She stepped inside beside her caretaker but before the gate closed, she turned to smile and wave goodbye. The boy left with a light heart because the little girl was as wonderful as he had ever dreamed.

Each day the boy would return. Sometimes the answer was no. But more and more the little girl would come out and spend time with him. The caretakers, seeing that he was a good boy, allowed them to explore farther from the castle walls. But each night he would dutifully walk with her across the drawbridge and she would go inside.

Sometimes on their adventures they would meet people who had seen the little girl out before. The boy was never jealous. The little girl would interact and play with them. Sometimes the boy would join them and sometimes he would not. But he was never far away. If someone ever threatened her or tried to hurt her, he was quick to be at her side to defend her. He was even strong enough to protect her and allow her the safety to cry without judging her.

Time passed. The caretakers and the little girl become comfortable with the boy. When he asked if he could take the little girl on more than a day trip away from the castle, the caretakers called a conference between them. This was a new and different request. They asked the little girl how she felt about being away from the security of the castle walls. After much discussion it was decided that the boy had proved himself a trustworthy and honorable protector. If the little girl wanted to go, then she could. The first night away was scary for the little girl. But over the course of many months with a few nights away she became comfortable with the boy as her security.

The castle still stands and the caretakers are ever vigilant. From time to time the little girl returns. Sometimes just to walk the familiar halls and enjoy the sunny courtyard. Once in a while she will run back with a tear-streaked face. Her caretakers will take her in and comfort her. When the boy asks, they tell him, "Not yet" and he will wait. When she is soothed the caretakers will open the gate and she will again join her playmate in exploring the hills with the security that her castle will always be there when she needs it. And when she does, her friend will always be just across the drawbridge waiting for her to come back out to play.

The End

****

Brent read the story and replied with all the right things. He thanked me for sharing it with him and told me he understood. He talked about how honored he was to be trusted by the little girl.

It was all lies, nonsense, and manipulation.

He would later use that story against me, saying I had "daddy issues."

But I didn't know any of that yet. I was just doing my best to be open and honest about who I was and what I needed to be in a healthy relationship.

Chapter 31

Never Get Married Because You're Afraid to Be Alone

At work, Brent hired Terri to be my direct supervisor. He had worked with her before and I found out later she had never been in a leadership position.

Brent told me he "kinda fudged" her experience to give her the job.

At first, Terri stayed out of my way.

She was based in Detroit, and I had been running the Charlotte center for a while. I didn't need a supervisor; unless something went sideways and I needed backup from someone with authority.

That was fine until Terri learned that Brent and I were seeing each other.

Suddenly, she was out to get me.

GM had a policy that I couldn't report directly to Brent once our relationship was discovered. (Things like that are always found out eventually).

Officially, I now reported to someone else. Unofficially, Terri still had dotted-line authority over my day-to-day work.

She started showing up on my vendor calls and making snide comments on conference calls while I was troubleshooting outages.

If she could sneak into a call, she would listen in silently and then call me afterward to berate me about everything she thought I did wrong.

It got so bad I finally told her that if she wanted to be on all of my calls, she could run them, and I'd go do something productive.

She started nitpicking everything I did and giving me poor performance reviews.

I vented to Brent. Not because I wanted him to do anything, I was just talking to my fiancé about my horrible boss.

But he started having conversations with Terri, who still reported to him, about her needing some leadership training.

She accused me of funneling "private conversations to management" without cause and said she was documenting it as "insubordination."

I told Brent he had to stop using what he learned in our personal conversations at work. He told me that as a leader he couldn't do that. So, my only option was to stop talking to him about what was going on.

The guy I officially reported to didn't want anything to do with what he called "girl drama," and told me I needed to figure out how to work with Terri or find a different place to work.

The job had always been really stressful, but now it was off the charts.

When I got back to work after getting engaged, no one seemed particularly interested in seeing the ring.

I thought that was odd because it was a stunning piece of jewelry.

I finally asked Tina if she thought it was weird. She shrugged. "Oh, we've all seen it. Brent was showing it off to everyone before you left."

I couldn't explain why but I felt like I had been cheated out of something. It seemed childish to be upset that I didn't get to have people gushing over my ring.

That was the first time I noticed that Brent was all about being the center of attention, making sure that things looked impressive and that people were in awe or jealous of him in some way.

As the wedding date got closer, that behavior got worse.

He bragged about the restaurant we booked, showed our invitations to people who weren't invited, and went on about the expensive flowers I had supposedly picked. (He had more to do with the cost than I did.)

I even started hearing about our honeymoon plans from people I barely knew.

For him, the wedding and all of the stuff surrounding it were opportunities for him to brag and show off.

I was having second, third, and fourth thoughts about marrying him.

But then he would do something that was kind or thoughtful like send me flowers or buy me clothes. (Boy did that man love to buy women's clothing!)

Now I recognize it for what it was: love bombing. But back then, it just felt like emotional whiplash.

When he did act like he loved me, it was amazing and that made it easier to overlook the times he was mean, hurtful or used me to make himself look good.

Then I got an email from someone calling herself "Stephanie." (I found out about a year later that wasn't her real name, but I'm going to use it throughout the book.)

In the email, she explained that she used to date Brent and thought it was only fair that I knew what I was getting myself into.

She included a screenshot from a casual hookup website.

It had Brent's full name and a vague description: height, weight, hair color, lived outside Detroit.

Under "What are you into?" it simply said: "Anything discreet, no strings."

Stephanie included the link, but since I was on a work computer, I didn't click it.

She closed with, "Don't bother to confront him. He'll just deny it. Do with that what you will. Good luck."

But I still naively believed I was in a relationship where we talked about things and told the truth.

I printed the screenshot, just the image, not the full email, and tried to have a conversation with Brent about it.

Just as Stephanie predicted, Brent denied everything. He even got angry and insisted that Dale (yes, my ex) must have created the account and sent it to sabotage us.

By the end of the conversation, I was trying to calm him down because he was threatening to call the police.

It was the first time Brent used his the-best-defense-is-a-good-offense strategy on me. But it would become a staple in his bag of tricks anytime I caught him lying.

****

When I told my oldest younger brother that I was getting married again, the first thing he said was, "Don't expect Mom and Dad to pay for another wedding."

What a strange thing to say. They only paid for about half of my first wedding. Why would he think I would expect them to chip anything in for a second one?

My mom was surprised. Rightly so. I had barely talked about Brent at all. When she asked me how long I had known him, I told her the truth: we met about a year before getting engaged.

Never mind that our first "business" dinner wasn't until about seven months later.

I insisted on a small, intimate wedding because it was a second marriage for both of us.

(At least, that's what I thought. He had actually been married twice before. He just failed to tell me about the second one.)

We invited all of his family and just the adults from mine. I'm not sure why his niece and nephew, both under ten, were welcome, but my teenage siblings weren't. But that's how it ended up.

The invitations clearly stated: "no gifts, please."

My dad called to tell me that flying out was their gift, and that they would not be bringing anything else.

Of course, that was fine.

I wasn't surprised when Brent's family brought gifts. Things we didn't need (I wrote kind thank-you notes anyway).

Brent told me to only invite friends I thought I would still remember in twenty years. A strange edict. But that did mean we didn't have to invite all the people we worked with, some of whom were annoyed not to be included.

I just dug that wedding album out of a box to remember who was actually there.

My parents. My oldest younger brother and his wife. My middle sister, who was pregnant. Carmen and her husband. My cousin, who we had flown in to do my hair and makeup (she did a great job). Tina and a coworker named Chris, who I rented a room from in Charlotte after my house sold.

There is also an attractive young woman with short brunette hair I can't place. I recognize her face, but I can't remember who she is.

On Brent's side, it was just his family. He never had friends, something he used to lament like he was the victim. The truth was, he was a horrible person, and people didn't stick around once they realized he was using them.

Chapter 32
My Second Wedding

The night of the rehearsal dinner, Brent laughed and carried on like he was having the time of his life.

He put his credit card on the hotel bar and told everyone drinks were on him.

He, my cousin, and a few others stayed up way too late, partying on his tab.

I went home to get my beauty rest.

****

The morning of the wedding, I got a call from the florist. The purple and white orchids for my bouquet had not come in. All she had was solid purple ones.

That was disappointing. My dress was solid purple, and I had wanted the flowers to contrast with it.

But what was I going to do, throw a tantrum? That wouldn't make the right flowers magically appear.

I suggested she do what she could by incorporating white ribbon, and it would have to be good enough.

I think she was relieved I wasn't a bridezilla. Good thing she called me and not Brent. She would have gotten a very different response.

As it turned out, the right flowers did arrive. I was pleasantly surprised not to have to explain to Brent why I had the "wrong" ones.

My cousin, my middle sister, and Carmen came to my house to help me get ready. The photographer showed up to document it, and overall, we were having a great time.

As it got closer to the time we were supposed to leave, I started wondering where the limo was.

I had never ridden in a limo (still haven't). Brent was delighted to be the first to "treat me like a princess."

The day before, I called the limo company to confirm the details and remind them the driver should take the long way around. Otherwise, he was going to get stuck in NASCAR traffic.

The woman who answered had been snarky, and I hung up with a bad feeling that the limo was going to be a no-show.

There is a picture of me sitting in my living room, completely ready to get married, talking to Carmen's husband while we waited.

I called the limo company office.

No answer.

There was exactly zero chance that I was going to be late to my own wedding because of a missing limo. I simply don't do late, and Brent would be furious.

But there was a logistical problem.

The plan had been for me, my sister, my cousin, and Carmen to ride in the limo to the ceremony. Then Brent and I would take the limo to the hotel after the reception dinner and a car service to the airport in the morning.

If I drove myself to the ceremony, we would have to figure out how to get the car back to my house.

Carmen and her husband had driven their minivan, so they could put their kids' car seats in the back and my sister and cousin could ride with them.

I asked the photographer if he had room in his car.

He said he would have to move some equipment, but we could make it work.

Twenty minutes past the scheduled pickup time, I left a message on the limo service's answering machine letting them know the limo hadn't arrived, and I was leaving.

(Remember my fifteen-minute rule for guys being late to pick me up for dates? It seemed reasonable that I shouldn't wait longer than that for someone I was paying.)

Later, I heard from neighbors that a limo sat in front of my house for a while that evening.

Carmen called them while I was on my honeymoon. She had to fight with them but she was able to get our money refunded.

The driver had gotten stuck in race traffic and tried to argue that it wasn't his fault because he didn't know.

Too bad. I had warned them that it was going to be a problem. They did not adjust accordingly.

****

I arrived at the restaurant just five minutes later than expected.

I was surprised to see Brent pacing; phone pressed to his ear.

Apparently, there was an outage at work, and Brent was on a conference call.

I had told my boss I was getting married and made it clear: "Don't call me."

Brent told me he had done the same. But clearly that was a lie. He was not so critical to anything that he needed to be on a call right then.

I decided not to confront him about it.

When Brent saw me get out of the photographer's car, he strode over and hissed in my ear while I was smoothing my dress, "Where's the limo?"

He had put the outage conference call on speaker, so I just shrugged rather than trying to talk over it.

"How are we going to get to the hotel?" His voice sounded like he thought I had sent the limo away and ridden in a dirty, beat-up sedan instead to spite him.

"I don't know. Maybe the driver will come here after he realizes I'm not at the house. If not, we'll figure it out."

I paused to see if he wanted to add anything.

When he didn't respond, I continued, "Are you going to be done soon? The officiant's already here."

He ignored me, unmuted his phone, and started aggressively laying into a tech on the other end.

I turned and walked into the restaurant to check the music and greet the people who actually cared about me.

The place looked beautiful.

One section held the flower arch and chairs for the ceremony; the other was set for the four-course dinner we had planned for the reception.

Brent came in a little while later. He wanted to tell me what was going on at work, but I cut him off: "I don't want to know. It's not my problem tonight, and I don't want to think about it."

When the music started, my emotions overwhelmed me. Tears started to roll down my cheeks as I walked down the short aisle and I wept the entire time we exchanged vows.

Afterward, my dad asked why I had been crying. I told him it was because I was so happy.

That was a lie. My intuition had been screaming; one last desperate attempt to stop me from making a giant mistake.

Sadly, I didn't listen.

During dinner, Brent gave a touching toast, gushing about how I was the perfect partner for him and how lucky he was. Everyone raved about how magical the entire evening was. (Brent was always good at putting on a show.)

At the end of the night, we climbed into the back of Carmen's minivan and they took us to the hotel.

The limo never did show up.

Chapter 33
My Second Honeymoon

Brent had been bragging for weeks about the incredible honeymoon he'd booked: Le Toiny Hotel and Beach Club on the exclusive island of St. Barts in the Caribbean.

We had to get up early to meet the car and catch our flight from Charlotte to Miami, then on to St. Barts.

I was surprised when we checked in for our flights that he had booked coach. With all the money he had been throwing around, I had assumed we would be flying first class.

I thought it was fine. The flights were short and we were going to a beautiful place.

But Brent complained through both flights, like I was the one who had booked him in coach.

Worse, Brent's luggage did not make the transfer in Miami.

I remember standing in the small baggage claim area in St. Barts and wishing it had been my luggage that was missing.

I would have just gone with the flow and figured it out.

Brent was angry and yelling at anyone within hearing range, including me.

The airline attendant told him that getting it on the next flight down was the best he could do.

I suggested we check into our villa, have some lunch, and then look for a shop where he could buy some stylish island wear.

He was still mad but he stopped screaming about it.

And his luggage was delivered that evening with an apology note from the hotel. Like it was their fault the airline screwed up.

But it made Brent feel important, and that's all that mattered.

****

The villa was the most luxurious place I had ever been in my life.

227

There was champagne on ice, surrounded by the most amazing-looking fruit.

A private courtyard. A plunge pool framed by fuchsia bougainvillea overlooking the breathtakingly blue Caribbean Sea. A shaded lanai where silent staff set out breakfast every morning.

However, it is possible to be miserable anywhere if the company is bad enough.

This was the first time Brent and I had spent seven days in a row together and I quickly realized that every little thing would set him off. He would rage or pout like a child over nothing.

That first afternoon, he sat nude on one of the stark white lounge chairs without putting down a towel and left a brown streak. I cringed every time I saw it for the rest of the week. But I pretended not to notice.

He rented a Jeep because he thought it would be cool to use it to zip around the island, but then was mad that it was a stick shift and he kept stalling it on the hills.

It also annoyed him that it was usually raining at the top of the mountain when we went from one side of the island to the other, and that he would get wet if the top was open.

I started bringing an extra towel with us, just in case.

He wanted to go to a nude beach. (It is technically illegal to sunbathe nude on St. Barts, but they generally tolerate it.)

Then he was mad: "Only people who shouldn't be are nude." And even worse: "Everyone is looking at you."

I was only topless, but I was wearing a very tiny bikini bottom that *he* had bought for me and I had a competitive beach volleyball player body.

Yeah. People were going to look. But let's not confuse the situation with facts. He was mad at *me* about it.

He wanted to go to Colombier Beach, which is only accessible by boat or by hiking down a very steep goat path.

As we walked, the rocks slid under my feet and I fell, catching myself with my hand, unfortunately right in a cactus. Of course, never one to interrupt someone's plan, we continued down to the beach, played in the water and hiked back out.

That afternoon we asked the concierge if there was a doctor in town who could help us. They sent someone to our room, but she only spoke French.

In the end, the best she could do was give me a hypodermic needle so I could dig the cactus spines out myself. Sadly, she did not have tweezers, which would have been far more useful.

I was still pulling cactus out of my hand weeks later. I even joked at work that I had smuggled pieces of plants through customs. But I never complained about it, because what was the point? That would just annoy Brent.

We did buy an absolutely gorgeous cocktail dress while we were there. Solid black and fit me like a glove.

The sales guy turned to Brent and said, in a French accent, "Enjoy it now. She'll only look good in it for a few years."

I was offended at the time, but the joke's on him. I looked amazing in that dress for at least fifteen years.

****

I remember lying in bed, looking out at the sea, the mosquito netting billowing in the breeze that was drifting through the open doors, thinking, *"This should be amazing. But I'd almost rather be home than here, dealing with Brent's bad mood."*

It was the first time I was unhappy in one of the most beautiful places on earth. It would not be the last.

Chapter 34
Mistake in Progress

When we returned from our honeymoon, we got on separate flights in Miami. He went to Detroit, and I flew back to Charlotte.

I was going to stay in Charlotte until my house sold. Then I would ask GM for a job transfer to Detroit and move in with him.

I wasn't thrilled about moving to Detroit. My experience of it was that it was cold, gray, and sad.

But he convinced me it made more sense for me to move than for him to try to find a new job, so I went along with it.

We saw each other every other weekend, with each of us flying once a month. It wasn't ideal, but it seemed to work.

On my first trip to his place after we got married, I asked if I could use his computer to check my email.

He was in the kitchen doing something and said, "Sure," without even looking up.

I walked into his office, turned on his computer and opened a browser window.

I clicked on the search bar. When the list of recently visited sites popped up, my heart stopped.

The third one down was Match.com.

I stared at it, my fingers hovering over the keyboard.

We had literally just gotten married. Why was a dating website in his recent search history?

I clicked on it and his profile loaded.

Just like the screenshot that Stephanie had sent me, the details were vague. Except on this site, it said he was looking for a committed relationship.

I forgot about checking my email. I just sat there staring at the screen, trying to process what I was seeing and what it meant.

My house was on the market. I was in the process of upending my life for him. Breaking up now would be complete chaos.

(I should have done it anyway.)

I got up and walked halfway back to the kitchen. "Hey. Can you come in here and look at something for me?"

He dried his hands and walked toward me, annoyance on his face.

I walked back into the office in front of him and, looking at the computer monitor clearly showing his Match.com profile, said, "Help me understand."

He looked at it and scrambled into the chair and closed the browser.

"Why are you snooping on my computer?" His tone was already sharp.

"I wasn't snooping. I just opened the browser and that was in your recently visited list." I kept my voice even, not wanting the situation to escalate.

"That's old. I haven't been on that site in months." He shut down the computer and shoved the chair back aggressively enough that I had to jump out of the way so it didn't run over my bare toes.

"Brent, that's not how recent history works. Just tell me the truth about what's going on so we can figure it out."

He jumped up in a rage. "First you snoop through my computer, sticking your nose where it doesn't belong." His eyes narrowed. "And now you're accusing me of what? Huh? What exactly are you accusing me of?"

I felt like a scolded child. "I wasn't snooping, and I'm not accusing. I'm just asking to understand."

"There is nothing to understand. Stop snooping on my computer." He brushed past me and back to the kitchen like that was just the end of the conversation.

I followed him, trying again. "I thought we agreed before we got married that we were going to be totally honest with each other and have the hard conversations."

He spun around glaring, his voice loud and commanding. "If you are accusing me of something, just come out and say it."

"You've obviously been on that dating website since we got married. I want to know what's going on."

He stalked toward me. "I *told* you, that is old and you shouldn't be snooping."

I held my ground, "I know that isn't true."

"Believe me or don't. That isn't my problem." He dismissed me with a shrug and walked away.

We didn't speak the rest of the night. The next morning, he acted like everything was normal.

That was the beginning of him gaslighting me so badly, I started to question whether I could trust my own memory of conversations and events.

****

A few weeks later, we got an offer on my house. It was less than what I had originally paid, but since I was so close to having it paid off, I would still walk away with a hefty check from the capital I had built up.

I started making plans to ship everything to Detroit and move in with Brent.

Then the bottom fell out.

He got laid off.

GM said it was "restructuring."

Brent said it was because of our relationship, and that I was lucky he loved me, because I had cost him his job.

I felt guilty, like I'd done something wrong, as if I had forced him to pursue and marry me, and now I was to blame for him getting fired.

We reworked our plan.

He was going to start job hunting, which meant he could end up living anywhere. It didn't make sense for me to move until we knew where he would land.

But the sale of my house was closing in less than a month.

We could ship my stuff to Detroit and store it in Brent's basement but I needed a place to live.

I approached my friend Chris at work and asked if I could rent his spare bedroom month-to-month.

He happily said yes.

I didn't realize one of our coworkers, the same one who'd dropped his crying employee in my lap during her boyfriend-and-a-gun incident, was already living in that bedroom.

But because he wasn't paying rent, Chris asked him to leave without even mentioning it to me.

I felt bad that I had accidentally put the guy on the street.

I ended up living with Chris for about six months.

In that time, Brent got a job on Long Island, New York that paid him more than the job at GM and agreed to pay his moving expenses.

They wanted him to start right away, so he packed some of his clothing and his two cats, handed the keys to his house to a realtor and moved into a long-stay hotel near his new job.

He always bragged about the "great deal" he'd gotten on his three-quarter-of-a-million-dollar house.

I thought it was dumb that he lived in a six-bedroom, five-bathroom house by himself. He didn't even put blinds in most of the house.

That became a problem when we tried to sell it. It wasn't brand new, and buyers expected things like window treatments, fresh paint, and landscaping.

None of that had been done.

We sat on that house, paying the mortgage, for a long time waiting for it to sell. When it finally did, I learned he had an interest-only loan on the damn thing.

Which meant he had zero capital in it. And because we had to sell it for less than he paid, we had to put money with it to get rid of it.

That is when it really struck me: he made a *lot* of money, but he was spending every cent. He had no capital outside of a small emergency fund.

A stark contrast to my smaller income, but capital-rich, financial situation.

****

Now we had a problem with my job. It no longer made sense for me to request a transfer to Detroit.

233

In Charlotte, I had built a strong network, and was being headhunted for jobs.

On Long Island, I would be just another pretty girl with a high school diploma. Finding a white-collar job might be tough.

We were thinking I might just stay in Charlotte until Brent got settled, but then Terri announced that my job was moving to Detroit.

They gave me forty-five days to "think" about it. Terri, smug as ever, said, "I'm guessing you'll just quit and move to New York."

I wasn't going to make it that easy for her. I replied, "I don't know, it might make sense for us to keep Brent's house in Detroit until the market gets better. I could live there for now. He and I will have to talk about it."

I knew that was completely unlikely, but I waited forty-four days to tell her I wasn't moving to Detroit and would accept their proposal of November 30th as my last day at GM.

I reached out to HR because Thanksgiving weekend fell at the end of the month that year, meaning the last working day was the Wednesday before the holiday.

They told me to plan on turning in my company cell phone and pager (the super clunky kind you could text on) that Wednesday.

The week before Thanksgiving, Terri flew down to do my exit interview. It was completely pointless. She wasn't going to report anything useful I said to HR anyway.

Besides, I already had a reputation for being *"dramatic."*

A few months earlier, an executive gave a speech about how "we're all on a cruise ship heading for the same destination, and we each have to do our part."

When he opened the floor for questions, I stood up and said, "On this cruise ship, management is on the deck having cocktails at a jazz party. I'm in the engine room bailing water. We're sinking, and you don't even know it."

That didn't go over well. And the leadership team didn't care what I thought now, either.

At the end of our perfunctory conversation, Terri asked me, "When will you be back in town?"

She knew I was flying to Georgia to spend Thanksgiving with my in-laws.

I was flying back on Sunday. But that was none of her business so I said, "I don't know. I might go to Long Island with Brent. Why?"

"You need to bring back your phone and pager."

I narrowed my eyes. "HR told me to leave them here when I walk out of the building on Wednesday."

"You can't. I have you scheduled to be on-call over Thanksgiving."

I wanted to laugh in her face. Did she really think that an employee whose job they had just eliminated was going to spend her holiday weekend on-call?

"You can schedule me on-call if you want. My phone and my pager will be left here."

She said, "We'll see about that," stood up, and walked out in a huff.

I learned that she called HR and tried to get them to force me to cover the on-call shift. They told her she had no leverage and to find someone else to cover or do it herself.

She then tried to say I had to pay them back for twelve hours of vacation time I had taken but not yet earned.

I countered that we had always done lieu-time, but if they wanted to be sticklers about twelve hours of vacation time, I was going to need to submit hundreds of hours of overtime I had racked up being on-call over the last eleven months.

I don't know exactly what HR said to Terri, but I heard through the grapevine that she was pissed I "won."

Good for her. I didn't feel guilty about it. Not even a little bit.

Chapter 35
Moving to Long Island

The weekend after Thanksgiving with Brent's family, I packed everything I still owned in Charlotte into my car, except the couch Chris was keeping, said goodbye to my friends, and planned to drive to Long Island on Saturday.

But a snowstorm was moving across the Northeast, so we decided I should wait and leave Sunday morning.

I started what should have been a twelve-hour drive at 4 AM.

Brent hadn't given me any insight into what to expect, only that there had been "some" snow but not to worry because "it should be cleared" by the time I got up there.

I never carried cash. I just kept my debit card, driver's license, and a ChapStick in a small change purse. So, when my brain was like, *"I should stop at the ATM and get some cash,"* I pushed back.

"It is 4 AM, cold and dark. Stopping at an ATM might not be safe."

"I really think having some cash is a good idea."

So, even though I had no clue why I was doing it, I stopped and withdrew forty dollars.

Thank goodness I actually listened to my intuition that morning. Charlotte didn't have toll roads back then so it never occurred to me that I would need cash to pay tolls.

I didn't even know how the New Jersey Turnpike worked. When I pulled up to the toll booth and the woman handed me a ticket, I asked, "What do I do with this?"

She looked at me like I was stupid but replied, "Give it to the person at the other end when you get off. They will tell you how much you owe."

The drive from Charlotte to the middle of Long Island cost me exactly forty dollars in tolls. I have no idea what I would have done if I hadn't stopped to get cash that morning.

And "some snow" was actually about ten inches. The roads were plowed but slushy and the farther north I got, the worse they got.

I was never so happy to arrive at my destination as I was that night.

Brent had rented a small apartment, furniture, kitchen supplies, towels, sheets, basically everything you needed to live, since all of our stuff was still in his house in Detroit.

But he hadn't moved in yet. He was still living out of the long-stay hotel.

We had planned for me to meet him at the apartment; we would unpack my car, and then spend the night at the hotel. He had taken a couple of days off so we could get him moved into the apartment.

When I arrived, there was an unmade bed with a box of linens sitting on it, a couch, and two bar stools.

The rest of the stuff was supposed to be delivered the following Tuesday.

Brent hugged me, but it was obligatory rather than him being excited to see me.

He said, "Took long enough. I have been sitting here with nothing to do."

I apologized and tried to explain how hard the drive was because of the snow, plus I made a wrong turn in New York City and missed the tunnel.

He wasn't listening.

Instead, he started randomly yanking on stuff in the trunk, trying to jerk it free.

I had packed the car like a game of Jenga. Everything had to be just so to make it fit and it had to be taken out in order, top to bottom.

"Be careful! You're going to break something." I might have said it with more urgency than I meant to.

Brent put what he was holding on the ground behind the car. Looked at me and scoffed, "Fine. Unload it yourself."

Then he walked into the apartment empty-handed and slammed the door.

I stared after him in shock. Was he really going to leave me to deal with this myself after I just spent almost fifteen hours driving in super stressful conditions?

I waited but he didn't come back.

Resigned, I started carefully trying to unpack the trunk. Things had shifted precariously when he yanked stuff out and I was concerned it was going to come crashing down.

When I carried my first load up the stairs, I found Brent in the position I would come to recognize as his default "I'm annoyed" posture.

He was lying on the couch on his back, naked, his head on the armrest so he could watch me. His knees were bent with one ankle crossed over the other knee, his junk hanging wrinkled and limp between his legs.

He was looking at his toes as he picked at them. He was flexible enough, from years of being a swimmer, to actually chew on his toenails. If he was really mad, he would do that. (Skeeved me every time.)

I looked at him in disbelief. "Are you really not going to help me?"

His eyes flicked up toward the ceiling. "Obviously I can't do anything right, so no."

I tried to explain that it wasn't that he couldn't do anything right. That the car just needed to be unpacked carefully. But he didn't move.

I lost count of how many times I trudged up and down those stairs before my car was finally empty and we could head to the hotel for some sleep.

****

The next morning, I was surprised when his alarm clock went off. I assumed we would sleep in since he had the day off and I was exhausted.

He got up and got in the shower before I could say anything.

When he came out of the bathroom, he started putting on business clothes.

I looked at him, confused. "Are you going to work?"

"Yes. I am going on a business trip. I'll be back on Wednesday or Thursday."

"I thought you had to be out of the hotel today?" I was genuinely perplexed.

"I do."

"How does that work?"

"You'll just have to do it. It's not that hard. There isn't that much stuff here."

"So I'm supposed to pack everything, including the cats, into my tiny car and move us into the apartment myself?"

We had shipped my BMW Z3 up weeks before, and it was parked in the hotel garage.

He glared at me and snapped, "Why are you making this a thing?"

"Because this wasn't the plan. When did you learn you had to go on a business trip?"

His response was clipped. "Last week."

"And why didn't you tell me?" My voice was rising.

"Look," he turned around and glared, "This is how it is. Figure it out."

I sat in bed stewing until he grabbed his watch and wallet from the small desk.

He started shifting things around on the desk. Then stopped, straightened and spat at me, "What did you do with my ring?"

All I could say was, "What?"

"My wedding ring. It was right here next to my watch and it's gone. What did you do with it?" His tone was caustic and accusatory.

"I didn't do anything with it. Why would I touch your ring?"

"Well, it's not here and I didn't move it so…."

I sighed as I got out of bed. "Did you check the floor?"

I got down on my hands and knees and looked around the legs of the desk. When I moved the trash can, I heard a tiny, metallic "clink."

A trash can with just paper in it shouldn't make that sound. I turned it over and dumped the trash out of it.

His ring rolled across the carpet.

"You threw it away!" he growled, looming over me.

"I did not throw away your ring. That doesn't even make sense."

"Then how did it get in the trash? How did you know it was there?" He said it like it was a gotcha moment.

"If I had to guess, one of the cats was probably up there playing and knocked it off the desk. I knew it was in there because I heard it when I moved the trash can."

I picked the ring up off the floor and handed it to him.

He swiped it out of my hand. No thank you. No acknowledgment that he'd yelled at me for no reason. Nothing.

He left without kissing me goodbye. He just said, "I'll call you." And closed the door.

****

I spent the day making multiple trips on still-slushy streets, the first one in a sports car meant for sunshine.

Then I switched to the Saab I had driven up the day before. It was safer and had more room for Brent's stuff.

Since there was no food in the house, I had to figure out how to feed myself. Fortunately, I thought to ask the front desk where I could find a grocery store before I left the hotel.

I was halfway through shopping when I remembered the kitchen stuff wouldn't arrive until the next day.

Fast food wasn't my thing, so I tried to figure out what I could eat from the grocery store without utensils.

It was a long and emotionally exhausting day, and I still had to make the bed before I could go to sleep.

As I dumped the box of linens out, I wished I had thought to wash them. Even without detergent, it would have been better than having to sleep with the cardboard smell.

But I was too tired to care for very long.

The delivery guys arrived the next morning with supplies to create a fully stocked kitchen and bathroom.

When they left, I was surrounded by dozens of boxes that needed to be unpacked.

Fortunately, they had included dish and laundry detergent because everything needed to be washed.

The floor was covered with packing paper, empty boxes, and stacks of dishes when the doorbell rang and made me jump.

I wasn't expecting anyone. Was I supposed to answer it or not?

I thought about Brent insisting that living on Long Island wasn't like the "friendly South." That I needed to be smart and keep my head on a swivel if I didn't want someone to kill me. (It actually wasn't like that at all.)

He had even made me get rid of the custom license plate for my little car. (It was: CA BLOND. I especially enjoyed having that tag when I was playing beach volleyball. It was very me.)

The doorbell rang again and a man's voice yelled a business name I didn't recognize, followed by, "cable company!"

Hmm. Maybe Brent scheduled a cable install.

I was more afraid of Brent's reaction if I missed the install than I was of opening the door. So I picked my way through the mess and went downstairs to see who it was.

Fortunately, it was just a really nice cable guy who chatted with me while he installed our TV and internet.

****

Brent had left me his personal cell phone so he could reach me "if he needed anything." We were going to get me my own when he got back.

He told me to answer it only if it was his work cell phone number. Everything else I should let go to voicemail.

At the time, I just accepted his instructions. But looking back, it's weird. Why wouldn't he want his wife answering his phone?

I know now it was because he was cheating. But back then, I was clueless.

That evening, he called to let me know he wouldn't be home until Thursday night.

I was disappointed that I was going to be alone in the apartment for two more full days. I was almost done unpacking and putting things away. Once that was done, I wouldn't have anything else to do.

And I was starting to get lonely. I was used to working full-time, going to the gym, and playing volleyball. Sitting alone in an apartment with two cats and nothing to do wasn't me.

Brent didn't even acknowledge my concerns.

I mentioned that the cable guy had come by and all he said was, "Oh good."

"You didn't tell me he was coming. I almost didn't answer the door."

"Sorry. I forgot." His tone was completely dismissive.

I would learn quickly enough that Brent loved to brag about having a memory like a steel trap but would flippantly say he "forgot" or "didn't remember" things whenever it suited him.

****

Despite my disappointment about him being gone and setting up the apartment alone, I had a surprise planned for him when he got home.

I had a sexy negligée I had been saving for the first night we slept in our own place as husband and wife.

On Thursday afternoon, I ventured out in search of a bottle of champagne and some champagne glasses.

I removed the wire from the champagne and put the bottle in the fridge, then made sure my teddy was fresh and wrinkle-free.

I wasn't sure what time he would be home. He hadn't told me when his flight was landing. So I showered, shaved, dried and styled my hair, did my makeup and spritzed on his favorite perfume early.

By five, I had my outfit on, covered by a bathrobe, and my high heels waiting at the top of the stairs.

Two sleek champagne glasses waited on the counter, ready for me to pop the bottle and pour the bubbly.

I stood by the window, peeking out at our empty parking spot, waiting for him to pull in.

A little after seven, I saw his headlights sweep across the grass.

I ran to the bedroom and threw my bathrobe on the bed.

Then I dashed to the kitchen and wrestled with the champagne cork. I finally got it open and carefully poured the golden liquid, trying not to let it bubble over.

I was just stepping into my heels when I heard his key in the door.

He threw the door open so hard that it slammed against the wall as he stormed in.

He looked up at me and growled, "It's fucking raining and you've got the fucking door locked. Are you stupid?"

I stood there, dumbfounded. He barreled up the stairs; his computer bag crashing into the wall with every other step.

His shoulder hit me as he reached the top.

I stumbled back, champagne sloshing onto my chest and pouring down on my shoes.

He stomped into the office to dump his computer bag on the floor, then spun around and said, "I'm hungry. What do we have to eat?"

He didn't wait for me to respond. He just started rummaging around in the fridge, bitching that I was useless and hadn't bought anything he wanted.

I slipped out of my heels, set the mostly empty glasses on the bathroom sink, and walked into the bedroom to get my robe, tears in my eyes.

I had never been so humiliated in my life. I felt foolish. Stupid. Small.

I dumped the untouched bottle of champagne down the sink the next morning after he left for work.

Brent never acknowledged my effort to have the house completely set up and then do something I thought most men would have been thrilled about.

I would never wear that lingerie again.

Chapter 36
Just Go to School

Shortly after I moved to Long Island, I had an interview with someone Brent knew. I thought it went really well. But the feedback the guy gave Brent was, "We only hire people with college degrees."

He didn't even bother to call me back. I felt dismissed; just like when the doctor had called Hunter instead of me to talk about *my* health.

I wasn't sure what I was going to do because sitting around the house all day with two cats was not going to work for very long.

I shouldn't have worried; fate had plans for me.

The first week of January, Brent and I were driving back from somewhere when we saw a sign for an open house event at Stony Brook University.

Brent looked over at me and said, "Why don't you just go to college? We don't need your silly money anyway."

I let the insult wash over me and said, "Why don't we stop and get some information?"

"Now?"

"Yeah. Why not?"

Brent made a U-turn. We followed the signs and walked in just as the people behind the table were packing up their flyers to leave.

We learned that if I could get a copy of my high school transcripts and my SAT score, assuming I qualified for admission, I could start classes as soon as the end of the month.

I had my SAT score (which actually wasn't that impressive), and getting my transcripts was as easy as making a phone call to my high school, where my dad still worked.

It took less than a week for me to get an email saying I had been accepted, I wrote a check using the money I had gotten from selling my house. And just like that, I was a full-time student.

Other than a Spanish class I took at the local community college when I was in high school, I had never been to college. I had no idea if I was going to be able to do it.

Because the high school I went to wasn't great, I hadn't done academic math in years, and I wrote like a business person, I had to take developmental courses that first semester.

Taking twelve credits was considered a full load, so that is how many I signed up for.

That was the first and last time I did that.

Every semester after that I took at least eighteen. And in grad school it worked out that I took twenty-seven credits once. (They changed the rules about the maximum number of credits you could take after that.)

That's how I ended up getting all three of my degrees in six and a half years.

That first semester I got three A's and an A-.

I should have gotten an A in the fourth class, a Russian Literature course, but the professor told me she only gave A's to students who could read Dostoevsky in the original Russian.

If I had that course later in my college career, I would have pushed back. But at the time I didn't know if I was an A student in college or not.

It all worked out though. I had an introduction to computer science professor who gave me an A- because I worked hard and came to his office hours. Realistically, I probably earned a B.

Shortly after my first semester ended, Brent and I went on a cruise for our first anniversary.

I remember sitting on the balcony, watching the ocean roll by, listening to Brent tell me how amazing it was to be married to me.

A week after we got home, the bottom dropped out of my marriage.

Chapter 37
Betrayal and Bad Advice

During my first summer semester, I took an evening calculus class that was brutal.

The grad student teaching it would stand at the board solving problems, pausing only to say, "And then..." at the end of each line.

When he solved the problem, he would turn around and say, "See. So simple."

I cannot tell you how many times I said, "No. Not simple. I don't understand."

That is the only class I ever took where I left a third of the final blank, and because the curve was so steep, I still got an A.

Two weeks into that class, I got another email from Stephanie.

The subject was: *You need to know*

The email told me that Brent was having an affair with a woman at work.

Stephanie gave me the woman's name, a physical description, told me she was getting divorced, going back to her maiden name, and that she had a child.

But the most damning evidence she provided was the password to Brent's personal email account.

She said Brent had given it to her when they dated years ago and had never changed it.

Then she warned me: "If you sign into that account, you are going to see some very graphic conversations and some not very nice things said about you. Use it wisely."

My hands went ice cold. I stared at the words, but all I felt was my world crumbling.

I had sold my house, quit my job, and moved seven hundred miles north for that man. We had been living together for barely six months.

What was I going to do?

I couldn't bury my head in the sand. If my life was going to explode, I wanted to see it coming.

I don't know how long I sat there looking at the screen, but eventually, I opened a browser and went to the Yahoo email sign-on page.

I was surprised that I didn't need the password. Brent had left his account signed in.

My mouse hovered over his inbox. Was I sure I really wanted to know?

I clicked to open it.

It was all there. Lines of emails with flirty and graphic subjects. I scrolled to the bottom.

It had started with her work email, but within two days, they switched to her personal account labeled simply "AMQ."

I started reading. It seemed like my heart stopped beating. I started to shiver

He was saying the same things to her he had said to me when we first started talking. Things like:

"Have you ever felt this intensity this quickly before?"

And "Dittomore!" when he wanted to agree with her.

The sob story about how he didn't get to go to his favorite grandfather's funeral (the truth was, there hadn't even been a funeral).

I watched him morph into exactly who she wanted. He was even working out with her, something he *hated* doing.

He was talking about how he wanted a baby. He had expressly told *me* he wanted no part of having a child take over his life. (Likely because I didn't want children.)

I realized I was never going to be able to read all of it at once, so I started printing it all out. I didn't know what else to do.

Then I called Carmen.

I didn't have access to any money without Brent noticing. So, I asked her if I could borrow enough to pay a lawyer a consultation fee and to hire a private investigator.

I learned later that she tore up the photo from my wedding she had on her shelf the moment she hung up the phone.

She was angry for me when all I could do was survive.

And she sent me $5,000 without even blinking an eye, telling me to pay her back when I could.

Then, for six weeks, I read and printed out the emails between Brent and his new lover. Hot, steamy, shameless, stomach turning.

I saw them make plans to meet up while I was in calculus class.

I lost weight I couldn't afford to lose.

I noticed a pattern. Sometimes he would lie to her, usually telling her I was "being a bitch" and he needed to be at home to smooth things over, while also lying to me, saying he had to work late.

I hired a PI to follow him.

That's how I found out he was spending time at the Suffolk County Vietnam Veterans Memorial Park, a known hookup spot for gay men, barely five minutes from our apartment. I won't be any more graphic than that.

It's also how I got pictures of him and AMQ together.

I learned that in New York, I was allowed to voice record in the car Brent was driving because it was registered in only my name.

I put a voice-activated tape recorder under the passenger seat before I left for calculus. The sounds on the recordings are disgusting.

I went to the doctor and found out I had an STD. Thankfully, it was curable.

I started going through the various tabs, search engines, and browsers on our shared home computer and found ridiculous amounts of active porn, sex-chat, and hookup accounts.

I then took the email printouts, screenshots of the porn sites, the pictures and report from the PI, the audio files, and a letter from my doctor to a lawyer.

That is when I got the absolutely worst advice I've ever been given in my life.

The lawyer told me, "You've been married barely a year. You aren't going to get much in the divorce.

"The courts don't care that you uprooted yourself for him.

"They don't care that he's cheating on you. They don't even care that he's given you an STD.

"I recommend you figure out how to make it work for at least five years. Ten would be better."

I could hear the blood pounding in my ears. Stay? She was confirming that I couldn't make it on my own and that being treated like garbage was safer than being alone.

The *one* good thing she told me? Move the money from the sale of my house into a bank account in only my name.

I did that the same day.

Then I had to think about her advice.

I couldn't get a job. I had exactly one semester of college. I was living in a state where I knew no one.

I called my parents.

I don't remember the details of that conversation, but I ended up flying out to California. My mom went with me to UC Davis to see if I could transfer my credits.

The visit was awful.

The student giving the tour was rude, unable (or unwilling) to answer my questions, and wouldn't tell me who I could talk to about getting real answers.

I went back to New York dejected.

The whole time, I was still signing into Brent's email at least once a day to print out messages between him and AMQ.

The affair was heating up.

The breaking point came one night during yet another fight with Brent. I don't even remember what it was about.

He was in his normal ass-in-the-air, ankle-on-his-knee position, and I was standing at the end of the couch.

He said something that made me grit my teeth and walk away.

In my head I was running through scenarios. *Do I tell him I know about the affair and the gay hook ups? Is now the right time? What if everything implodes if I do? Where will I live?*

Then he said the most fateful line: "Maybe I should just divorce you and take half of the money from your house."

If you had been in the room, you would have seen my warrior bitch rise, sword in hand and ready to strike.

I spun around, venom lacing every word. "I know about your whore, bitch Alice. I know what you're doing at the Vietnam Memorial. Stop doing that nasty shit in my car. It's gross! If you want a divorce, fine.

"But know this,"

My eyes narrowed, and I vowed, "I will make every picture, every email and every dirty secret you have ever had part of the public record."

I stormed out of the room adding, "And don't think you're going to sleep next to me tonight!" as I slammed the bedroom door.

I know now that shame is the most effective weapon you can deploy against a narcissist. I had unknowingly just delivered it with surgical precision.

Chapter 38
Brent's Emotional Collapse

Brent didn't try to join me in the bedroom that night. But at four in the morning, when I got up to use the bathroom, I heard a weepy, broken voice say, "Robyn?"

It sounded like begging.

I stepped around the corner. "What?"

He was curled up on the couch in a fetal position.

"I'm sorry. I'm sorry I'm an awful person. I know I need to do better. I don't want to lose you."

His voice was raw from crying.

I was still clinging to the fantasy that he had promised me before we got married.

I still believed that if I could just explain what I needed, he was willing and able to give it to me.

I didn't yet realize he was a narcissist and that they don't change.

So, I stepped farther into the room and said, "If you want to try to make this work, I have conditions."

"Anything, I'll do whatever you want."

"You need to end it with Alice immediately. You're going to move out, and we're going to live separately for at least six months.

"You're going to go to Sex Addicts Anonymous and deal with your porn addiction.

"You're going to pay for my living expenses, my college, and create an expense account that you will fund monthly.

"We will start going to couples counseling.

"And in six months, we will see where we are and how I feel. I reserve the right to bail out and file for divorce at any time.

"I will be keeping all the documentation I have and will not hesitate to use it.

"Am I clear?"

His voice was tiny and defeated. "Yes."

"Are you willing and committed to doing all of it?"

"Yes."

"Also, we will no longer be having sex. You have proven that you do not care about my health, and I'm not willing to risk it. And that may never come back."

"I understand."

"I'm going back to bed. We can discuss this more tomorrow."

I then went back to bed and he stayed on the couch.

The next day, he sent this email to the AMQ address (reprinted exactly, including typos):

Subject: I am swamped...

...today so it is hard for me to respond to emails.

Also, I will not be able to work out in the morning. I have a late appointment tonight and wont' be able to make it in in time...

I had a personal collapse last night... I believe that I told you that I am scared about any new relationships and last night I realized why. I am not who you, or I, think I am. I have many, many personal flaws that I haven't been able to reconcile and/or rectify and these flaws would make me participating in a successful relationship impossible and I don't want to enter into such a relationship until I resolve them.

Basically I didn't sleep last night because I was going through a time of tremendous personal introspection and pain. I know now what I have to do — I have to go through extensive personal and spiritual counseling before I will be ready, or able, to participate in a relationship. If I don't do this I will continue in my present serial relationship mode where I lose interest in a relationship extremely quickly. This is what happened with Robyn and with my past several relationships. I can't put anyone else through that again. It is too devastating to them and to me.

To resolve these issues I have already begun setting up counselling sessions with a spiritual leader and a psychiatric counselor. I know that I must go *through this or I will be unable to function as an independent person.*

This is an incredibly hard decision for me because I am admitting to myself, essentially for the first time, that I am really, really, really, screwed up and that I am not able to fix it on my own. That goes against ever fiber of my being but it is the God's honest truth...

I wanted you to understand where I am and know that I am doing what is right. I need to be emotionally and spiritually healthy in order to begin to live my life again.

Her reply:

You know, it's OK not to be strong all the time, please don't be so hard on yourself Brent. You're not screwed up, you just need some time to rest and take care of yourself so you can get back on your feet again. Just know that you are not alone here, you have many many people who care about you and that's what we are all here for — for you to reach out when/if you need anything...

Please let me know if you need anything... and anything goes from one end of the spectrum to the other. Just name it and don't hesitate to ask...

Alice

You'll notice that nowhere in there did he tell her he wanted to work things out with me. He did not tell her that I had busted them and had evidence that would drag her name and reputation through the mud.

Looking back, I don't think this was actually the end of their relationship.

I stopped checking his email for a while and when I did again, he was carrying on with a different woman.

But in the meantime, we did do all the things on my list.

Unfortunately, the counselor he found for us was completely useless.

He told me at one point I needed to stop emasculating Brent.

(That was before I realized I'm not emasculating. He felt emasculated. That's on him.)

I replied that he should stop acting like a helpless little girl, calling me to change his flat tire, deal with spiders in the house, and do home repairs.

That didn't go over well.

(It did lead to a new rule for dating Robyn when we finally did get divorced: You must be more man than me.)

I shared that I knew he was diabetic before we got married and I knew he would likely lose his legs and his eyesight, among other things, at some point. I committed to "in sickness and in health" anyway because I loved him.

And I kept trying to make the craziness work.

That had to count for something.

There is one other appointment with that counselor that stands out.

I was at home working on a paper for school and Brent was at work. We were supposed to meet at the counselor's office.

When I looked at the clock, I had about an hour before I had to leave, so I decided to continue writing.

I got so absorbed in it that I didn't look up again until it was fifteen minutes *after* the appointment started.

If I left then, I would arrive with only twenty minutes left in the session. So, I called.

The counselor picked up, and they both jumped in, berating me for not taking it seriously, for not really wanting to make things work with Brent.

I will admit now that at an unconscious level, that could have been true.

What struck me was that neither of them called to check on me.

Their first concern wasn't, *Is she safe? Did she get into an accident?*

They assumed that I had purposefully and with malicious intent chosen not to show up.

And that told me more than anything else that Brent didn't know me.

Integrity was, and still is, one of my core values. If I say I'm going to do something, I do it. If I commit to something, I show up.

I asked if we could do the forty minutes left in the session with me on the phone.

That was rejected by one or both of them.

So I hung up, and Brent continued that session by himself.

I don't remember if we had more sessions with that guy after that or not.

We might have decided that it made more sense for us to just see our individual therapists.

I was seeing someone through the school counseling center and I realize now the poor girl (who was about five years younger than me) was in *way* over her head.

Can you imagine being twenty-seven years old, a grad student with no life experience, and having someone sit across from you and unload everything I've written so far in this book?

She was worse than a deer in headlights, and couldn't even begin to offer support or advice.

I stopped going when I came in for a session and there was someone completely new who hadn't even read the notes. Apparently, the person I was seeing had rotated to a different location.

The new young woman looked at me, all sweet and innocent, and said, "So what are we helping you with?"

I couldn't. I saw no point in starting over with her. There was no way I could get real help from a rotating cast of "kids" who had no life experience beyond college.

Chapter 39
Trying to Create Normal Out of Stupid

Even after Brent moved out, I kept trying to build something out of the wreckage that was our marriage.

One of those attempts was ballroom dance lessons.

I had wanted to learn to ballroom dance for a long time and had looked into joining the ballroom club at school. But they met at ten o'clock on a weeknight.

I have always slept from ten to six, so clearly that wasn't a thing for me.

Instead, I looked for lessons that Brent and I could take together.

That was a mistake.

He yelled at me the whole time, then stormed out halfway through the lesson.

I followed him into the parking lot in tears, where he continued to yell at me.

Then he got in his car, and screeched the tires as he drove away.

Too embarrassed to go back in, I sat in my car, thankful we had met there and I didn't need to call a cab.

As I drove back to the apartment, I thought about the mess that was my life and how out of control I felt.

The next time I talked to Brent, we went on like nothing had happened.

I never brought up ballroom dancing with him again. But I did get to take lessons and become pretty good at it when I went to grad school.

****

Brent claimed that he had been asked to be a leader for his Sex Addicts Anonymous chapter. His trunk was full of boxes of pamphlets and handouts about overcoming porn and other sex-related addictions.

I don't know if it was true that he had been given a leadership role. I once heard him lie to his mother about the weather. But he must have at least been attending at some level to end up with all those boxes.

He was also supposedly continuing to see his therapist. Obviously, I had no knowledge of how those sessions went. Assuming they were actually happening.

Through it all, I continued to go to school, take an overloaded course schedule, and somehow get A's.

I think I knew the marriage wasn't salvageable. That it was only a matter of time before the whole thing imploded on itself, no matter how hard I tried to contort myself into his warped world.

I did eventually find a new counselor for myself.

She was a sweet woman who listened and nodded, but she didn't give me any tools or useful suggestions.

Her favorite thing to say was, "Hmm... what do *you* think you should do?"

It made me want to scream, "If I knew the answer to that I wouldn't be here!"

Now I use that useless question as an example when talking to potential clients about how the world of coaching and therapy is a very deep pool full of very shallow people.

It's hard to find someone who really gets you and is both willing and able to support you.

I speak from experience. Both as someone who has done a lot of work with her own coaches and therapists, and as someone who now does this work as a coach and confidante. It is 100% worth it to keep looking until you find the right person for you.

It will make all the difference in the world.

The next therapist I tried shared three things that have stuck with me and that I now repeat to my clients:

1. It's not your fault when someone lies to you.

2. You are not to blame for believing them.

3. It's not okay for someone to make decisions in your life because it makes their life easier.

Those are heavy things.

I blamed myself for believing Brent's lies for a long time. Especially after it became clear that he was more likely to lie than tell the truth.

I wanted SO badly to reclaim the fantasy we were supposed to be creating, that I believed his lies for years. And when I stopped believing them, I still let them slide to my detriment.

Brent would make choices that only considered his needs, and I would have to adjust.

This therapist helped me start to see how wrong that was.

She helped me put a small crack in the belief that my wants and needs didn't matter.

She was also the one who pointed out that having and spending money isn't love.

The amount of expensive jewelry, clothing and shoes he bought for me instead of saying he was sorry was in the tens of thousands of dollars.

There was a tiny glimmer of the woman I would someday become starting to emerge.

But then Brent got fired, and any thought I had about me and my needs screeched to a halt as I tried to protect his ego from the reality that he was an ass and deserved to be fired.

****

I had seen it coming.

I could tell by the self-confident, bragging stories Brent was telling me about work that his boss was over it.

Brent talked like he was irreplaceable. He was convinced his boss was an idiot and that it was only a matter of time before the boss got fired and he took his job.

I tried to suggest that maybe he could be kinder in his delivery when he disagreed with his boss.

But he would just laugh in that self-assured, everyone-but-me-is-stupid way that narcissists do, and tell me he had it under control.

I was in the middle of a biology exam, trying to identify various kinds of oak leaves and bark (thrilling stuff), when my phone started ringing. I ignored it. Then it rang again. Then again.

The professor snapped, "Whose phone is that?"

"Mine. I'm sorry."

"Turn it off."

By the time I got to my bag, it was ringing again. Brent knew I was in class, but when he wanted attention, he demanded it.

After class, I called him back. He didn't even say hello. Just: "I got fired."

I was not surprised but I acted shocked.

I said all the right things.

I dealt with him sobbing, and saying he was a failure.

I got him calmed down; told him I thought he should look for consultant work since he seemed to be getting fired every two years and said we would figure it out.

Then I went to my next class.

****

When I met up with Brent that night he had gone from blindsided and shocked to angry.

He was so loud and obnoxious at dinner that I wanted to disappear into the floor. The best I could do to make it up to the wait staff was to sneak an extra twenty-dollar bill onto the table as we walked away.

Over the next few days, we decided that it made sense for us to move back in together.

Brent said all the right things about loving me and pointing out how much work he had done on himself (likely lies).

He told me he really wanted to live with his wife and to build our life together.

I still hadn't worked through my money trauma from childhood, so I was stressed about all the expenses: rent for two places, the remaining mortgage balance from his Detroit house, and storage space for the stuff we had to get out of his basement.

Moving back in together was financially smart and a step toward a normal relationship.

So I agreed, and he found a lovely two-bedroom townhouse, plus a storage unit, for less than what we were paying in total rent.

The timing of him being unemployed also worked out well for me because I was getting ready to apply to grad schools.

Since he had time and was trying to show he could be a good husband, he helped me research schools and submit applications.

Then multiple things happened all at once:

- I got into my first-choice of grad school. Rutgers, in New Jersey.

- I learned that Brent was having another affair with a different woman

- Brent took a consulting job in London, England.

The barely contained chaos that was my life was about to get worse.

Chapter 40
Maybe an Open Marriage Will Work

I found out about Brent's second affair (at least the second one I knew about) when I signed into his email right after he had finished telling me I was the most important thing in his life.

By then, I had figured out his backward tell: the sweeter and more sentimental he got about our relationship, the more likely he was actively chasing someone else.

In the email I opened he was complaining that I refused to let him have anal sex with me.

Oddly, the woman was defending me, saying anal sex wasn't exactly comfortable for most women.

It was a bizarre conversation to drop into midstream.

But this time, I couldn't even be mad. He had shown me who he was. My job was to believe him. And remember.

At about the same time, he had an interview that required him to travel and stay overnight.

The next morning, I called his hotel room. A strange man's voice answered, groggy and confused.

I asked for Brent. There was a long pause and then the line went dead.

When I called back, I didn't get an answer (shocking no one).

I called Brent's cell phone. He didn't answer that either.

That is when it started to dawn on me that he would have relationships with women, but one-night stands with men.

When he returned from that trip, he told me he had been offered a job that would require him to travel, flying out on Sundays and returning on Fridays.

That was fine by me. If he wasn't home, we couldn't fight. But I wanted to stop living the lie that we were in a monogamous relationship, when very clearly the only one being monogamous was me.

So I sat him down and said, "Let's call a spade a spade. I know you're having another affair with a woman and that you're hooking up with men.

261

"Clearly, monogamy isn't something you are going to do. If we want to stay in whatever-this-is, let's just agree that we are in an open marriage."

He agreed, but I could tell he didn't like that it gave me permission to have other partners too.

I only had two rules:

1. Be nice to me.

2. Don't lie.

I made it very clear that I wanted him to stop telling women I was an awful bitch just to get them to feel sorry for him.

Then I asked, "Do you want to know if I start seeing someone?"

I believed that if we were going to be friends through this craziness, maybe we could talk about our lives. He wanted no part of that.

His response was clipped. "No."

"Fine. I will keep it to myself."

(I would eventually go out with a few guys. But I had too much going on to deal with another relationship.)

I never imagined myself being the kind of person to accept something so convoluted and drama-filled. But in that moment, it felt like control. Like I was steering, not careening down hill without brakes.

Of course, it was an illusion. But the hell I knew felt safer than facing the unknown alone.

****

There was a glimmer of good news in the chaos that was my personal life: I was accepted into Rutgers' Doctorate of Psychology (PsyD) program, with a concentration in high performance and sport.

I honestly thought I hadn't gotten in. They'd said they'd call by a certain date and that date had come and gone.

When I finally did get the call, my impostor syndrome flared up hard.

Harry-ette, my internal saboteur, convinced me the admissions committee had chosen every other student invited to interview day, and they'd all turned Rutgers down.

So in a last-ditch effort to fill the cohort, they'd lowered their standards just enough to let me in.

I lived under that shadow for my first three semesters. I was sure someone would review my file and realize I didn't belong. (I learned later that's a very common feeling among grad students.)

That belief finally got a little crack in it one day when I walked into a professor's office, almost in tears.

I held out a research paper she had assigned and said, "I've read this three times, and I'm just too dumb to understand it."

She took the paper, glanced at the title, and said, "Robyn, if you've read it three times and don't understand it, it's not because *you're* dumb. It's because it is poorly written."

I wish I remembered her name, because in that moment, she changed my life and I would love to be able to thank her for it.

It had never occurred to me that someone in a position of authority, someone with a published paper, could explain things so poorly that it wasn't *my* fault for not understanding.

Years of guilt and self-doubt lifted in an instant.

It might be them, not me.

Wow.

After that, I started to feel like I belonged, at least academically. The program itself was full of internal politics and drama, which was darkly funny given they were training organizational psychologists to help companies *with* internal politics.

It was a classic "doctor, heal thyself" situation.

Even after being scapegoated and barred from the program's "cornerstone" course, I still earned both my Master's and Doctorate in just four academic years.

But before any of that could happen, Brent moved to London, and I had to move to New Jersey.

****

The conversation about Brent taking the consulting gig in London was straightforward. It wasn't *if* he would go; just how to make it work.

He suggested I apply to Cambridge for grad school, but that didn't make sense on several levels.

First, the job was only guaranteed for six months. He could end up anywhere in the world after that, and I would be stuck alone in a foreign country trying to finish a degree. There was no way to know he would end up living in London for more than four years.

Second, Cambridge didn't offer a program that fit what I wanted to do nearly as well as Rutgers did.

Brent also said it was better for our tax status if I stayed in the U.S. I don't know if that was true, but I believed it at the time.

The job started immediately, so Brent packed his suits and left. We would see each other about every six weeks, alternating which of us would fly.

That left me to find a place for us to live in New Jersey and to handle the move.

We decided to buy a house to establish residency so I could pay in-state tuition, even though I was deeply uneasy about putting my capital into a joint asset.

It took several trips between Long Island and New Jersey to find something I thought Brent would accept.

When he came back from London the first time, he looked at one house, and we made an offer.

The next time he returned was for moving weekend.

Unfortunately (but not unexpectedly), he was rude to the movers, calling their boss and loudly complaining about how incompetent they were while they were still unloading the truck.

It was so bad that I heard one of the guys complain, "I shoulda stayed in school so I could afford to have other people snatch my stuff rather than snatching stuff for assholes."

In response, they literally dropped a box of my crystal from the truck bed onto the driveway.

I heard it shatter and my heart broke. But I said nothing.

I had bought that crystal myself, long before I met Brent. The movers thought they were punishing him. He deserved it. He was being an ass.

But in reality, they only punished me. He couldn't have cared less about my things.

And I being verbally berated and abused by him that day too.

While trying to get boxes where they belonged, I found a small one I didn't recognize. It had men's rings and watches in it.

Brent liked to collect watches, so it was odd that these were crammed in with random junk.

I brought it to him; partly curious, partly wondering where it should go.

He said the watches had belonged to his father (who was still alive). One ring was from his first marriage. But there was another men's wedding band. It looked barely worn.

When I picked it up and asked him about it, he took it from me, inspecting it, then shrugged. "Hmm. I don't know where I got this. Or why I have it."

I thought that was weird. But I knew better than to press him.

Years later, I learned where he got that ring.

He had actually been married between his first wife and me. With one little glitch.

They had a big wedding and reception. Then a honeymoon. All the things you would expect from a marriage.

A few weeks later, the officiant called and said she'd accidentally let her license lapse and that they weren't legally married.

Her advice was that they pop down to the Justice of the Peace to make it legal.

But Brent kept putting it off. Then one day he came home and told his "wife" he was moving to Denver for a new job. But she was welcome to live in "his" house until it sold.

He had told me when we were dating that he had a "crazy ex-girlfriend" who tried to sue him when he did the nice thing of letting her live in his house after he moved to Denver.

Apparently, all of that slipped his mind when I asked about the extra wedding band.

****

Luckily, Brent didn't stay long after the move. He left while most of the house was still in boxes. My youngest sister flew out from California to help me unpack, paint, and get settled before classes started.

But before she arrived, I had to deal with getting the cable, internet, and phone installed. That turned out to be a story of a lifetime.

Chapter 41

Held at Gunpoint by Cops in My Own Kitchen

The day our cable was supposed to be installed started like any other.

I woke up alone. Took my morning shower. Tossed my hair up so it would be out of the way. Fed Brent's cats, who at that point were more mine than his, even though I'm allergic to cats.

Then I went back to the task of unpacking boxes and organizing the house.

When the doorbell rang, I went to answer it and noticed the van, branded with the cable company logo, parked in the street in front of the house.

I wondered why he didn't park in our oversized driveway, but didn't give it much thought.

When I opened the door, the cable guy introduced himself and I invited him in.

We went through the order Brent had placed. A cable box in the living room for the TV, internet in my office upstairs and Brent's office in the basement, plus the home phone.

Once we confirmed what he was supposed to do, we went into the basement to find where the cable and phone lines came into the house.

After that, I left him to it and went back to what I was doing before he arrived.

It didn't take him long to come back upstairs to find me. He needed to know where I wanted the boxes to come out of the wall.

Back into the basement we went to discuss the pros and cons of different options, and how hard it was to run the wires. I ended up staying to help. He needed an extra set of hands and I am quite handy.

We chatted about what we were doing, his life, and my plans for grad school. Typical conversations you might have when working side-by-side with someone.

When we got to the part where he had to cut the wire coming into the house so he could splice in the phone line, the house alarm started blaring.

I was stunned. How could we have tripped the system when I hadn't even chosen an alarm company yet?

I dashed up the stairs and into the laundry room where I had noticed an alarm panel.

It was covered in blinking red lights.

I had no idea what buttons to push or what code to put in.

I picked up one of the remotes sitting on top of the panel and just started pressing buttons.

Finally, the earsplitting noise stopped.

I turned to the cable guy, who was standing next to me at that point and said, "Sorry. I haven't even set up our alarm yet. I have no idea how to run it."

He shrugged, and we went back downstairs to finish the job.

It had to have been less than seven minutes later when I heard an aggressive male voice yell, "Franklin Township Police!"

What the hell?

I sprinted back up the stairs and as I reached the top, turned toward the front door.

The foyer was empty.

I turned around to find two fully uniformed and angry-looking cops standing in my kitchen with their guns drawn and pointing at my chest.

The first thing that came out of my mouth was, "Close the backdoor. You'll let the cats out."

It's darkly funny that in that moment, my biggest concern was how angry Brent would be if I lost his cats.

The cop closest to me gave a small nod to the guy behind him, who holstered his gun and closed the back door.

The first guy kept his gun pointed at me but lowered it to my knees.

I stood, looking at him with my hands at my sides, fingers splayed wide.

Finally, the first cop spoke. "We got a call from the alarm company that the house alarm was tripped here."

"I'm having cable installed. We had to cut the phone line to splice it in. I don't even have an alarm company. I have no idea who called you."

He holstered his gun.

"Do you have proof that you live here?"

I thought about mortgage and deed paperwork that was still sitting on the kitchen island. But then realized, I had already changed the address on my driver's license.

Because I needed to establish residency, I had made a point of going to the DMV to update my license before the ink was even dry on the purchasing paperwork.

I replied calmly, "My driver's license is in my purse, right there on the counter. Is it okay if I get it for you?"

He replied with a single nod.

I decided not to stick my hands in my purse with my back to him. Instead, I turned around so he could see me dump everything out onto the island.

I picked up my wallet, pulled out my license, and handed it to him.

He looked at it briefly and then handed it to the guy standing behind him, who took out a small notebook and started copying something into it.

The first guy then explained that when the cable company had called the number on file, they hadn't gotten an answer, so they had called the police.

When they arrived, they saw my car with New York plates, walked around to the back of the house, noticed the damaged weather stripping on the door, and assumed someone had broken in.

In reality, the previous owners had a dog who scratched at the door and I hadn't gotten around to fixing it yet.

(Did they think the cable van parked out front was cover for some covert gang of New York-based thieves?)

Because the door was unlocked (I never made that mistake again) they had let themselves in.

We managed to piece together that the people who had sold us the house, hadn't told their alarm company or the phone company that they were moving. The cable guy and I had tripped the alarm by cutting the phone line because it was still live.

What a fiasco.

The second cop handed me my license back and asked, "Do you have children?"

I thought that was a strange question but responded, "I don't."

"That's good. I can tell just looking at you that you wouldn't want your kids in the Franklin school system."

It took me a second to figure out what he was implying. Then I had to stop myself from rolling my eyes as I thought, *"Racist much?"*

It was that moment the cable guy decided to walk up the stairs.

As soon as we heard footsteps, both cops drew their weapons and pointed them at the door.

I stepped between them and the door, hands out, fingers spread wide, and said urgently, "It's just the cable guy!"

I have realized over time that my confidence that they weren't going to shoot me at any point in this interaction is white privilege. If my skin had been a different color, the outcome could have been very different.

As it was, it's just another one of my crazy life stories. But I do regret not calling out the cop's racism in the moment.

The cops left the way they came in, through the back door, telling me that additional false alarms would cost a hundred dollars.

I called the realtor, who called the previous owners and had them cancel their alarm service. They also sent me their passcode, just in case I ever needed it.

I never used the alarm in that house. I was too afraid that I would set it off again.

Chapter 42
When Crazy Becomes Normal

It was only a couple of weeks after we moved in when my grad school classes started, and life fell into a rhythm.

I was in class or doing homework during the week. On weekends, if I was home alone, I did yard work or managed whatever home improvement project Brent had decided to start.

He hired contractors to completely remodel the kitchen, and then the master bathroom, without ever asking how it would be for me to live without them.

He paid to redo all of our landscaping without telling me it was happening.

Guys just showed up, and suddenly I was managing a project I knew nothing about.

When Brent was home, six days every three months, my life screeched to a halt. Everything became about making sure he didn't lose his shit over some minor inconvenience.

I can't even tell you the number of times he would watch TV in his classic pose, junk showing while picking or chewing on his toes, while expecting me to sit there (even though I hate watching TV) so he could spend time with me.

Even my classmates knew better than to call me when he was home. There was no point. I wasn't ever going to be available.

If I had a break in my classes, I would fly to London to see him. But he was always working, so I had to entertain myself. I got to the point that I could easily find my way around the city without a map.

Sometimes I would get last-minute calls to drop everything and fly over for the weekend to help host a wine tasting or client dinner party.

Those were hard, because I would fly out on the red-eye Friday night and then back on Sunday, to be back in class on Monday.

We spent Thanksgiving and Christmas with his family and went on high-end cruises twice a year.

When I say it like that, it sounds reasonable. But there was always a layer of crazy simmering underneath it all.

****

Brent loved to dress me up and show me off. Nothing made him feel as good as when someone would say, "You have the most elegant woman in the room."

It wasn't uncommon for him to buy clothing, shoes, and jewelry, particularly when he was feeling guilty about something. I learned to gush about each new thing so he didn't get mad that I "wasn't thankful enough."

He also enjoyed bragging about taking extremely complicated, exotic vacations.

But he was a horrible traveler. Very much the quintessential American tourist. Everything had to be all about him all of the time or he would be angry.

I had to keep him from getting into a fist fight with a woman and her family on a train platform in Europe because he didn't like where she put her luggage.

He screamed at a busload of tourists when we were in Scotland because they were "ruining his picture."

And he was always mad at me.

Conversations like this were common:

Him: "What do you want to eat?"

Me: "Doesn't matter. Whatever makes you happy is good."

Him: "You always make me choose! Why can't you ever be involved in the process?"

Me: "Okay. Let's go to xyz place."

Him: "Why would you choose that? That's stupid. I don't want to eat there."

I would keep suggesting different places while he berated me until he would get frustrated and tell me where he wanted to eat and I would agree. But at that point, dinner had been ruined.

When we were in Tahiti it escalated even further.

Early in the afternoon we rented an ocean kayak and paddled around the small island where we were staying in an over-water bungalow.

When we left on our little adventure, the tide had been in and it was easy for both of us to get in the kayak and set off.

When we got back, the tide was out and there was a "shelf" in the beach where the water went from about three feet deep to being only a few inches deep.

I was in the front so I could get out in the shallow water. He was in the back where the water was deeper.

He didn't want to get wet and told me to pull the kayak up onto the sand. There was no way I could pull his two-hundred-pound self, plus the kayak out of the water.

Instead, I suggested we back onto the beach so he could get out and then I would just get out in the deeper water. He rejected that idea and stood up, annoyed, to try to walk to the front.

Unfortunately, he lost his balance, wildly windmilled his arms while throwing the paddle and fell out of the kayak. Rather than just getting his legs wet, he was now completely soaked.

(I swear I didn't laugh. But it was hysterical.)

He stormed onto the beach and sat on a coconut while I pulled the kayak out of the water and swam out to retrieve the drifting paddle.

He had complained before about me not taking enough pictures of him, so I snapped a picture of him fuming on that coconut.

His sister made us a calendar of our holiday photos that year. "Pissed on a Coconut" made the cut as one of the photos she thought was the best. (Of course, I never mentioned that I called it that.)

That evening, still annoyed that I had "made him get wet," he asked what I wanted for dinner. Knowing it was a trap, but having no way to avoid it, I responded, "What did you have in mind?"

He said, "What about the buffet at the main lodge?"

Silly me. I thought it was an invitation to have a discussion. I said, "I'm not really hungry enough to make it worth $75 for the buffet."

He lost his mind, ranting about how I never wanted to do anything he wanted to do and how much he hated being on vacation with me.

I backtracked right away. "I'm sorry. We can totally do the buffet. That's great."

"No! I don't want to do it now."

He stomped back toward our bungalow while I trailed after him asking, "Why are you behaving like this? Let's just go eat."

He spun around, contempt spewing from him. "I have your passport in my bag and all the credit cards are in my name. I'll leave you on this island and cancel everything."

I froze in panic. One of my deepest fears was being abandoned or lost. He knew that and was purposefully being cruel.

I spent the rest of the evening trying to mollify him.

The next day he was still so angry that he refused to leave the bungalow.

He spent the entire day in bed, watching cricket (which he didn't understand) commentated in French (which he didn't speak).

I wasn't allowed to leave either, but at least I could swim around the bungalow and look at the fish.

What a waste of a perfectly good exotic vacation.

I did learn from that experience though. I got a copy of my passport (which I kept hidden in my things) and a credit card that was only in my name.

The next time he threatened to abandon me, we were in Grand Cayman. I simply said, "Are you going back to New Jersey or London? Since the room's paid for, I'm staying here for the week."

That didn't go over well. He didn't actually leave, but I did end up on a sunset cruise by myself that night.

I was thrilled to have even a tiny bit of control when he lost his temper.

****

The next vacation drama happened when we were four days into a two-week Mediterranean cruise.

Brent got an email from his sister saying his father had suffered a stroke. I knew in my gut we were going back to Georgia for a funeral.

I'm not sure if Brent was in denial or if he truly thought his dad was going to recover, but he said, "You should stay on the cruise. It's paid for. I'll just go back and see Dad."

I thought about the nightmare Brent would be traveling back to the States, and how awful he became anytime things got hard. He would be unbearable at a funeral.

There is part of me that wishes I *had* stayed on the cruise. I would have had more fun alone in those ten days than on every vacation I ever took with him combined.

But I didn't even hesitate. I said no. I would go with him and support him through whatever happened. Always the dutiful wife, even when it hurts.

I repacked our suitcases while he worked out logistics with the cruise line.

He came back with a plan: get off the boat at the next stop, take a car to Rome, fly to London, spend the night at his apartment, then fly to Atlanta in the morning and drive several hours to his parents' place.

Because of the time difference, we didn't get to talk to his family while we were in London.

When we landed in Atlanta, he called his sister and she told him they were at the funeral home making arrangements. She didn't realize he hadn't been told that his father had passed.

Right there on the plane, Brent lost it.

Obviously, he was grieving. But it came out as anger, directed at me.

He hadn't packed a suit, which I thought was stupid. We had been in his London apartment. He had time to unpack from the cruise and repack for this trip.

Of course I didn't tell him what I thought. I just went into problem solving mode.

He didn't want to hear that we should look for something for him to wear before leaving Atlanta, since there was nothing but a Walmart in the small town where his family lived.

The morning of the funeral, he was still trying to find something to wear, while I did his mother's hair.

She didn't feel up to going to the salon, so I offered to wash, dry and curl her hair. Even though she never really liked me, it still felt like the right thing to do.

I had a black cocktail dress I had packed to wear for dinner on the cruise. It was really too sexy for a funeral, but it was the only thing I had with me that was remotely acceptable.

****

In contrast, when my grandfather died several months later, I went to Illinois alone.

I was glad Brent didn't insist on coming. I knew I would be taking care of my dad while I was there, since my mom was staying home with several of my siblings.

I fell easily back into the "woman's" role of nurturer and caretaker. I made sure Dad's shirt was pressed and that he was getting enough to eat.

It was also the first time I'd seen Hunter in years. He tried to be funny and flirty. I wanted no part of that.

But when I dropped one of my earrings down the hotel sink, Dad called Hunter, and he came, took the drain apart, and fished it out.

He doesn't have a bad heart, even if he makes horrible life choices and was a terrible partner for me.

The situation didn't get really uncomfortable until Dad and I arrived at the funeral home.

Just as we pulled up, Brent called.

I told Dad to go ahead and that I would catch up in a minute.

I listened to Brent talk about nothing important for a few minutes and then tried to wrap up the call so I could get inside.

He got angry, telling me I never treated him like he mattered. That he should always be my number one priority. And if I didn't want to spend time with him, maybe we should rethink our marriage.

I just couldn't. I didn't have the energy to have a stupid blow up with him.

Finally, I said, "Look, I have to go bury my grandfather. We'll have to do this later."

He was still yelling when I hung up and turned off my ringer.

When I looked at my phone later, my voicemail was full of ugly messages and there were more texts than I could count of him bitching about how awful I was to him and he couldn't believe he had put up with me for so long.

I remember thinking about the contrast: how I had treated him and his family with love and respect when his dad died, and how he was treating me while I said goodbye to my grandfather.

The next time we talked, Brent had gotten over himself and was back to being a reasonable human.

I sometimes wonder what sparked that meltdown. It could be that, for a couple of days, I was focused on my father and not meeting Brent's narcissistic supply needs.

****

When I got home, I told an acquaintance how insane Brent had been while I was at the funeral. I expected sympathy, understanding, maybe commiseration.

What I got instead was the best advice I have ever been given.

He said, "Robyn, you *are* resilient. Stop making decisions that make you prove it."

I was incensed. How dare he suggest the chaos in my life was *my* fault when Brent was so clearly unhinged?

But as I replayed his words in my mind over the next few months, I started to realize: I *was* making choices that kept Brent in my life.

Maybe there was some truth in what he said. That I was forcing myself to do hard things, then wearing the pain like a badge of honor. Like a martyr.

Maybe it was time to start making different choices.

Chapter 43
Hunter Wants to Try Again

Something I never expected after returning home from my grandfather's funeral was a phone call from Hunter.

When I first heard his voice, I had to ask, "How did you get this number?"

"Your dad gave it to me. You know by God's law, you're still my wife."

My stomach flipped and I wanted to gag.

I suddenly remembered my dad telling me, years ago when Hunter and I first split up, that I would always be his wife in God's eyes.

But he had added that it would be sinful and dishonorable for me to have sex with Hunter if I ever slept with another man.

It was a strange conversation, but it did explain why my dad gave him my number when he asked.

Hunter was still talking, something about living in Florida in a house that had an indoor/outdoor pool that went under the wall in his bedroom.

I stayed on the phone out of morbid curiosity. I didn't understand why he had called me.

And then he said it.

I was standing in my master bedroom in the house I shared with Brent and Hunter said, "I think we should try again."

I laughed. He had to be joking. There was no way he really just said that to me.

Then he added, "I'm serious."

"I'm sorry. I thought you were kidding."

"No. I really think we should try again."

"You know I'm married, right?"

"I know your marriage sucks."

Well, he wasn't wrong about that.

I changed tactics.

"I'm not the same girl I was when we were together. I'm getting a doctoral degree now."

"That's okay. I don't mind."

You don't mind? That was his response? How did he miss that I was trying to point out that we weren't compatible?

I tried something else.

"When you threw me out, you said, *I don't love you. I don't want to be married to you, and I don't want you living in my house.* Never mind that the house was just a slab of concrete, plywood walls, and a tin roof. I had to cut the grass in the bedroom because it would grow under the wall."

"That was a long time ago and water under the bridge. You should let it go. Besides, it wasn't even true. I love you. I've always loved you. And you are the only girl I have ever loved."

"You loved me? Then why did you throw me out?"

Now I was invested. I simply had to know what kind of crazy story he had to justify his behavior all those years ago.

"Do you remember Muscle Mike, Tiny and the guys they hung out with?"

"Yeah. I remember them."

"Did you know they were part of a cocaine ring?"

"I didn't know it was a ring. But we were at parties all the time with cocaine on tables, so I'm not surprised."

"Did you know that cocaine ring was part of the cartel?"

My blood froze. "What?"

"Yeah. Those guys were in deep with the Mexican cartel."

He said it casually; like he was telling me someone we knew and spent time with bought milk.

"I had no idea."

"It's just as well you didn't. They were dangerous men."

"I bet."

"They ended up stealing my identity. They bought a whole fleet of trucks. I almost ended up in federal prison because of it."

"Federal prison?"

"Yeah. I was lucky. The undercover fed realized I was just the fall guy. She convinced me to go on vacation the week she knew they were going to get busted.

"But then I had to spend almost two years completely off the grid so we could figure out where they were using my identity.

"It was a mess."

He didn't continue so I prodded, "I'm sure it was. But what does that have to do with me?"

"Oh, right. When the guys in the cartel realized I had good credit, they started poking around and testing how hard it would be to steal my identity. But apparently you noticed and blocked stuff. I don't really know what happened."

I had to laugh to myself as I thought back to the end of our marriage. I had fixed Hunter's credit only to have it stolen by the cartel? That was ironic.

Then I remembered a weird phone call I had gotten from the bank about a transfer. I had just said I didn't recognize it and canceled it. There had also been some fraudulent charges on a credit card. I hadn't thought it was a big deal at the time.

Hunter was still talking, "So I guess they realized you were going to be a problem and wanted you out of the way."

Being in the way of the cartel didn't sound ideal.

"They convinced me you were holding me back. That I could do better than you. So I told you to leave."

I had to stop him, "Hold on. You're telling me that our marriage ended because the cartel didn't like me?"

"Yeah, pretty much."

"You told my dad you threw me out because I was lazy."

"Yeah. I don't know why I said that. You were the hardest-working woman I've ever met. Every woman I've dated since you hasn't been willing to work at all. They're just gold diggers."

I did not want to get off track.

"So let me get this straight. My dad married me off to you, which you accepted because I was good stock, and then you threw me out because the cartel convinced you that you could do better?"

"Robyn, it was a long time ago, and I made a mistake. I'm just telling you because I'm clean now, I have been for several years. I want you to understand what happened, that I have always loved you and I want to try again."

My brain was trying to grasp the pieces of the puzzle I didn't even know existed that were now falling into place.

So many things made sense, even the Apple Strudel Heist suddenly didn't seem as funny and random as I had always thought it was.

"Look Hunter, I'm not interested in trying again. You weren't a good partner for me all those years ago and we have grown even further apart since then."

I don't remember exactly how the call ended.

When I finally hung up, I was sitting on the floor beside my bed in stunned silence

The cartel had inadvertently freed me from a marriage I was only in because I grew up in a cult.

My mind absolutely could not process it.

In a weird and twisted way, I could thank the cartel for getting me out of the cult.

****

I still hear from Hunter randomly, usually via text.

He once sent me a picture of a box of sex toys and asked me to meet him at the beach.

When I told him, "No, thank you," he replied, "You're no fun."

I told him I was plenty of fun for the person I was in a relationship with, and that he was not that person.

I also reminded him that he never wanted to have sex with me when we were married. He told me that was because of the drugs, and I should "let it go."

I think that is his favorite line whenever I try to talk about his past behavior.

He then texted me a picture of his two dachshunds lying next to his bare thighs (his gut the only thing keeping it from being X-rated) with the message, "Check out my wieners."

He hasn't grown up at all since I met him when I was sixteen.

Most recently he sent me a text telling me I should be careful about going into New York City because of gang activity. I haven't gone into NYC in years, and I'm not sure why he would feel the need to text me about that.

I have been asked why I don't block his number.

Part of why I haven't is that the saga is hysterical at this point. There's no emotional damage being done, so why not play along?

Another part is that he is family, so maybe there could be a reason we would need to be in touch? Unlikely, but I make that up.

He will probably show up at my father's funeral. When that day comes, I don't want to be dealing with bad blood between us.

Before you ask. Yes, my current husband knows all of this. I have nothing to hide. He's confident in our relationship, and whenever I say, "I heard from Hunter again," he just rolls his eyes, laughs, and asks, "What did he want this time?"

Chapter 44

Putting the Dr. in Front of My Name

Funerals and strange phone calls from my ex-husband aside, I was laser-focused on getting all the boxes checked to complete my doctoral degree.

My dissertation was titled: *A Case Study of the Design, Implementation, and Formative Evaluation of a Team Development Program for a Women's Swimming and Diving Team in a NCAA Division I University Setting.*

That is an impressively academic way of saying I created a team and leadership development program for a swim team.

My lead professor (also called my chair) would redline and rewrite my work, then redline and rewrite his own rewrites. It was a painful process, and considering how many of us read it over and over and over, it still has a shocking number of typos.

I will be forever grateful that my chair had a policy not to let his students schedule their defense (the last step in the process) until the dissertation was truly doctoral level and he was ready to approve it.

He also had a rule: anyone could attend a defense, but only people who had read the entire dissertation were allowed to ask questions.

That meant once he scheduled my defense, I knew I was going to pass.

I was surprised when my mom wanted to fly out to attend.

After my presentation, my chair told her she raised an amazing woman and that she should be proud of me. It felt good to hear him say that and I assume she was, or she wouldn't have flown out to be there.

I had one small disappointment: I couldn't graduate that December because I was missing a few internship hours.

I had it all planned out: half of my internship was in sport psychology and the other half in business psychology.

But some wires had gotten crossed, and I ended up having to pay for one more semester of credits so I could get the additional hours I needed.

With all the i's dotted and t's crossed, I didn't feel the need to attend graduation. But Brent told me it was important that I walk across the stage.

So, I bought a cap and gown and filled out the paperwork to do it.

It should have been a happy day. Both of my parents came out for it (again, I was pleasantly surprised they wanted to) and Brent made a point to be home.

But it started out badly and got worse from there.

Before the actual graduation ceremony, we had to attend a brunch held by the psychology department.

I warned Brent, who was diabetic, that the food would be awful and he should eat before we left the house.

The graduate program I attended was notorious for being cheap when it came to feeding students and faculty. I knew there wasn't going to be anything he wanted to eat at brunch.

I also knew that if he didn't eat, he would be worse than his usual, unbearable self. He blew me off, told me to stop being dramatic, and just sucked down his morning Diet Pepsi.

"Brunch" turned out to be dry muffins and some fruit. Shocking no one, he didn't want to eat any of it.

And of course, there were speeches. Lots of boring speeches by people who thought what they had to say was important.

I had been asked to write and then read something positive about "those who supported" me through grad school.

Clearly, my parents and Brent hadn't been much support. But it seemed obnoxious to stand up and say "I made it in spite of you."

I wrote something ridiculously flowery and glowing and felt like a fraud reading it. But I thought that was better than starting a war.

Brent paraded around like a peacock, shaking hands and accepting congratulations like *he* was the one graduating.

But once the speeches started and he had to just sit at the table and listen, he leaned over to whisper-yell in my ear that he was hungry and this was stupid.

No shit, Sherlock. I tried to warn you. What's the professional way to say "I told you so"?

There were early indications that this was a likely outcome.

After surviving an insufferable Act One, we still had to endure the whole production of me walking across the stage to accept a blank piece of paper (my real diploma would be mailed later).

I had to leave my parents in Brent's care, or maybe the other way around, and find my way through the cattle call of ropes and arrows to where graduating doctoral students were supposed to sit, then find my place in alphabetical order.

We were told to remain in our seats until all graduates had walked. That meant all of the graduate and undergraduate students.

That was going to be an hours-long process of calling names after the graduation speeches were done.

Brent started texting me as soon as I got to my seat.

"It is too hot."

"This is taking too long."

"I'm thirsty." (Code for him wanting more Diet Pepsi.)

I had no idea what he expected me to do.

When it was finally my turn to hear my name called and walk across the stage, I was an anxious ball of nerves.

Not because I was graduating, that part was fine.

But because Brent had me on blast and it was overwhelming.

When I got back to my seat, where I had left my phone in my bag, there was a text that said, "Let's go."

I texted back, explaining that I was supposed to stay until the ceremony was over.

He replied, "I am going to lunch. You can either join me or find your own way home."

There was no way I was going to put my parents in a situation where they had to decide between leaving with Brent and staying behind with me.

So I gathered my things, awkwardly made my way to the end of the row, and walked out of the event.

When I met up with Brent and my parents, he was all but sprinting for the car.

I was in heels, which were sinking into the grass, and my parents couldn't keep up either.

At one point my dad asked if they could get a picture. Brent huffed, snatched the camera from him, snapped one picture of me, my mom, and my dad, and shoved the camera back at him.

That blurry picture is the only evidence that I wore a cap and gown that day and earned my doctoral degree.

When we got to the car Brent growled, "Take off your cap and gown. It will be embarrassing to sit in a restaurant with you wearing that."

I wanted to wear it at lunch. I wanted to be proud. I wanted a chance to enjoy my accomplishment. Maybe even be the center of attention for a brief moment.

But it wasn't worth the fight. I took it all off and tossed it in the trunk as he rushed us to get in the car. Then he drove like a crazy person to get to lunch.

All of that could have been avoided if he had just eaten breakfast, like I suggested.

I think that is the first experience my parents had with Brent being an ass for no reason.

It would happen again before the end of their trip.

****

Brent scheduled his flight to London for the same morning my parents were headed back to California.

Mom and Dad's flight was early enough that, even though Brent was flying internationally, he was going to have a longer-than-necessary wait at the airport if we all rode together.

I suggested he take a car service, but he insisted on riding with us.

When we got to domestic security, I was saying goodbye to my parents when Brent said, "I'm going to head over to the international terminal."

I said, "Give me a minute and I'll go with you. We can have coffee before your flight."

His response was clipped. "I have work to do."

I knew that meant he didn't want to spend time with me, probably eager to catch up with whatever sexual conquest he was currently chasing.

All I said was, "Oh. Okay. Have a good flight. Call me when you land."

He gave me a perfunctory kiss on the cheek and purposefully strode away.

My dad frowned after him and asked, "When will you see him again?"

I shrugged. "I'm not sure. In about six weeks or so."

I was so used to being treated like a second thought that I didn't even notice that the man who had vowed to love me had chosen to leave me before he had to.

My parents didn't say anything else. But I could tell by the look on my dad's face as he watched Brent's back disappear that he was thinking, *"That's not how a man who loves his wife behaves."*

And he was absolutely right.

Chapter 45
Then My Panties Started to Disappear

After the fiasco of my graduation, the next time I saw Brent was for a Caribbean cruise, supposedly to celebrate me. I just wasn't allowed to talk about finishing grad school.

We wouldn't want to take the spotlight off of Brent.

But I had been on enough elaborate trips with him to know how to play the game. Fine. Whatever.

A few days into the cruise, we found our way to a quiet beach on St. John. The sand was warm, the breeze smelled like the ocean, and the water looked like a postcard.

We spread the oversized ship-branded towels on the sand, swam for a bit, then stretched out to enjoy the sun.

Brent was sitting up, watching people walk by when he said, "What are you going to do next?"

I rolled over so I could look at him.

"When we get back to the boat?"

"No. With your life."

I blinked. That was a heavy topic for the beach.

I chose my words carefully. This could go sideways fast.

"Well, my sport psychology professor suggested I turn my dissertation into a book."

He snorted. "*You're* going to write a book? Who would want to read anything you have to say?"

His voice dripped with derision. I ignored it in hopes of avoiding a fight.

"It would be intended for female athletes, their parents and coaches."

"Who gave you permission to write a book?"

Suddenly I was a teenage girl again; being shamed for daring to dream beyond the role the cult had assigned me.

My throat constricted. He was using my past trauma like a knife and twisting it deep into my most painful wounds.

I almost whispered, "Permission?"

"You didn't ask me if you could write a book." He said it with dismissive authority, like it was an undeniable fact and I was too stupid to realize it.

But then I reined in Harry-ette. I was not going to let Brent use her to drag me down that road.

"I don't need your permission to turn my dissertation into a book. Where did that even come from?"

My voice was incredulous. Clearly, he had lost his damn mind.

"You need to get a job. I'm tired of supporting your lazy ass."

I almost laughed. "My lazy ass? You mean the one that flies back and forth to Europe to grease the wheels of your business deals while managing your entire life in the States?"

"I paid for your education and I want a return on my investment."

"Correction. We agreed to use our family income to cover my tuition because we used the capital from the sale of my house in Charlotte as a down payment on the house in New Jersey."

He glared. "I'm going for a swim. Then we're leaving. Don't follow me."

What a lovely, peaceful day at the beach.

Geez.

I got up and started folding the towels, making sure to keep the one in the bag sand-free so he could dry off.

Sooner than I wanted him to, he came storming up the beach.

"Why did you pick up the towels?"

His voice was sharp. It was an accusation, not a question.

"Because you said you wanted to leave when you got out of the water."

"I wanted to sit on the beach and dry off first. I'm not going to leave soaking wet." He sneered.

"Okay. I can put the towels back down."

I pulled out his towel and spread it on the sand.

"Never mind! Let's just go."

He grabbed the edge of the towel and yanked it up, flinging sand all over me.

I thought about offering him the clean towel but he was already stomping away from me and I knew if I didn't catch up before he waved down a taxi, he would leave without me.

I picked up the bag, stuffed our water bottles into it, grabbed his sandals, and sprinted after him.

Lucky for me, years of beach volleyball had made me quick in the sand and I was right behind him before he even reached the road.

****

I started to notice that Brent was suddenly having a hard time introducing me.

For years it had been, "This is my wife. She's just a student."

I was no longer "just a student," and when titles were being used, "Mrs." was no longer correct.

I was now, "Dr."

That became a problem at an event in New York City a few weeks after the cruise.

We were standing in a circle of maybe six people when someone walked up behind me and said, "Dr. [our last name]?"

I turned around. "Yes?"

But they were looking at Brent. Who does not have a doctorate.

There was a flash of confusion on their face, but they recovered quickly and said one of the guests of honor had asked to meet me.

I excused myself and followed them across the room.

Riding the elevator to our room at the end of the night, Brent stared blankly at the mirrored doors.

When he spoke, his voice was flat, like he was giving an order with no room for argument.

"You can't use your title when we attend events. It makes me look stupid."

I wondered how being married to someone with a terminal degree made him look stupid. But I didn't ask.

"I am not going to use Mrs." I wasn't making a counterargument. It was a statement of fact.

His jaw clenched as he turned to glare at me.

In heels, I was eye-level with him. I stared back, daring him to die on that hill.

The elevator doors opened and he walked out without saying another word.

I followed behind him, smirking. I'll take that as a win.

****

On the train home from NYC, I knew we needed to have a come-to-Jesus conversation. The contempt between us was palpable.

If we were going to survive, something had to change, especially now that it looked like his job might transfer him back to the States.

I turned toward him to lean against the window and pulled my jean-clad knee onto the seat.

"Brent, we need to talk."

His thumbs paused typing on his phone.

I continued, "Do you want to stay married to me?"

He set his phone down in his lap and looked at me before responding.

"I do."

"Then we need to spend some time together that isn't at business events or on vacation and talk about what this looks like going forward."

He nodded. "I was thinking the same thing. If things go like it looks like they will, I'll be working out of Philly within the next month. I'll be home every weekend."

I tried not to cringe. The energy in the house always turned black when he was there.

He had complained that it didn't even feel like home to him. I knew that was because he didn't actually live there. He treated it like a hotel where he stayed a few days every couple of months.

The thought of him in my space every weekend made me sick to my stomach.

I sighed, "Do you have any suggestions?"

"What if we committed to having brunch together every Sunday? We could make a game of it. Try different diners."

With someone whose company I enjoyed, that would have been fun. With Brent it sounded like a chore.

But I smiled and said, "That's place to start. Should we do that this weekend?"

He smiled back but it didn't reach his eyes, "That would be great."

Then he picked up his phone and went back to typing.

****

Around that same time, my panties started to disappear.

Not my favorites, but ones I wore often enough to notice they were gone.

At first, it was just a vague noticing. I was doing laundry more often because I seemed to have fewer pairs.

Maybe they had slipped behind the laundry basket. Or fallen between the washer and dryer. Or maybe I left them in my luggage the last time we traveled.

When it became obvious that something was up, I started actively looking for them. They were nowhere.

Just — gone.

I thought about the last time there had been contractors in the house.

When we had our bathroom remodeled, I caught a guy stealing my underwear out of the laundry basket.

But that had been several years ago.

We hadn't had anyone, other than our housekeeper, in the house in almost a year. And I had no reason to believe she had suddenly developed a fetish for my underwear.

I could not come up with any logical explanation for where my panties could be going.

It was especially disappointing because I couldn't get the European brand I liked in the States, and I no longer had a reason to be in London every few months.

I finally had to shrug it off, but it nagged at me. Like a seed stuck in your teeth you can't quite dislodge.

Then we went to Florida to visit Brent's sister.

It was just for a long weekend, so we decided not to bring our laptops. His sister had a computer we could use. That would be good enough.

On the second night, I asked Brent if he needed anything, and if not, would he mind if I checked my email?

He shrugged and without looking up from his phone said, "Fine."

I walked up the stairs, sat down at the small desk and clicked on the light. The computer had been in sleep mode and came up quickly.

I typed in the password that was on a sticky note next to the mouse, opened a browser and navigated to Yahoo.

My fingers froze above the keyboard.

Instead of the sign on screen, I was taken to an email account called Mike33333333.

Staring me in the face was a subject line: "Does your wife wear thongs?"

What the actual hell?

I clicked to open the email and scrolled to the bottom to start at the beginning of the conversation.

It was Brent, calling himself Mike, having a graphic sexual conversation with a man he had apparently met online.

It was clear they had been meeting up for a while. I will spare you the particulars.

The part that stood out to me was Brent describing, in detail, pairs of my underwear that were now missing.

He asked the guy if his wife wore thongs.

The answer was no, but that his teenage daughter did, and he could get some of hers.

Apparently, they were taking mine, and his daughter's, dirty underwear and putting them on their faces or sticking them in their mouths during sex.

Sometimes they were wearing them.

Suddenly, I was thankful they were missing, and that he hadn't been just putting them back in the wash.

I forwarded a few of the emails to myself to add to the folder with the emails from AMQ and what the PI had found years ago. Then deleted them from his sent folder and went back downstairs.

I forgot to check my own email.

For the next two nights I slept on the floor in the closet with a blanket and a pillow. I just couldn't bring myself to sleep next to him, and talking to him about it while we were at his sister's house was a recipe for a nightmare.

He flew from Florida back to his corporate apartment in Philadelphia and I went back to our place in New Jersey, so the conversation had to wait until the following weekend.

When I confronted him, he absolutely lost his mind about me "snooping."

I pointed out that it wasn't snooping when he was dumb enough to leave his email with a fake name signed in when he knew I was using the same computer.

Then he yelled that we had an "open marriage" and he could do whatever he wanted.

I rolled my eyes and said that did not include using my panties during his sexual exploits. And it was somehow even more creepy that they were doing the same thing to a teenage girl.

Looking back, I know how much I contorted myself, justifying insanity to make a deeply unhealthy situation "work."

That conversation ended with him agreeing to stop stealing my underwear. And they did, in fact, stop disappearing.

But there was nothing that would help this marriage survive us living on the same continent when he couldn't even abide by two of the most basic rules: be nice to me and don't lie.

Chapter 46
I'm Done

Less than a month after the missing panties conversation, Brent called to say he was trading in our Infiniti QX4 for a Mercedes convertible.

That made no sense. The Infiniti had all-wheel drive and was the only vehicle I drove in the winter.

I pointed out that a sports car would be useless in the snow.

He just replied, "I already made the deal. I'm picking up my new car this weekend."

There was nothing I could do. The title was in his name. He could do whatever he wanted with it.

Never mind that I expected we would have a conversation about change like that.

I spent Friday afternoon clearing our personal things out of the Infiniti, once again questioning the viability of the relationship I was in.

On Sunday, Brent went to pick up his new car. I expected him to come back for me so we could go to brunch.

After several hours of puttering around the house, I called to ask what was going on.

He had decided to "drive around" in his new car and "forgot" about brunch.

I wondered if he was meeting up with the guy from the missing panties situation, but bit my tongue.

The following weekend while we sat across from each other in yet another diner, Brent gushed about what a great wife I was.

After we ordered, he started the conversation, "I know I'm hard to live with."

I looked at him but didn't reply.

He continued, "You really are the perfect wife for me. You put up with my quirks."

I would have called them character flaws, but didn't correct him.

"You're beautiful, fun to travel with, smart."

I wondered what he was buttering me up for. I didn't know what "love bombing" was yet. If I had, I would have recognized it instantly.

As our food arrived and we ate, he kept going on the same track; talking about how much he loved me and how I was the best thing to ever happen to him.

I had seen him say the same things to other women. I wasn't impressed. But I saw no reason to start a fight, so I just smiled and went along with it.

But from the moment we sat down, his phone buzzed nonstop with incoming texts.

He would stop talking, pick it up, and start typing, saying, "Sorry. There's an outage at work."

Or "Damn. I don't know why they can't figure this out themselves."

Or "Sometimes I think I should fire the whole lot of them and hire new people. They're all so dumb."

He always thought he was the smartest guy in any room. I didn't feel the need to stroke his ego, so I ignored his commentary.

He didn't seem to notice.

When our waitress brought the bill, he set his credit card on it and announced, "I'm going to the bathroom."

He walked away, leaving his phone sitting face up on the small table.

Not twenty seconds later, it buzzed. I unconsciously looked at it.

The messages were very clearly not about work. Even upside down, I could see my name a few texts down.

I reached over and picked up the phone and read, "I can't get divorced because Robyn's being such a bitch. She's trying to steal the house."

The reply that had just come in said, "She's so pathetic. I can't believe she's such a gold digger."

I scanned through the text conversation.

The entire time he had been sitting across from me, telling me how amazing I was and how thankful he was to have me in his life, he had been texting his current lover about how horrible I was.

This broke both of my rules about being nice and not lying.

Worse, he was using lies about me to make her feel bad for him. It made me feel dirty.

I put his phone on the table where he had left it.

He came back, sat down and picked up his phone to reply.

I said very simply, "I'm done."

He replied, "Me too. We can go as soon as she comes back with my credit card."

"No. I'm done with this relationship. I know you're not texting about work. If you feel like we can't get divorced because I'm trying to steal the house, let me put your mind at ease. I don't want the house. We can sell it and I'll move back to California."

His face flushed red, then purple. He exploded out of his chair, slamming the table with his legs hard enough to pitch everything toward me.

His unfinished orange juice glass crashed to the table, then rolled off the edge and hit the floor.

My mostly full glass of water tumbled into my plate, sending a dirty wave of ice, water, and leftover syrup toward my lap.

I scrambled to get out of the way.

He stood over me screaming, "We are in a fucking open relationship. That means I can fuck whoever I want and you can fucking deal with it!"

Everyone in the diner turned to look as he stormed out, leaving his jacket on his chair where it had fallen on the floor.

The room seemed ridiculously still when he slammed the door into the wall on his way out.

I could hear the water dripping from the table and splashing in the growing puddle on the ugly diner carpet.

A waiter was the first to move.

He picked up the chair, set it upright, and asked, "Are you okay?"

I watched Brent jerk open his car door, get in, start the car and tear out of the parking lot.

297

I sighed. "Yeah. I'm fine. Thanks."

Our waitress came back with the bill and seeing the mess, just stood there saying nothing.

I held my hand out to her, "You can give me that."

I glanced at the ticket, added a generous tip, and handed it back.

The normal busy-diner buzz started to return as I gathered my things and Brent's jacket.

I walked over to an empty stool at the counter and asked the woman taking orders if I could get an iced coffee to go.

Something about having the cold glass in my hand while I waited for a cab felt… grounding.

****

When I got home, Brent was nearly finished packing to head back to Philly.

His clenched jaw made it clear that conversation wasn't on the menu, so I went to my office while he stormed through the house, throwing things into his suitcase more aggressively than necessary.

Within the hour, he yelled up the stairs that he was leaving.

I stepped out of my office and looked down into the foyer at him. "Okay. Drive safely."

He narrowed his eyes and inhaled, but must have thought better of it because he didn't say anything.

Instead, he spun around and stomped through the laundry room into the garage, slamming the door behind him.

I heard his fancy little sports car fire up and watched through the arched window as he sped out of the driveway.

I realized I hadn't heard the garage door close, so I went downstairs and peeked into the garage. Sure enough, it was still open. I clicked the button to close it and breathed a sigh of relief.

I would have a week of not dealing with him in my space.

I spent that week, and the next interviewing divorce lawyers and moving into the spare bedroom.

But Brent was acting like everything was normal. Like I hadn't told him I was done playing this game.

A few weekends after the diner blowup, he stood in our living room and said, "I think we should move to Tampa."

This was the first I had heard about any move, and Tampa seemed random. (Later, the connection to the sports car would click.)

I'm sure I looked as confused when I replied, "Tampa? Why Tampa?"

Apparently that was the wrong answer, because he immediately escalated to yelling: "You never want to do anything I want to do!"

"I'm not saying if I do or don't want to move. I'm just trying to understand how you came up with Tampa."

"You know what? Maybe we should get divorced!"

"Okay."

He looked shocked. I think maybe he expected me to argue with him about it.

Then he said the words that burned into my brain. Words that showed just how little he thought of me.

"You'll never make it without me. You're going to live under a bridge in a box." He spat the words at me as his face twisted with contempt.

My reply was emotionless. "Should we both hire lawyers, or can we divide everything without a war?"

He snorted. "I'm hiring a lawyer. Do whatever the hell you want. I don't care anymore."

****

That Sunday, instead of driving to Philly, he was flying to London. Until then, I'd always gotten up to drive him to the airport.

I guess he assumed I would keep being his chauffeur, because when he was ready to leave, he just yelled from the foyer, "I need to get to the airport!"

I stepped out of the guest bedroom, still in my pajamas.

"Since we're getting divorced, I don't see why I should keep saving your company money by donating my time."

"Great. So what am I supposed to do now?"

"You could drive and park your car in long-term parking." I knew damn well he wasn't going to do that, but it was funny to say.

He just glared at me.

I continued, "Or you could stop being an ass and ask me to take you."

I could tell it was killing him, but he gritted his teeth and said, "Will you please take me to the airport?"

"Sure. Just let me get dressed."

When I dropped him off, I said, "I suggest you book a car service for when you get back. I won't be here to pick you up."

I never drove him to or from the airport again.

Chapter 47
Divorcing a Narcissist

I need to tell you something: I was scared out of my mind at this point in my life.

I didn't have a job; just a half-finished book and a piece of paper that said I owned an LLC.

Other than being arm candy and making sure Brent's corporate dinners and events went smoothly, I hadn't worked in seven years.

The capital I brought into the marriage was tied up in our house, a joint asset that he could argue he deserved half of.

But I had a few things going for me.

While Brent had been blowing money on renovations, landscaping, and outrageous vacations, I quietly put extra toward the mortgage principal, creating capital he hadn't been able to spend.

I knew I was resilient. Resourceful. I had no idea how I would make it on my own. But I absolutely believed I would figure it out.

Even though Harry-ette kept replaying, *"You're going to live under a bridge in a box,"* a small part of me knew it wasn't true.

The thought of being free from Brent's lies and manipulation felt like swimming out of deep, black water with seaweed wrapped around my legs, lungs burning.

I just had to keep going and I would be able to take my first real breath in years.

****

Unfortunately, the lawyer I hired turned out to be worse than useless. He sat next to me in the meeting with Brent and his lawyer, but did nothing.

Brent screamed and was so hateful that his lawyer finally pulled him out of the room and started running messages between us.

If I had been less scared, more willing to fight, or had a better lawyer, I would have gotten a better settlement.

As it was, I got the bare minimum.

One of my biggest frustrations was that our marriage contact was completely unenforceable. He had written and signed vows that he would be faithful.

I had undeniable proof that he wasn't.

It was a clear breach of contract and should result in consequences.

The state of New Jersey didn't think so.

But when Brent said he was going to sue me for my tuition, I told his lawyer I would compile a list of everything I did to keep his life running smoothly while he lived in London.

Off the top of my head, I listed several:

- Caring for his two cats, including vet visits and grooming

- Paying his bills on time, without fail

- Managing his household, including overseeing renovations and doing small repairs

- Picking up and dropping off his dry cleaning

- Dealing with car maintenance

- Driving him to and from the airport

- Handling his speeding ticket. Including court correspondence and getting the case dismissed

- Hosting and attending his business events

- Accompanying him on vacations that he chose and booked without my input

I looked her in the eye and said, "If we add up what he would have paid for those services, it will come out to more than my tuition. He's welcome to pay me the difference if he wants to go that route."

After she walked out, my lawyer told me that my degree wasn't on the legal list a spouse could expect repayment for anyway.

That demand mysteriously disappeared when she came back.

I did, however, have to pay him $5,000 to buy him out of my "business," which was nothing more than a piece of paper saying I owned Champion Performance Development, LLC.

After hours of back and forth, we finally had something we could agree on and my lawyer said he would write it up.

Two weeks later, my lawyer sent me a boilerplate divorce agreement that had none of the stipulations I had fought so hard to create.

When I asked him to revise it, he kept screwing it up.

I asked for an editable version so I could fix it. He refused.

I was beyond annoyed. He was charging me by the hour to create a document that was absolutely useless.

When I called him to express my frustration, he told me the retainer I had paid him was gone and that he was firing me as his client.

I ended up suing him and getting most of my money back. Just one more layer of stress in an already insane situation.

In the end, Brent's lawyer wrote up the agreement, and I hired someone just to review it.

It stated that we could both keep living in the house until it sold.

But Brent decided to start building a house in Tampa. (I'm pretty sure he already had his sights on a new wife down there.)

He started bringing home floor plans and bragging about what a great house he was building; trying to get my opinion on options.

I finally said, "I don't care. I'm not interested. Stop asking for my input."

He acted like I had hurt his feelings. But really? Why did he think I was still going to stroke his ego?

We got an offer on our house. It was for less than I thought it was worth, but he accepted it without even consulting me.

I called his lawyer and said I expected Brent to pay me the difference between what we had agreed was our lowest sale price and what he had accepted.

To her credit, that happened without an argument.

Two weeks before closing, I signed a lease on a townhouse.

Then a hurricane hit. The buyers of our house lost their business in the flooding. Their mortgage company backed out, and the deal for them to buy our house collapsed.

It took several more months for us to get another offer.

In that time, I got a call from the realtor for Brent's house in Florida. They said they needed my signature to close because his deal was contingent on the sale of our place.

I made it crystal clear. I wasn't signing anything tied to his house. I wasn't involved, and I didn't want my name anywhere near that mortgage.

Of course it turned into a fight. To this day, that address still shows up on my credit report. I can't get the credit bureaus to comprehend: I never lived there, never signed anything, and my name doesn't belong on it.

****

As Brent's Florida move got closer, he bragged that he might be taking a consulting job in Dubai. I immediately asked what he was going to do with his cats.

"I'll just leave them at home like I used to." He said it straight-faced and dead serious.

When I met him, his cats were less than two years old. He would often leave them for as long as ten days. Food, water, litter box in the bathtub and basically, "good luck."

I rolled my eyes. "They're not young anymore. They need care now. You can't just leave them home alone while you're in Dubai."

(Not that I think it was okay that he was leaving them before.)

"Then I'll take them to a shelter. They're purebred; someone will scoop them up."

They were absolutely beautiful cats, but I knew damn well no one would adopt them. Plus, they loved each other. I simply couldn't let that happen.

"Brent," I spoke to him like he was a child, "they're old now. No one is going to adopt them."

"Well," he waved his hand dismissively, "I can't keep them."

I gritted my teeth and snorted, "Fine. Even though I'm allergic, I will keep them. But," I paused and took a deep breath through my nose, "you have to pay me cat support. Sixty dollars a month each."

He agreed. And he did actually pay me "cat-amony", even though it wasn't part of our court order, until he got remarried (poor woman). I guess his new wife put a stop to it.

I still had those cats when I met Russ. And in the two or three years he knew them, he loved them more than Brent ever did.

****

The silver lining of signing a lease months before I had to move was that I could take my time, moving a little bit each week.

When the house finally sold, I left detailed notes on the kitchen island: how the heated floors worked, that the garage was on the same GFCI as the basement (I learned that the hard way after losing a full freezer of food), and how to run the sprinkler system.

I even left my phone number.

I have done that for every house I've sold, left the kind of information I would want if I were moving in.

I have never had a seller do that for me.

But even after settling all of that, I still had to wait for a judge to finalize the divorce.

****

It took almost eight months. Then his lawyer "forgot" to tell us for another three. But in the end, I was finally free.

My only real regret? I kept his last name.

I didn't want to go back to my maiden name. I wasn't that girl anymore.

My youngest sister and I spent an entire evening, and a bottle of wine, trying to come up with a name that was unique, easy to say, and sounded good with "Doctor."

We didn't find one we liked. And since my college degrees were under his name, I decided to just keep his.

That was a mistake.

Over the years, I kept trying to come up with a new name. I considered using my middle name as my last name. But then would I just not have a middle name?

I cringed every time I had to say or spell his name. It wasn't mine, but it was what everyone called me.

Because I didn't change it during the divorce, I assumed it would be hard and expensive. And I let that stop me.

Time made it harder. My books. My TEDx talk. My business branding. I would lose all of that if I changed my name.

But I told my sister, "Don't you dare bury me under that name."

Then, about three months ago, someone said something that took my breath away: "Robyn, you can't build a life you love on a name you hate."

Gut punch.

When I started writing this book and realized: *This book is mine. It is my story. I don't want his name anywhere near it.*

I filed the paperwork with the court. It was a mess. Maiden name. First married name. Maiden name again, but this time they dropped the space. Second married name. And now, finally, my name. The name I chose.

The last name on this book is my birth middle name. I gave myself a new middle name.

Just today, I mailed in the passport paperwork. And I have the first available appointment with Social Security in a month.

It is work. It does cost money. But eventually, it will be totally worth it.

****

I thought about ending this book here. But then you would miss the growth I had to do to make a business work, and the sweet, funny story of how I met Russ.

Let's keep going. There's more to tell.

Chapter 48
My Personal Trauma Almost Tanked My Business

You would think that once I was free from Brent, life would be smooth sailing.

But I was still carrying a mountain of trauma.

Harry-ette was still dragging me down, loudly whispering that I couldn't, I shouldn't, and who the hell did I think I was?

My schooling gave me the foundation to *do* the work. But what they didn't teach me was the first clue about how to run a business.

I really thought I was going to be able to say, "I have a doctorate in business psychology with a concentration in high performance and sport. If you want to achieve great things, I can help you." And people would just… hire me.

Turns out, that's not how it worked.

I paid to attend workshops and seminars that told me the answer was to write a book.

"Once you publish a book, people will see you as an expert and business will just flow to you!"

I published my first book and started doing speaking engagements for "exposure."

I gave people *lots* of information. They loved me. They told me I was great.

It turns out that "exposure" is what they put on a death certificate when you die outside, not how you pay bills.

I knew I could help people. I did it all the time when they came up after events with questions, and I could see the light bulb moments happening right there in front of me.

But I had no idea what I was actually selling. I would ramble about services and things I *could* do without clearly defining what they would actually get.

And confused people don't buy.

I spoke at national coaches' association events. Coaches of female teams understood what I did and were interested in how I could make their teams better.

But most of them didn't have the budget to hire me.

A male coach told me he loved what I did and he had budget, but bringing in a "pretty girl," would "distract his players." (I was over 40 at that point. I don't think that was the problem.)

I was told I should create a weekend seminar so coaches could come to me. That would be cheaper for them and more lucrative for me.

Since I had no idea how to put on a seminar, I decided to hire a marketing team to help me.

And that is when I got my first slap in the face about how underhanded and unethical some "business people" are.

****

I started looking for a marketing team in what I thought was the right place.

I was at a networking event with a friend and she introduced me to a friend of hers.

In the course of the conversation, I learned that she had worked closely with a marketing guy named Theo. She raved about him and offered to make an introduction.

I accepted, thinking that I was getting an honest referral from a friend of a friend.

My first mistake was not verifying that.

She wasn't actually a friend of my friend. She was just an acquaintance.

She had never worked with Theo. She just knew him and knew he gave a 10% kickback for referrals.

But I didn't know any of that.

When I made the appointment to meet Theo, I was excited thinking I had found the answer to my struggling business.

He said all the right things, trotted out amazing stories about how his work had created huge revenue gains for other businesses, and outlined how he could make my weekend seminar an incredible success.

Then he told me the price tag: $20,000 for four months' worth of work.

My stomach dropped. *Holy shit. That was a lot of money!*

Back then, I didn't know there were two types of fear.

Trauma-based fear that you have to walk through.

And intuition-based fear that you should always listen to.

I had only ever heard people say, "Success is on the other side of fear."

I knew I had money trauma. My parents had hammered frugality into my brain and Harry-ette thought I might end up living under a bridge.

I had scraped by when I was married to Hunter. And Brent had done nothing to make me feel safe about money by always threatening to take my capital.

I thought if I put on my big-girl pants and paid Theo, my business would skyrocket.

You have to spend money to make money after all, right? (That isn't actually a hard and fast rule.) I just had to overcome my fear.

But this is where I ignored my intuition, even though it was screaming at me:

I asked Theo, "Why do people stop working with you?"

His response, "They run out of money and can't keep going."

If I had been listening closely, I would have realized that a marketer's job is to help a business make enough money to cover his fees and then some. If people were running out of money, he wasn't doing his job.

But I couldn't hear that over the trauma-based fear I was trying so hard to stamp down.

I asked Theo for references and called every one of them. I asked if he had good integrity. I asked if he was a man of his word. I asked if he was selfish or generous.

Of course, his references all said the right things. They all raved about what a good guy he was. I still don't know if they were lying or if he had them fooled.

I believed all of them. It scared the hell out of me, but I walked through my fear and I signed the contract. I didn't have $20,000 to throw away. I was barely paying my rent.

Not only did he fail to help my business, he actively set me back.

A few weeks in, one of his employees asked to meet me privately for lunch.

She told me in confidence that she had warned Theo they had no experience with what I wanted and couldn't deliver on it. That he should refund my money and walk away.

His response to her had been, "We don't refund money. Just fake it."

I took the contract to a lawyer and asked if I could get out of it. He told me if I hadn't paid Theo, I likely could have just not paid him and backed out.

But because he already had the money, getting it back would cost more than just walking away.

I'm guessing Theo already knew that.

I called the woman who had referred him to me, and she said, "Oh, I don't know. I've never worked with him. But he paid me $2,000, so..." She shrugged.

It didn't matter to her that he had stolen my money and given me nothing in return.

It was a valuable, albeit expensive, lesson about fear and intuition.

At the time, I felt like a fool, humiliated. Now it feels more like the tuition I had to pay for the wisdom I gained. (That doesn't let Theo off the hook for being a horrible human.)

Now, years later, I understand the two types of fear, and I am able to explain it to my clients in a way that they can use it to avoid making similar mistakes. I can help them because I've been there and I've gotten it wrong.

However, Theo gave Harry-ette a lot of new ammunition. My impostor syndrome turned up to eleven.

I didn't know then that the only people who don't have impostor syndrome are likely impostors.

I was questioning if this was what I was supposed to be doing with my life. If I could really make a business work.

I cried to my youngest sister. Told her how hard it was, how my savings account was bleeding out, how I had no clue what to do next.

She said to me, "Robyn, you are the most educated, underpaid person I know. Why don't you just get a job?"

And then I remembered all the jobs I'd had. How unappreciated I was. How little control I had. And how many loyal people I had seen get laid off with the weak excuse of "restructuring."

No. Just no. I wasn't going to do that. I knew I was smart. I could figure this out. And I wasn't going to have to live under a bridge to do it.

Still, I couldn't help wondering: How could I be both brilliant and so completely clueless and lost at the same time?

Thankfully, I had no idea how long and how many setbacks it was going to take for me to "figure it out."

****

It was during the mess with Theo that I met Russ. I'll tell you that funny story in the next chapter.

Once Russ realized he actually wanted to go out with me, his amazing skills as a graphic designer who can write code and his willingness to help me with no strings attached started to heal my trust in human beings.

After Theo, I pivoted to include working with both businesspeople as well as athletes.

I started speaking at Chamber of Commerce events.

I still couldn't clearly explain what I did. But I got a few clients anyway.

I started to make enough to break even, but it wasn't enough to feed me yet.

The people I had worked with when I was in grad school still wanted me to work for internship-level pay (or even for free).

I thought I needed to get out of New Jersey. Get a fresh start. Move closer to my family.

I was flying to Las Vegas for speaking engagements. Maybe it made sense for me to move there.

Russ drove me to the airport, and I met my sister and spent a long weekend looking at houses.

Businesspeople told me the book I had written for female athletes was great, but that I needed to write one for business. So I took everything I had learned since I turned my dissertation into my first book and wrote a second one.

Russ designed the cover (I still love it) and did the page layout.

I invested the money to self-publish because I knew how to do that and I knew I could get it to market faster than if I went with a traditional publisher.

I thought *this* book would be the answer. It was going to be the thing that made getting steady clients easier.

It wasn't.

I continued to struggle.

What was I doing wrong? Why couldn't I make this work?

I know now that a lot of the things I had been successful at in my life, I had done by brute force. I could outwork, out-hustle, have more grit, and be more resilient.

But that hard-driving, balls-to-the-wall style wasn't working now.

I needed someone to help me. Maybe a business coach.

Remember how I told you that the coaching and therapy world is a very deep pool full of very shallow people?

I was about to learn that lesson again.

And I decided not to move to Vegas, not yet, because: Russ.

Let me share how he became part of my story before we go any deeper into how I had to deal with my trauma and what I learned to be ready to have a successful business.

Chapter 49
I Had to Ask Him Out Four Times

The first memory I have of Russ is of him loudly arguing with another guy in the gym about football. I was one and a half seconds from telling them to shut up or take it outside when Russ broke it off.

I'm guessing our relationship would have gone very differently if I had called them out for being obnoxious while I was trying to bench press.

I had joined that particular gym because Gio, a guy I had been seeing, was a member there. When I broke it off with him to spend time with Russ, he said, "I knew I shouldn't have *let* you join that gym!"

"Let me?" Clearly, he wasn't the right guy for me. Dodged a bullet there.

As is the case with most gyms, I was one of only a few women who worked out regularly in the weight room.

At first, everyone ignored me. But showing up six days a week meant people started to recognize me, say hello, and eventually chat.

I know my way around a gym, and guys typically respect that. Plus, I can hold my own if they get mouthy. (You might remember that from my volleyball stories.)

It didn't take long for me to learn a little bit of backstory about everyone. And because everyone wears weightlifting gloves, blunt questions about relationship status were the norm.

I became friendly with all the regulars and learned Russ was the only single guy who worked out in the mornings like I did.

There were whispers about him being gay, simply because no one had ever seen him date anyone.

I didn't get that vibe from him, but even if he was, he could hold a conversation and seemed kind. That's good enough for a gym friend.

When I learned he had been working for himself for almost twenty years, I thought it might be useful for us to do some business networking.

One day I suggested, "Hey, we should get coffee sometime. We could talk about our businesses."

This man looked me dead in the eye and said, "I don't think our businesses can help each other."

Oh. Okay.

A strange response, since I thought all business owners were always looking for more business connections.

But whatever.

(When I mentioned to him that I was writing this story, he told me for the first time that he had been really disenchanted with business networking at the time, which is why he turned me down.)

The next time I suggested we do something was right after I heard him talking to someone else about a wine he had tried over the weekend.

When there was a break in the conversation, I said, "You know, I got several bottles of wine in the divorce and I don't have anyone to drink them with."

His response: "That's too bad," as he picked up a heavier set of dumbbells.

I just shrugged and did another set.

I wasn't hurt or put off. I wasn't trying to get him to date me. In fact, I assumed he wouldn't want to date me because I'm three inches taller than he is.

I just thought it might be nice to have someone to do stuff with.

Apparently, the stuff I was asking him to do wasn't his thing. That wasn't about me.

We both had a pattern of warming up on an exercise bike for thirty minutes and then heading back to lift.

So, we fell into the habit of riding next to each other and chatting when we could.

One morning, while we were riding, I mentioned that I had booked my flight to go house hunting in Vegas. The fact that I was planning to move had been a common topic, so he shouldn't have been surprised.

But as we got off the bikes and walked back toward the weights, Russ said, "I'll miss you when you move to Vegas."

I stopped putting my lifting gloves on and looked at him.

I was incredulous. "Miss me? How can you miss me? You won't even have coffee with me."

He told me later that was an aha moment for him. But he didn't do anything about it at the time.

Our next pass and a miss came at a networking event.

Russ told me that he was a member of the local Chamber of Commerce and that they were having a networking event that was open to guests. His tone made it clear that he wasn't asking me out, just mentioning it, one business owner to another.

I was always looking for new networking spots, and it might be nice for him to see me not looking like a gym rat for once.

I asked him to email me the details and made plans to attend.

The evening of the event, I arrived a little bit after the start time, in hopes that he would already be there and maybe introduce me to a few people.

When I walked in, I saw him standing in a small group, holding an appetizer plate and a glass of wine.

I walked over to greet him.

With an overly flirty smile, I said, "Hi! It's so good to see you." And because his hands were full, I leaned in to kiss his cheek. (Forward, I know.)

I was wearing heels, which made our height difference even more obvious, so he couldn't really dodge me without actually ducking out of the way.

He introduced me to the people in the group, and after a bit of small talk, I excused myself, saying to him, "Maybe we can grab a drink after...?"

He nodded, and I left to do my networking thing.

As the evening wound down, I started to look around for Russ to reconnect about that drink.

He was nowhere to be found.

I asked a few people and was told, "I think he left."

Now we know that Russ has a much shorter social battery than I do. It's not uncommon for me to find him sitting in a chair by himself waiting for me to finish talking to the last person when we go out.

But at the time, I just assumed that drinks after an event weren't his thing either.

As I left, I noticed postcards tucked under the windshield wipers of all the cars. When I got to mine, I leaned over to grab it.

It was an announcement for the grand opening of a new pub, offering two free drinks and an appetizer if you brought it in. I tossed it in my passenger seat without much thought.

The next morning at the gym, I gave Russ a little bit of a hard time about leaving without saying goodbye.

He told me I was in a conversation when he left, and he didn't want to interrupt.

I then asked if he had seen the postcard about the pub grand opening.

He didn't know what I was talking about. Apparently, he had left before his car got one.

I told him about it briefly, tilted my head, and smiled as I said, "It might be fun to do."

He shrugged, picked up his dumbbells, and said, "Maybe," as he started his next set.

But two days later, he walked up and said, "Can you send me the details about that pub thing?"

I thought, *"He's going to take another girl!"*

But I said, "Of course."

When I got home from the gym, I grabbed the postcard from the passenger seat and went inside to send him an email.

I was planning to share the exact email I wrote him, but sadly, the old Sony laptop it's on won't even turn on.

So you'll just have to believe me when I tell you it was a long, flirty email.

I even shared their website, poked a little fun at how awful it was, and told him they clearly needed a good graphic designer. (Remember, he's a graphic designer who builds websites).

A few hours later I got his reply.

It was exactly two words long: "I'm in."

I sat there staring at it and wondering, *"What the hell does that even mean?"*

Did he want to go? Did he want to go with me?

I replied, "Does that mean you want to go?"

"Yes." Clearly a man of few words.

"Should we ride together?"

"Sure. I can pick you up."

I knew him. But I didn't know him *that* well. I wasn't ready to give him my address.

After several more back-and-forth emails, I learned that he lived between me and the pub, so we decided I would drive to his place and then we would go together from there.

When I mentioned the plan to Gio (who I was still friendly with), he said bitterly, "You must be pretty sure he's not a serial killer."

I remember rolling my eyes and telling him I was pretty confident Russ wasn't a serial killer.

On the evening of the grand opening, I went all out.

Hair. Makeup. Lashes. Skinny jeans. Fitted leather jacket. Four-inch heels. (I had told him I was going to wear heels and he didn't seem to care.)

I was 100% the blonde bombshell I could be and I knew it.

I rang his doorbell at exactly the time I had committed to arriving.

When he answered the door, he looked at me and said, "Are you ready to go?"

I thought, "No. I came *here* to get ready."

But out loud I just said, "Yep."

We walked to his car and he opened the door for me. (Something he still does.)

The ride was short and the conversation was easy.

When we got to the place, the parking lot was already pretty full and Russ asked if I wanted to be dropped off at the door so I wouldn't have to walk in heels. I told him I was okay to walk.

I didn't want to stand outside waiting for him, risk some other guy chatting me up, and annoy Russ before we even got inside.

As we walked toward the door, a pickup truck slowed down and the guy inside stared at us long enough to make me feel awkward.

Then he came to a stop and said, "Hey, Russ! Is that you?"

As we got closer, Russ greeted him and introduced me.

Then the guy said, "I'll see you inside," and drove off.

As we walked up the steps into the place, Russ said, more to himself than to me, "That was weird. I barely know him and he never speaks to me at networking events."

I didn't need to reply because he turned to talk to the hostess.

She told us we could sit anywhere we wanted in the bar area.

We chose a high-top table in the middle with a good view of everything.

When our waitress came over, I showed her the postcard as she gave us menus.

We had just gotten our drinks when another guy who knew Russ walked up to our table. (Russ just told me his name was Carl. I'm impressed he remembered.)

Russ was polite and introduced me, but then the guy called a man and a woman over from the bar, and all three of them stood at our table talking like it was a networking event.

I think the woman realized we might be on a date because she eventually wandered off, taking the second guy with her.

Carl stood there talking, moving from topic to topic without breathing for forty-five minutes. He even ordered himself more drinks, ate some of our appetizer, and ignored his female friend when she came back and tried to get him away from us.

When he finally came up for air, he looked at me, looked at Russ, then back at me, and said, "So what's the deal with you two?"

I had no idea how to answer that. Were we on a date? Were we friends hanging out?

I think Russ said something like, "We just thought we'd check out this new place."

Carl, now a little tipsy, finally went back to his friends at the bar.

I looked at Russ and smirked. "Well, he had a lot to say!"

Russ shook his head in disbelief. "I don't think he's said that much to me in all the time I've known him put together."

Then he casually added, "Do you want to get some burgers?"

My stomach knotted. I hadn't planned on dinner. That sounded like a date. Plus, my business wasn't doing that great, and I was being really careful with money.

He must have sensed my hesitation. Without looking up from the menu, he said, "I'm buyin'."

It seemed rude to make him leave, and I was enjoying his company, so I smiled and picked up the menu.

When our orders came, I looked around for ketchup for the fries. None of the tables had any. When we asked our waitress for some, she brought two tiny ramekins.

Russ joked that there must be a ketchup shortage and they were rationing it.

About halfway through our meal, a guy sitting at the table behind me tapped me on the shoulder. When I turned around, he said, "Do you have any ketchup?"

I explained that they didn't have bottles on the tables; he'd have to ask his waitress.

When Russ and I were both done with our burgers but still picking at the fries, I excused myself to go to the bathroom.

When I walked back out, I almost ran directly into a huge, Marine-looking guy.

And when I say "huge," you have to remember that I was in heels. I was over six feet tall myself, and this man towered over me.

I stopped short, said, "Oh, sorry," and stepped to the side to go around him. Except he stepped with me.

I now had my back against the wall and an alarmingly large man boxing me in.

He looked down at me. "What's going on with you and that guy?"

I froze in place, on the verge of panic.

When I didn't respond, he moved closer and continued, "Because if he's not interested, I am."

Nope. Nope. Hard nope. That was way too aggressive for me.

I said, "Yeah, I'm not," and ducked around him to go back to the table.

Russ had been watching the whole thing from his seat, and as I came back, he asked, "Do you know that guy?"

I was freaking out, afraid Russ was going to think I was flirting.

"No. I don't." I didn't explain any further.

A few minutes later, the guy walked past our table and sat down in a booth across from a woman. I realized pretty quickly that he had left his date at the table to stalk me to the bathroom.

Double nope.

After putting his credit card on the bill, Russ got up to go to the bathroom. I was people-watching when the guy behind me tapped me on the shoulder again.

I turned around and he slurred, "Do you have any ketchup?"

I squinted at him. "I told you..."

He interrupted me. "I don't want ketchup. I just want to talk to you. Is that guy your boyfriend?"

What the hell is going on with everybody tonight?

I stumbled through some kind of response, trying to get him to stop talking to me before Russ got back.

I didn't succeed. I was still turned around in my seat when I saw Russ walk out of the bathroom and catch my eye.

My inner monologue was screaming, *"He is going to leave me in this bar because all these guys won't quit talking to me!"*

(Obviously I had a lot of relationship trauma that I was attributing to him that night.)

Russ paused next to me and said to the guy, "Did you need something?"

The guy mumbled something about ketchup as I turned back around and Russ sat back down.

Before he could say anything, I started apologizing, "I'm so sorry. I don't know what everyone's deal is tonight. I promise I'm not flirting with them."

Then Russ said one of the most iconic, swoon-worthy lines ever: "Robyn, when you bring the best-looking woman into a bar, she's going to get hit on. I don't care, as long as you leave with me."

I was stunned into silence, and I did leave with him that night.

Chapter 50
Our First Date and Beyond

After that not-a-date the first week of February, Russ decided he actually did want to ask me out.

But should he ask me out for Valentine's Day? Would that be weird? Would I think he wasn't interested if he didn't?

I learned later that he asked several female friends at the gym what he should do.

He ended up sending me an email asking if I wanted to go out for Valentine's Day.

I totally freaked out.

Too much pressure too fast.

I wanted to go out with him but not on Valentine's Day!

I called my youngest sister in a panic.

She was a calm voice of reason: "Robyn, Valentine's Day is less than a week away. There is no way he's getting reservations anywhere. You are not going out on Valentine's Day. Calm down."

And, of course, she was right.

We went out the Saturday after instead. But when the waiter said, "Happy Valentine's Day," my stomach clenched.

At the end of the night, Russ asked if I wanted a ride to the airport for my trip to Vegas. It seemed like a lot to ask of him.

(I didn't know then that hyper-independence is a trauma response to not having people you can depend on, particularly in childhood.)

I asked him if he was sure he wanted to do that, and he responded, "If I didn't want to, I wouldn't have offered."

Wow. Refreshingly honest communication.

Less than two weeks later, he dropped me off at the airport and picked me up when I came back.

On the ride home, we talked about my plan to move in about six months when my lease was up.

He told me there was no reason we couldn't enjoy spending time together in the meantime.

Casual, fun, honest.

I was up for that.

We also decided that we weren't going to tell people at the gym we were "dating." We had both seen too many gym couples break up, causing the drama of everyone picking sides and having opinions.

That ended up being funny because over the next month or so, a guy named Joe kept telling Russ he should ask me out, while at the same time telling me that Russ might be a great "gay friend" for me.

About six weeks after our not-a-date, it seemed appropriate to "out" our relationship when Joe invited both of us to his birthday party.

Russ and I arrived together, holding hands.

Joe spent all night telling people that he was the reason we were together. I just rolled my eyes and let it go.

But after the beer had been flowing for a bit, Joe walked up to me and said, more loudly than he might have meant to, "Why are you wearing heels?"

He jerked his head toward Russ, who was standing behind me talking to someone else.

I didn't even get to open my mouth.

Russ turned around and responded, "Because she looks damn good in them."

I just smiled and said, "Yeah. That."

Russ took my hand, reached up, and gave me a quick peck on the cheek.

****

Here are a few funny stories about our first few months together:

> One Saturday early on, I told him I was going to go for a bike ride, and he asked if he could join me.

I told him, "I'm going to ride thirty miles. Can you keep up?"

He didn't respond with the usual shock I get when I say how far I ride. Instead, he just said, "Yeah. I should be fine."

He did those thirty miles without blinking an eye.

The first time Russ came with me to Costco, I went to pick up the Costco-sized cat litter, and he said, "Let me get that."

I replied, "I can do it." (Hyper-independent trauma response again.)

He responded, "I know you can, but when you're with me, you don't have to."

I felt seen, respected, and cared for all at once.

Russ related this story to me:

When he told his mom about me, she said, "Be careful. She's after your money."

He replied, "I am too. Where is it?"

His mom grew to love me, and I loved her.

As an Italian mom, the biggest compliment she could give me was letting me cook in her kitchen, which I did many times in the twelve years I had with her.

The last thing she said to me before she passed was, "Robyn, you know I love you."

I do. And I love you too, Mom.

Russ and I were going to stay with friends, and as he was unloading the car, Charlie said, "Do you need a hand?"

Russ replied instantly, "Yes. Please clap."

And Charlie did.

I laughed so hard my eyes watered. Russ's quiet, dry sense of humor slays me.

****

Before I ever got Russ to go on our not-a-date, I had done a speaking engagement at a softball coaches convention in Florida, where I met a guy named Peter.

He was younger than me and keenly interested in chatting.

When he learned I lived in New Jersey, he told me his parents lived there and asked if he could take me out when he came up to visit them.

I agreed, mostly because it seemed unlikely to ever actually happen.

He had called me a few times since then, wanting to have conversations that were much too intimate for how little he knew me.

When he kept pressing me, wanting to know how I shaved "down there," I finally said, "If it is ever appropriate for you to know, you won't have to ask."

That shut him up.

Russ and I had been dating almost three months when Peter called to tell me he was coming to visit his parents and to schedule our "date."

I told him I was seeing someone, but if he wanted to have lunch as friends, I was open to that.

He kept bringing every conversation back to sex. But I had said I would see him, and didn't want to go back on my word.

One lunch shouldn't be a big deal.

I told Russ the whole story, including how Peter made me feel like I needed to be on high alert, and how I felt obligated to follow through on my promise to see him.

Russ didn't say much about it right then.

But later, as I was pulling into the parking lot at the hair salon, my phone rang.

When I picked up, Russ said, "I need to say this. Of course you can choose to do whatever you want. I'm not telling you that you can't. You're a grown woman and get to make your own decisions. What you choose to do won't impact our relationship. I just want you to know that this whole thing with Peter makes me uncomfortable and I'd rather you not go."

He said it all in one breath, like he needed to get it out before I could interrupt.

I said, "Okay. Thank you for letting me know."

And we hung up.

But I thought about it the whole time I was getting my hair cut and highlighted.

If he had tried to forbid me to go, I would have responded with indignation and said, "Just watch me."

But he didn't do that. He told me how he felt, what he would like to see happen, and then left the ball in my court to make a decision.

I had never had a man, from my father through everyone I had dated or married, be so respectful.

I didn't know then that *this* was what secure masculinity looks like.

When I got back to my car, I called Peter.

I told him I was dating someone and although the relationship was new, I really respected him and because of that, I needed to cancel our lunch plans.

I expected him to be disappointed. What I did *not* expect was the onslaught of anger he spewed at me.

"This always happens to me. This isn't fair! I met you first. I can't believe you're backing out on me. You promised…"

I let him rant for a bit. Then I interrupted him.

"Peter. Peter. This is ridiculous. I'm going to go. Take care of yourself."

I think he tried to reply, but I hung up on him.

When I told Russ I had canceled with Peter he said simply, "I'm glad."

A couple of years ago, I got a Facebook friend request from Peter. I ignored it. I don't need any part of that energy back in my life.

****

Russ and I were spending most of our time together. So much so that sometimes I had to tell him, "I need some me time," and I would go on a bike ride by myself.

It never bothered him. He would just say, "Okay. Have fun. I'll see you when you get back."

If we were teasing each other and I puffed up my chest and said, "Is that the way you want to play it?"

He would always say, "No ma'am" in a weirdly confident, powerful but yielding way.

He was (is) so different from the other men in my life.

There is a place in central Jersey called Old Man Rafferty's that became "our place" by accident.

It started when we went there one Thursday night to sit outside and have a pizza made in the stone oven.

The guy making pizza was friendly, the drinks were good, and the evening passed with the ease that comes with good company.

We went back the next Thursday.

And the next.

Pretty soon, we wondered if we were there too often because the hostess recognized us and the guy at the pizza oven knew our order.

But we kept going anyway.

One Thursday it was raining, so we ended up sitting inside.

The bar was full, and there was a group of people, including a husband and wife, sitting next to us on my left.

The woman kept looking at us, particularly at me.

I wasn't sure what her deal was. So I just ignored her.

Suddenly, she turned completely around to face me, so close that her knees were against my chair.

I looked at her in surprise, as she demanded, "Where is your husband?"

I realized the problem.

I often wore a simple band on my left ring finger because it reduced the number of men who interjected themselves into my life.

She had noticed that Russ didn't have a ring and made up her mind that I was cheating.

I didn't feel the need to explain all that to her, so I just pointed at Russ and said, "Right there."

Her husband, trying to turn her chair back toward him, said, "See? I told you. Now leave them alone."

I had thought she was just drunk. But the way he spoke to her made me wonder if something else was going on.

I went back to my conversation with Russ, but the interaction lingered at the edge of my mind.

When our meals came, I made room by pushing my unfinished appetizer plate up and over to my left. Not in the other woman's space, especially because she had her back to me. But also not directly in front of me anymore.

Before I could react, she grabbed an appetizer and stuck the whole thing in her mouth.

Her husband gasped, "No! You can't do that!"

She spit it out directly onto the bar and slouched like a child. "Why not? She's not eating it."

I realized then that she must have had a stroke or something because she didn't seem to have any impulse control.

I pushed the appetizer plate toward her. "You're right. I'm not eating them. You may have them. Try them with the dipping sauce. It's really good."

She gave me a child-like grin as her husband said, "You don't have to do that."

I looked over her head at him and replied, "It's okay. Really. Let her enjoy them."

He did, but he insisted on buying our next round of drinks.

Through the whole encounter, Russ was calm, unflustered, and just let me handle it.

When I asked him about it later, he told me, "You clearly had it under control. There was no reason for me to jump in. Besides, if you needed me, you would have asked."

Imagine that. A guy who doesn't feel the need to be a savior.

It was on the way home from one of those Thursday night dates that Russ said to me, "You know I can't move to Vegas with you."

I remember thinking, *"I never asked you to."*

But I didn't say that out loud.

He continued talking, "I'm my mom's youngest son. It would kill her if I moved that far away."

I might have said, "Okay."

It was the first sign that he thought we might be something more than just "light and casual."

By early summer, I had stopped looking at places in Vegas.

I told Russ I would put the move off for a year to give us time to decide if we were a thing. But I wasn't playing around.

This was an in-or-out situation.

We decided together that, since his lease was up around the same time as mine, we would move in together.

It had only been eight months since our not-a-date, but knowing sooner rather than later seemed smarter.

Chapter 51
Jump Over a Broom in Front of a Goat

Living with Russ was easy because he was a grown man who had lived on his own for a long time and was perfectly capable of taking care of himself.

When I told him, "I don't cook, I don't clean, and I don't have babies,"

He replied, "I cook. We can hire someone to clean. I don't want babies."

He did his own laundry, cleaned the bathroom when it needed it, and didn't expect me to be his mommy.

Plus, the cats loved him, and he loved them. (I think he cried more than I did when they crossed the rainbow bridge.)

Our biggest challenge was that he would jerk while he was sleeping, and a couple of times he hit me hard enough to knock the wind out of me.

We solved that by switching sides of the bed.

It hasn't been a problem since.

****

My father was a different issue.

He was not pleased that I was "living in sin," and made that very clear whenever we spoke.

I finally told him, "If it'll make your God happy, I'll gladly jump over a broom in front of a goat. But I see no reason to tell the government about my relationship with Russ."

He didn't love the snark, but he did stop complaining about my living arrangement.

****

By the time Russ and I celebrated the first anniversary of our not-a-date, it was clear I had to choose him over Vegas.

I was relieved not to have to deal with all the logistics of moving that far anyway. But that didn't mean I wanted to stay in New Jersey.

Russ agreed to move. His graphic design and website work could be done from anywhere.

I agreed to stay within two hours of his mother, with the commitment of living there as long as she was alive.

When I met him, he was having lunch with her and his brother every Sunday, and when we told her we wanted to move, her response was, "You're killing me. I'll never see you."

We promised we would come back at least every six weeks, and we kept that promise until she passed away last March.

We looked at all the surrounding states and settled on Delaware because the cost of living was lower than New Jersey.

We didn't know then that Delaware was so insular.

We once attended an event where the speaker was introduced: "He's not from Delaware, but he has lived here since 1978, so we'll give him a pass."

Unfortunately, that attitude extends to who they will do business with. We have been here for almost twelve years, and I have had only four clients who live in Delaware.

That hasn't been a problem, especially since the pandemic. Many of the people who choose to work with me are mobile and global and very comfortable doing business via Zoom, so I have clients from Europe to Hawaii.

****

It took Russ and me several months to find our house. We made offers on a few places that didn't work out, but eventually we got the perfect place for us.

It's in a quiet neighborhood with a yard where I can grow flowers and food, and Nebula has room to chase a frisbee.

It even has a driveway that faces south, so as long as there is less than three inches of snow, we don't have to shovel.

It's close to a bike trail and amazing places to hike.

Russ is always willing to drive me the forty-five minutes to the Philly airport when I need to fly, and he attends events with me when I speak locally.

Which reminds me of a funny story:

I was speaking at an event in New Jersey when a woman came up to me afterwards and asked, "How did you get him to ask you out? I hinted for months that I wanted to go out with him, and he never asked!"

I laughed and told her I had to ask him out four times. If I had waited for him to ask, I would still be waiting.

I have seen women hit on him right in front of me. I just chuckle to myself and think, "This will be interesting."

There was even a woman who hit on him at several networking events in a row until she finally realized that I always seemed to be around. Then she asked him, "What is your deal with her?" pointing over her shoulder at me.

Russ frowned. "She's my wife."

The woman spun around, glared up at me, and sputtered, "You should tell people you're married to him!" Then she stormed off, never to be seen again.

Apparently the wedding band he has worn since we moved to Delaware wasn't enough of a clue for her.

****

At the height of the pandemic, my mom and dad decided to visit all of their "outside of California" kids because flights were cheap.

But they had to get special permission from their pastor to stay in our house.

Staying in a house where people are living in sin apparently causes the sin to rub off on you. (I'm not exactly clear about how that works.)

Fortunately, their pastor told them that since Russ and I were committed to each other, had purchased a home together, called each other "husband" and "wife," and both wore wedding bands, we were married in God's eyes.

Turns out, we didn't need the government's piece of paper after all.

But then in 2022, I had what doctors thought was a health scare.

It actually turned out to be nothing. I just sprained my sternum painting our two-story living room and foyer. (Which I had told each doctor about, but none of them connected it.)

But before I figured that out, several cardiologists tried to convince me that I needed a heart catheterization.

I told them I was not going to start with the most invasive option and suggested a CT angiogram instead.

The cardiologist's response was condescending: "We can do that, but then you'll just need two procedures instead of one."

The angiogram showed my calcium score was zero. Clearly, heart disease was not the issue.

The cardiologist refused to turn her camera on for the Zoom call to talk about my results.

Her response was flippant: "Well, whatever it is, it's not your heart, so I can't help you. And if it were going to kill you, you'd already be dead."

Healthcare in the U.S. at its finest.

While we were dealing with all of that, I looked into what it would take to create a health directive and a will that would make sure Russ was the person making decisions for me if I couldn't do it myself.

I also wanted to be certain there was no question that he would get all of our assets if something serious happened to me.

Figuring that out was no easy feat.

Instead of jumping through all kinds of legal hoops with lawyers and tons of paperwork, we started having the conversation: Should we just tell the government about our relationship, i.e., get married?

I was not interested in doing any kind of dog and pony show, and Russ didn't care.

In doing some research, we learned that we could self-officiate in Washington, D.C., and we didn't even need witnesses. That sounded ideal.

We sent in the paperwork, had separate phone calls with someone at the courthouse (everything was still remote due to COVID), and received our marriage license.

Russ told his mom and brother about our plan. They were both on board and weren't disappointed that we were doing something they didn't have to attend.

I told two of my siblings after the fact, mostly so someone in my family would know and Russ wouldn't have to prove it.

I ordered a stuffed goat online and brought our kitchen broom.

We drove to D.C. with Nebula and spent the night in a hotel.

On the morning of March 20, 2022, at the U.S. National Arboretum, with the cherry blossoms just starting to bloom, we jumped over a broom in front of a goat with a dog as our witness as the sun crossed the equator from south to north (spring equinox), and declared ourselves married.

After we sent in our paperwork, the government agreed.

Interestingly, when Dad was creating our family tree, he asked about including Russ.

When I told him we use the date of our not-a-date as our anniversary, but also shared the date we told the government about our relationship, Dad used the first one.

Chapter 52
This Is My Circus. These Are My Monkeys.

Do you remember the girl who got married because she didn't know she could say no?

The girl who cut the grass in the bedroom of a shack on a catfish farm, believing hard things were just how life worked?

The girl who first caught glimpses of who she was while playing beach volleyball but still married a narcissist, thinking she couldn't make it on her own?

The woman who earned three degrees in six and a half years while flying to London to be arm candy?

But who still had to control the panic when that marriage ended, unsure if she could even feed herself?

Those experiences are still in me. Shaping, but not defining who I am.

And you know about Harry-ette. She is still here, and there are times she can still gut-punch me. But for the most part, she sits in the backseat and no longer gets to drive.

The Bitch, The Ego, and The Flirt still show up to protect The Little Girl. But they rarely need to. She's safe now.

There was a time I would have called the life I live now boring.

But this is what peace looks like.

That doesn't mean it's been easy.

****

In 2017, Russ and I decided to start a health and wellness business together. We called it the Whole Food Muscle Club.

I studied nutrition at the Center for Nutrition Studies at Cornell.

I wrote the content, and he designed our book: *How to Feed a Human the Whole Food Muscle Way*.

He built an amazing membership website. We did Facebook Live videos five days a week and Ask Us Anything webinars once a month.

He even got over his fear of public speaking to give talks with me.

It was slow to take off, even after we hired a marketing consultant and a PR person. (Yes, I'm a glutton. Clearly, I didn't learn after Theo.)

We had speaking engagements lined up and plans for a big marketing push.

Then COVID hit.

We watched as all three of our businesses crashed. Every gig we had scheduled for 2020 was canceled within a three-week period.

My business tanked.

Russ's clients stopped spending money on design, and nobody was building new websites.

We had to make some tough choices.

It didn't make sense to have three businesses on life support, so we closed the Whole Food Muscle Club, took the website down, and pulled the book off the market.

Russ worked on resuscitating his business, and I took a hard look at what I loved and wanted to rebuild in my business.

It was a blessing in disguise because that reflection time is what made me realize I really enjoy the intense connection of working with someone one-on-one.

It led to the client conversation that gave me the moniker "Mental MacGyver" and the realization that I've been through chaos, so I can lead others through chaos.

Another client told me that I work in the space between executive coach, therapist, and business strategist. Right where people feel the most alone and isolated. When I wondered aloud, "What does that make me?" he replied simply, "A professional confidante."

Those realizations reshaped my business.

It took years to rebuild our livelihood, and Harry-ette spoke up with a vengeance: "Nothing you create ever lasts. Why do you keep trying just to fail?"

When life goes sideways, I used to absolutely panic about not being able to put a roof over my head or food on the table. But I have always been able to figure it out, and I've gotten better about not losing myself in the fear.

I know what it takes to come through chaos and feel (mostly) safe living in peace. I am honored to share those lessons in my work and through my stories by being the person anyone can feel safe opening up to.

When I decided I wanted to sit in public with a sign that said, "Happy2Listen" and let strangers tell me their stories, Russ's only concern was that I do it in a safe place.

My goal was simple: to put the human back in the human race.

What if I could be the one person someone passed on their way to end it all and they chose to live another day instead?

I have even organized groups of people to join me in being emotionally available in public for anyone who might need to talk.

It's not Russ's thing. He's not the extrovert that I am, and doesn't feel qualified to help people like that. But he is always willing to drive me to places to be Happy2Listen and be a quiet supporter.

I have heard shockingly sad and gloriously joyful things, but they aren't my stories to share.

If you have the personality to do it, get a piece of cardboard, write, "Happy2Listen," and sit in a safe, public place.

You might be amazed by how human humans are.

****

I could likely write another whole book, maybe two, about the lessons I've learned, the mistakes I've made, and the quiet power I've found inside myself.

What I know for sure is that to figure out what *is* our circus, and which monkeys are ours, we have to have tough conversations with ourselves.

I would like to close this book by sharing some of the ideas that have helped me and that I use to help my clients.

Use them if you think they will help, and ignore them if you aren't there right now.

Let's start with one of the simplest and most powerful questions:

What do you want to be different?

I have found that if I ask, "What's your dream?" "Where do you want to go?" or "What's your plan?" the response I get is abstract, unattainable, and even heartbreaking.

Talking about what needs to be different reveals the foundation of what isn't working and a place to start to change it.

Is there water in the well?

When you learn there's no water in a well (i.e., someone doesn't feed your soul and instead sucks you dry), stop going there looking for a drink.

Ambivalent relationships are the most toxic.

Brent was the perfect example of an ambivalent relationship. Like many narcissists, he would oscillate between charming and cruel.

If you're never sure whether someone will praise you or tear you down, love you or hate you, protect you or throw you under the bus, there is no water in that well.

And they will feed your impostor syndrome.

If you want to continue loving them, love them from a distance.

We get to choose whether we bring the things we were told about ourselves into our future or not. And we can decide to remove people from our lives who create chaos.

Are you afraid to ask for help?

I shared with you how hard it was for me to accept help from Russ when we first started dating because for me, "help" always came with strings attached.

I wore my independence like a badge of honor.

I recognize hyper-independence in many of my clients because they feel guilty or even shameful when they need help.

If you have a traumatic past, hyper-independence might be a way you self-sabotage, even if you've moved beyond the trauma.

I had to learn to accept help when it was offered and to trust the people who love me enough to ask for help when I needed it.

It doesn't always come naturally, but I've gotten better at it.

Do you remember the best advice I was ever given?

"You are resilient. Stop making decisions that make you prove it."

Those of us who have been taught and expected to be nurturing (the healers, the givers, the always-see-the-best-in-others) forget that we need to be our number one priority.

We feel guilty when we don't give. And we rarely ask for what we want or need because we expect people to notice and give freely, like we do.

When we finally collapse and ask, the people around us (the takers, the energy vampires, the ones who thrive by using us) tell us we're selfish.

And we feel the burn of that shame in our soul.

I had to learn to ask myself, "Am I being resilient or stubborn? Is this my intuition or an internal saboteur?"

Recognizing the difference is part of what has allowed me to stop always doing things the hard way as if, that gave me some kind of extra honor.

Who do you think should be the center of the one life you've been given on this earth?

This was a hard question for me to start asking myself, and even harder to answer honestly.

If you want to stop making decisions that make you prove you are resilient, you need to sit with the anxiety this question creates and really, truly answer it.

And the only true answer is that *you* should be the center of *your* life.

That doesn't make you selfish or mean. You can still be kind and generous while not giving yourself away.

You aren't required to set yourself on fire to keep other people warm or break yourself into pieces to fix someone else.

What's in it for me?

Does it hurt your heart to think about yourself first? It did for me when I first started working on it.

You deserve to love yourself first.

If you asked that question, and the answer is, *"there's nothing in it for me,"* think long and hard about why you are doing it.

Being generous is wonderful. But when "altruism" causes you to lose yourself, it's a problem.

(I don't think altruism is a real thing.)

Unconditional love between adults leads to abuse.

Your love absolutely should have conditions, and you deserve so much more than "be nice and don't lie."

If someone has convinced you that you should love them "unconditionally," they are probably trying to keep you from creating healthy boundaries.

It has been helpful for me to remember that the only people who have a problem with my boundaries are those who want to cross them.

Does your inner critic have a name?

I gave Harry-ette her name long before I learned to recognize her in the moment. She came up for me while I was writing this chapter.

She said the chapter was crap. That nobody cared, that you, my readers, were only here for the drama and trauma, not the lessons.

Her delivery was wrong. Or at least, I'm choosing to believe it was. But I had to pick apart her message to find what was useful.

She was right about one thing: what I had written was too authoritarian. It was preachy, like I was trying to tell you how to live your life. It's not my place to dictate that.

I had to let go of the mean, hurtful words Harry-ette used so I could write something better.

If you name your inner critic, it might help you tease apart what is your voice and what is someone else's that you're just repeating.

****

I want so badly to end this book in a way that sparks the strength I know lives inside you. To provoke you to love being the amazing, beautiful, messy human you truly are.

I want to write something that speaks to your soul, so it doesn't take you as many years as it took me to love yourself and to give yourself permission to let go of the people who aren't allowing you to heal.

This is what I can say about the life I live now: *This is my circus. These are my monkeys.*

But I don't have to run a breeding program.

I don't have to keep making decisions that create chaos and make me prove I'm resilient.

I can heal my inner demons instead of giving away parts of myself to feel worthy of being loved.

While I was writing this book, a business coach told me I shouldn't release it because it would "pigeonhole" me as a "motivational speaker" and keep "serious business people" from wanting to work with me.

But I believe my story is more than motivational, and my education was meant as a gift to support that story, not hide it.

I believe that how I came through massive trauma, and what I learned from it, is the message I'm meant to share.

It's what gives my work emotional depth. It's what makes me different.

I won't let fear, or embarrassment, keep me silent anymore.

Would I want to relive the craziness of my life? Absolutely not.

But I love who I've become, so I wouldn't change it either.

I'm finally owning my truth and choosing to be the light in the chaos for others.

To tell the truth. To show up with intensity and call to those who are ready to step up and own their power.

We are here to help the willing, not convert the resistant.

For the first half of my life, I attended the school of hard knocks. It was about earning wisdom through chaos and trauma.

There are people in my past who I truly believed the world would be better off without. Some of them might have even deserved high-velocity lead poisoning.

But I've chosen to let go of that anger.

Because as much as it pains me to admit it, if we are going to grow, the world needs assholes.

They teach us what we need to learn, even if it's the hard way.

I'm grateful for those lessons and even more grateful I no longer need those people in my life.

I feel deeply for those still learning from them. Brent's current victim, in particular.

The second half of my life is about using the knowledge and wisdom I have gathered to help others, without apology.

Thank you for coming with me on this journey. I hope you discovered some of your own healing between these pages.

If this book touched you in any way, my deepest wish is that you will share it with others.

With love, gratitude, warmth, and a fierce belief that you matter in this world,

Dr Robyn

Acknowledgments

Writing a memoir means revisiting painful moments, triumphs, and versions of yourself you'd rather forget. I couldn't have done it alone.

To everyone who has ever heard part of my story and said, "You need to write a book" or "Your life should be a movie."

To **Leanne and Laurie**, who read the first error-filled chapters as I wrote them and encouraged me to keep going when I wondered if I was wasting my time.

To **Glady**, for line editing with precision and heart, and for being confident and vocal that this book mattered, especially when I wasn't sure it did.

To **Stephanie and her book club**, for being beta readers who asked the tough, necessary questions that made this book better and braver.

To **Carmen,** who lived alongside me through many messy chapters of my life and loves me anyway.

To **the therapists, coaches, mentors and passing acquaintances** who helped me make sense of chaos, offered me advice (solicited or otherwise) and shone light on the darkest parts of my life.

To my **parents**, who did the best they could with what they believed and who love me in their own way.

And of course, to **Russ.** Thank you for believing in me, for supporting me with your incredible talents (the websites, the cover designs, the layouts, the endless technical rescues), for being my biggest cheerleader, and for loving every version of me. You show me every day what it means to be an amazing partner and friend by always standing beside me.

Finally, to **you, the reader.** Thank you for trusting me with your time and for holding space for this story.

About the Author

You just read my story. The messy, unfiltered truth of it. What else could an "About the Author" page possibly tell you?

Here are a few things that didn't fit in previous pages:

There's a bonus chapter waiting for you at **ThankTheCartel.com**

Everything's Better in Black Stilettos is a slightly fictionalized glimpse into my life as executive arm candy in Brent's world: the galas, the power plays, the moments when I had to be both invisible and unforgettable.

You'll also find a photo gallery on the site. The faces, places, and moments that bring the stories you just read into sharper focus.

As for what I'm doing now? I've channeled everything I learned into helping others navigate their own impossible situations. You can find my work at **MentalMacGyver.com** and follow me on LinkedIn: https://www.linkedin.com/in/robynlynette/.

If my story stirred something in you, whether it's your own story you want to share, thoughts about what you just read, or an interest in having me speak, I'm listening: **Share@ThankTheCartel.com**